A Treasure g Text

19 Aug 95

Happy Birthday
Steve,

May you find plenty
of Treasure!

CC / Bobbie

RAM
BOOKS

Ram Publications

Hal Dawson, Editor

Buried Treasure of the United States
Complete field guide for finding treasure; includes state-by-state listing of thousands of sites where treasure is believed to exist.

The New Successful Coin Hunting
The world's most authoritative guide to finding valuable coins, totally rewritten to include instructions for 21st Century detectors.

Modern Treasure Hunting
The practical guidebook to today's metal detectors; a "how-to" manual that carefully explains the "why" of modern detector performance.

Treasure Recovery from Sand and Sea
Precise step-by-step instructions for reaching the "blanket of wealth" beneath sands nearby and under the world's waters, totally rewritten for the 90's.

Modern Electronic Prospecting
Explains in layman's terms how to use a modern detector to find gold nuggets and veins of precious metal.; includes instructions for panning and dredging.

Modern Metal Detectors
Advanced handbook for field, home and classroom study to increase expertise and understanding of any kind of metal detector.

Weekend Prospecting
Offers simple "how-to" instructions for enjoying holidays and vacations profitably by prospecting with metal detectors and gold pans.

Gold Panning is Easy
This excellent field guide shows the beginner exactly how to find and pan gold; follow these instructions and perform as well as any professional.

Treasure Hunting Pays Off
A basic introduction to all facets of treasure hunting...the equipment, the targets and the terminology; totally revised for the 21st Century detectors.

True Treasure Tales -- Gar Starrett Adventures
The Secret of John Murrell's Vault
The Missing Nez Perce Gold

Garrett Guide Series -- Pocket-size Field Guides
Find More Treasure With the RIGHT Metal Detector

An Introduction to Metal Detectors	Use the Super Sniper
You Can Find an Ounce of Gold a Day	Find Wealth on the Beach
Metal Detectors Can Help You Find Coins	Find Wealth in the Surf
Money Caches Are Waiting to be Found	Avoid Detector Problems

Sunken Treasure

How to Find It

by Robert Marx

RAM
BOOKS

ISBN 0-915920-74-3
Library of Congress Catalog Card No. 90-63186
Sunken Treasure: How to Find It
First Edition.
© Copyright 1990
Robert Marx

First Edition Printing, November 1990.

Book and cover design by Mel Climer
All photos by Tanit Corp., except Pages 170, 188 and Back Cover by John de Bry

For FREE listing of related treasure hunting books write

Ram Publishing Company

P.O. Box 38649 • **Dallas, TX 75238**

Dedication

There is something in a treasure that fastens upon a man's mind. He will pray and blaspheme and still persevere, and will curse the day he heard of it, and will let his last hours come upon him unawares, still believing that he missed it only by a foot. He will see it every time he closes his eyes. He will never forget it until he is dead and there is no way of getting away from a treasure once it fastens itself upon your mind.

Joseph Conrad

This book is dedicated to all those who, as children, devoured countless books about maritime history. It is for those who envied the exploits of the great seamen of the past, regretting they'd not been born in earlier times so they too could have sailed the high seas in quest of fabled riches. This is for those who have chosen to seek the ships sailed by seaborne explorers so long ago…those who have chosen to hold the past in their hands.

By Robert Marx

The Underwater Dig
The Lure of Sunken Treasure
Port Royal Rediscovered
Sea Fever: Famous Underwater Explorers
Shipwrecks in Mexican Waters
Shipwrecks in Florida Waters
Shipwrecks of the Western Hemisphere:1492-1825
Always Another Adventure
Pirate Port: The story of the Sunken City of Port Royal
They Dared the Deep: A History of Diving
The Battle of Lepanto:1571
The Battle of the Spanish Armada: 1588
The Treasure Fleets of the Spanish Main
Following Columbus: The Voyage of the Niña II
The Voyage of the Nina II
The Capture of the Treasure Fleet
Buried Treasure of the U.S.
Spanish Treasure in Florida Waters
Quest for Treasure: the Maravilla

Contents

Editor's Note

Placing a label on Robert Marx...even one so grandiloquent as *a legend in his own time* is no simple task. The man defies categorizing. He is a dedicated historian and marine archaeologist...yet a helluva diver and daredevil adventurer. He can be grimly serious about the profession of marine archaeology and recovering artifacts from beneath the sea...yet treat remarkable personal achievements almost flippantly. His sense of history is truly astonishing.

Bob is one of the most successful and well known specialists in the field of marine archaeology, and he has an equally strong reputation for his work in naval and maritime history. He studied at UCLA and the University of Maryland and served in the U.S. Marine Corps where he was a diver and worked on salvage operations. His feats are almost legendary...exploration of sunken ships he has discovered all over the world...the highly acclaimed underwater study of Port Royal in the Caribbean, ravaged by a 1692 earthquake...advising leaders of industry and government. His numerous books, articles and scientific papers are amazing in their descriptions of various projects in which he has participated.

Respected by archaeologists and sport divers alike, Bob has written more than 30 books and has published hundreds of scientific articles and reports. As his career has led him into a deeper interest in underwater archaeology, Bob has focused more of his personal attention on educating governments concerning the importance of not only protecting archaeological areas, but also actively supporting qualified projects.

Perhaps Bob Marx was described, if unknowingly, by a famous professional athlete who defended himself decades ago against the charge of boasting with the explanation, "If you done it…it ain't bragging."

Bob Marx has certainly *done it*!

To say that he is outspoken would be an understatement. Bob's countless friends and (occasional) adversaries are well aware of his strong opinions. Furthermore, they know all too clearly that these judgments are firmly based on personal experience and accomplishment. It is, therefore, hardly necessary to offer the disclaimer that the views presented in this book represent those of the author rather than those of Ram.

Association with Robert Marx is indeed a privilege for Ram Publishing Company. We are confident that this book will prove to be one of his most notable.

Hal Dawson
Editor, RAM

Dallas, Texas
Autumn 1990

Introduction

The fascination of the unknown...the lure of riches shrouded in history...these have long compelled man to search for such fabulous treasures as King Solomon's mines and the golden city of El Dorado. In fact, these and other mythical hoards usually have a basis in truth...yet their legends have become so blurred by time and overactive imaginations that separating fact from fiction has become impossible.

The romantic image of treasure is a compelling one. As long as mysteries remain to be solved and the lure of immense riches beckons, there will always be those committed to the quest and fascinated by the past.

Most people associate both buried and sunken treasure with intrepid explorers armed with faded parchment maps, each map marked with a cross to indicate a precise location...of a pirate cache on some palm-fringed island...or, of a Spanish galleon rotting on a tropical reef. As so many fabulous treasures have come to light in recent years, however, everyone realizes that what was once considered fanciful may now be reality. Of course, the *fact* remains that pirates almost never had any swag left to bury after their bouts in port with grog, girls and gambling.

Centuries ago treasure hunting was a hobby of the rich. Today, almost anyone with intelligence, determination and some know-how can find a treasure...especially those lost under water. And the search itself, following clues that unveil the past, can be exciting and fulfilling...even if treasure *isn't* found. People have been hunting for valuable artifacts of the past for more than 4000 years. For the

1

average guy who punches a time clock and keeps up with the rat race it is still one of the best ways to experience adventure and excitement...and possibly even become a millionaire. I know dozens of lucky souls who have accomplished this dream.

Just last summer off the East Coast of Florida a teenager with a surf board as a boat, an underwater metal detector and scuba gear, recovered over $300,000 worth of treasure from one of the 1715 shipwrecks...all in less than an hour. A month later another young diver spearfishing in the Philippines accidentally stumbled on a hoard of World War II gold ingots worth over $3 million. Although the press covers the more spectacular finds, hundreds of other discoveries made worldwide go unrecorded, often to escape confiscation by a government or other claimant or to avoid paying the lion's share in taxes.

After this book is published, I'm sure I'll hear from many professional treasure hunters and underwater archaeologists, as I have in the past when I wrote similar books. Their question will be...*Why write such a book and give away all of your secrets?*

My answer is that I am not greedy...and, **there's enough treasure out there for everyone to find.**

When I got started, there was no book or person I could turn to for help. Thus, I had to learn everything through years of hard work and frustration. After 40 years spent exploring more than 3,000 shipwrecks and numerous sunken cities in 58 different countries over the globe, I feel strongly about not wasting the vast amount of scholarship I've acquired in the school of hard knocks. I feel responsible for sharing this knowledge with others who love the sea and historical sailing ships. I want them to experience the same thrill of discovery and the joy of bringing the past to light.

I *welcome* others to follow in my footsteps...or I should say in the wake of my fins.

Spanish Galleons

A diver's dream of shipwrecks laden with sunken treasure conjures up images of bulky Spanish galleons, their holds crammed with gleaming riches...and, not without reason. Over the centuries more than 2,000 of them were lost in this hemisphere. Only a small number have ever been found. Along the east coast of Florida and down through the treacherous reefs of the Keys there is hardly a mile where one or more of these rich ships did not meet its doom.

Even with today's sophisticated navigational aids, the sea still claims more than its share of ships along the galleon routes, dotted with reefs and shallows and often swept by tropical storms as sudden as they are violent. In the days of dead-reckoning navigation...with inaccurate or nonexistent charts...on sail-driven wooden ships whose rigging and hulls were ravaged by shipworms and the corrosive tropical climate...the toll was far higher.

Billions of dollars in treasure from these ships lies waiting to be discovered.

Registers from the Royal Mints show that Spain extracted gold and silver worth a total of 4,035,156,000 pesos from her New World mines in the years between 1492 and 1830. Of this amount 493 million pesos, slightly over one-tenth, consisted of gold. The remainder was silver. About 40% was mined in Mexico. Almost all of the rest came from Peru, with a small amount from Colombia and Chile.

Gold and silver worth about 17,500,000 pesos were shipped to Spain in an average year. Only small amounts were left in the colonies for local use. There is no way to

3

determine the "unregistered" gold and silver mined during this period, but the amount is estimated at between one and two billion pesos. Some of this unregistered treasure was smuggled to Spain, but the majority was probably used to purchase contraband goods from other European nations, goods which came from the Continent aboard foreign ships.

Until the discovery of the New World by Columbus, economies of the European nations were stagnant, primarily because of the severe lack of precious metals, the main ingredients in meeting an expanding mercantile trade. One of the principal motives behind Columbus' voyage of discovery was his desire to find the riches of Zipango by sailing westward. He then hoped to return with great quantities of gold and silver to satisfy the needs of Spain and other European nations.

Zipango was none other than Japan. Columbus carried with him the account of Marco Polo, who on his travels heard of the fabled riches of the Golden Land where even the rooftops were golden (the gilded tiles of pagodas) Ultimately, however, treasure came not from Japan but from the mines of Peru and Mexico. The importance to Spain of this treasure from the New World can readily be understood from the following dispatch sent by the Venetian ambassador in Spain to the ruler of Venice, the doge, in September 1567:

"At the time of writing my last dispatch to you, I informed you that there was great anxiety all over Spain over the delay of the arrival of the treasure fleet from the Indies and, when the Genoese bankers informed the King that unless the fleet reached port shortly, that they would be unable to negotiate any further loans for him, Philip II fell into such a state of shock that he had to be confined to bed by his physicians. The King then ordered about 10,000 ducats, which was about all the treasure left in his royal coffers, to be sent all over his realm and distributed to various churches and monasteries for the saying of masses

4

for the safe arrival of the treasure fleet. I am happy to inform you that news has just arrived from Seville that the fleet has made port safely and there is now great rejoicing not only here in the Royal Court, but all over the land as well."

Spain, which exploited the New World so greedily, failed sadly to profit in the Old World. She neglected to understand the necessity of developing an economy based on goods and services like the northern countries, Germany, the Netherlands and England. But no nation ever amassed so much precious metal! In poring over thousands of historical documents in European archives, I discovered that the above account was by no means exceptional. In fact, it was almost a *yearly* occurrence over a period of three centuries.

The Indies treasure was so important that any delay in its arrival damaged Spanish credit disastrously and sent tremors of concern through all the major financial centers of Europe. Although generally between a quarter and a third of the returning Indies treasure was consigned to the Spanish Crown, it never seemed to be enough and the Crown was constantly in debt to international bankers. At times the Crown's share of the Indies treasure was pledged to these bankers for as much as four or five years in advance.

Treasure from the New World was of equal importance to all the other European nations, providing nearly 95% of the precious metals on which their monetary systems were based. There is a popular misconception that only Spain benefited, when in fact she benefited less than England, France, Holland and Italy. Throughout the 16th, 17th and 18th centuries, when heavily laden and usually cranky ships carried immense amounts of treasure, there was virtually no industry of any kind in Spain. She was totally dependent on other nations for manufactured goods, both for export to the New World as well as for domestic consumption. Therefore, nearly all her treasure had to be used to pay other countries for these goods.

The city of Seville held a monopoly on New World trade until it was superseded by the seaport of Cadiz early in the 18th century. During the first five decades following 1492, as the main terminus for ships sailing to and from the New World, Seville was the main commercial and financial port of Spain. Its location 60 miles up the Guadalquivir River offered no handicap since ships were then quite small and could easily navigate up the river.

Around the middle of the 16th century, however, when the first organized fleet came into existence, ships began to double in size. In addition, Seville could not accommodate large numbers of ships. As a result, even though the main control of the Indies trade remained in the hands of the merchants and royal officials in Seville, seaports of Sanlucar and Cadiz replaced Seville as the main terminus.

Both of these ports had drawbacks. Sanlucar, situated at the mouth of the Guadalquivir River, had a very dangerous sandbar over which ships had to cross when leaving port. During the three centuries when treasure ships plied between Spain and the New World, more than 200 ships were lost on this sandbar. Cadiz, although much larger than Sanlucar, was vulnerable to attacks by enemy fleets and prey to a dangerous wind called a levanter. As a result of these obstacles, over 500 additional ships of the Indies navigation were lost during that period.

In 1503, when Columbus was in the New World on his fourth voyage of discovery, the Indies trade was put on an organized basis at the orders of Queen Joanna with the founding of the House of Trade in Seville. Charged with promoting and regulating trade and navigation with the New World, making certain that all royal orders were

This large gold chain which was found by a pretty sports diver off the island of Grand Cayman came from a Spanish galleon that was wrecked in 1628.

carried out and collecting taxes and duties on both out-ward-bound and returning cargoes, the House of Trade also supervised the preparations and dispatching of all ships sailing for the New World.

Officials of the House of Trade first made their head-quarters in Seville's huge cathedral, much to the discontent of the local populace. But, construction was begun in 1572 on a new building nearby, which served as the home for the House of Trade officials until the Indies trade monopoly was transferred to Cadiz. Today this building is the Archives of the Indies, where millions of pages of priceless documents dealing with the ships in the Indies navigation are stored with other documents relat-ing to the New World.

In 1519, the year that Cortez sailed from Cuba to begin his conquest of Mexico, Charles I decided that the busi-ness of administering the affairs of the New World was taking up too much of his time. He created a new ad-ministrative body, the Council of the Indies, as part of his Royal Court. Its chief function was to keep the king ad-vised on matters concerning his New World possessions. The Council was also responsible for appointing royal officials to govern in the New World and commanders of the treasure fleets as well as for organizing the conquest of new areas. The Council played the role of middleman between the House of Trade and the king.

Still another administrative body, the Merchant Guild, was created in 1543 to aid in trade and navigation. Its officials were appointed from among the richest and most influential merchants engaged in commerce with the New World. The Guild's three main functions were supervision of marine insurance necessary to equalize losses from

Treasure to be recovered from sunken Spanish galleons can be a clump of silver pieces of eight, as shown above, or a large chest filled with gold and silver coins.

shipwrecks and ships captured by enemies or pirates, acting as a clearing house for all manufactured goods arriving from European nations for transshipment to the New World and maintenance of civil jurisdiction for its members, merchants and businessmen engaged in New World trade.

One of the earliest laws concerning Indies navigation was that ships must be of Spanish construction and ownership. Nevertheless, over the entire period of the Indies navigation, about half of the ships that sailed for the New World were of foreign construction. Rarely was there a sufficient quantity of Spanish-built ships available, even though the ownership aspect of the Spanish law was rather strictly enforced.

During the first half of the 16th century, ships were astonishingly small...most of them less than 100 tons and many as small as 30 to 40 tons, the size of Columbus' Niña, the smallest vessel on his first voyage of discovery. To obtain a better idea of the small size of these early ships, one has only to realize that a ship of fifty tons was 35 to 40 feet long and from 12 to 15 feet in the beam, while a ship of 100 tons was 50 to 55 feet in length and 16 to 18 feet in the beam.

These vessels were in a class called caravels but were often referred to in documents as *naos,* which merely means a ship. Caravels were first built early in the 15th century by the Portuguese for voyages of exploration. By making slight modifications in their sails and rigging, the Spaniards found them well adapted for transatlantic voyages. Although they were quite fast and much more seaworthy than any of the later classes of ships used by the Spaniards for Indies navigation, their relatively small size soon proved to be a handicap. It restricted the amount of cargo that could be carried and severely limited quarters for crew and passengers.

A much larger vessel than the caravel was needed by the early 1540s, when the New World's demand for imports from Europe and Spain's need for wealth from the New World had increased so greatly. At that time the standard sailing ship in Europe for carrying large cargoes, called a "carrack," ranged in size from 100 to 800 tons and was a large, round, bulky tub. Although capable of carrying large cargoes, its shape made it such a slow sailer that after several years of trial and error on the transatlantic voyages to the New World, it was found impractical and never used again.

The Spaniards next tried using galleys, which were larger and faster than caravels, but they too were impractical. Although larger than caravels, they could carry less cargo because a great portion of the space in the hold had to be utilized for carrying water and victuals required by the large number of slaves needed to propel them. Also, they were extremely hazardous in any kind of storm because they rode very low in the water.

By the early 1550s, when larger and larger quantities of treasure begun arriving from the New World, Spaniards were hard-pressed to find a suitable vessel. Not only did the vessel have to be larger in size but more defendable as well, since hostilities had broken out between France and Spain. Many of the smaller caravels began falling prey to French privateers. The solution was found by Don Alvaro de Bazin, Spain's foremost naval leader in the 16th century. By combining the carrack's bulkiness with the swift-sailing lines of the galleys and the sail patterns and rigging used on caravels, he invented the galleon, which became the standard class of ship used throughout the remainder of the Indies navigation.

The average size of a galleon was from 300 to 600 tons, but late in the 16th century many were as large as 1,200 tons. They were constructed with two or three spacious decks, large fore and stern castles, and carried from three to four masts. Though slower than caravels or galleys, the galleons could average about four knots on a transatlantic crossing when not overloaded and with their bottoms properly cleaned. This speed was more than twice that of carracks. Their disadvantage was the massive size of the fore and stern castles, which made the ships top heavy and placed them in great peril of capsizing in storms. Not until early in the 18th century was this danger properly understood and the castles reduced in size.

Although the galleon became the standard ship used in the Indies navigation, this vessel was called a galleon only when it carried a large number of cannon. When used as a merchant ship and carrying only a small amount of cannon, it was called a *nao*. Thus, on one voyage to the New World, a ship might be called a *nao* and on the next a galleon.

Besides the galleons and *naos*, other classes of smaller vessels, ranging in size from 40 to 100 tons, were also used in the Indies navigation. Although they were of many different types of construction and rig, including caravels, pinks, flyboats, sloops, and pinnaces the Spaniards referred to them all as *pataches*. They served various functions, such as reconnaissance vessels in convoys, advice boats between Spain and the New World and to carry small cargoes to such small outposts as St. Augustine, FL, which as a minor settlement did not warrant a larger ship.

Although the main terminus for Indies navigation was centered in southern Spain, very little suitable timber was available in this area. Thus, most of the Spanish ships were built in the provinces of northern Spain. After the turn of the 17th century a large number were also built in Cuba and other New World ports. Most of the masts, spars and other heavy rigging came from as far away as Russia and Poland with cordage and sails imported from Scandinavia and Holland. Until the end of the 16th century, when factories producing a good grade of iron were founded in Biscay Province in northern Spain, most of the metal fittings, anchors and iron cannon were imported from various countries of northern Europe.

Even the small caravels were obliged to carry several

pieces of artillery, the number depending on a vessel's size and function. For example, a galleon of 400 tons used as a merchant *nao* would be required to carry only 10 or 12 cannon, whereas the same vessel serving as a flagship of a convoy and entrusted with bringing back a large amount of treasure would be required to carry as many as 50 cannon of various caliber. Iron cannon, unless new, were used merely to fire salutes or as signals between ships They heated too quickly after firing and would crack or burst apart, often rendering more damage to those firing than those fired upon.

When the galleons superseded the earlier class of Indies vessel, it became standard practice for them to carry only bronze cannon, except when they were scarce. The largest bronze cannon used on the galleons in the 16th and 17th centuries was called a demiculverin. It weighed about 2 tons and fired an iron ball weighing from 7 to 12 pounds at a maximum distance of 1,000 paces at point blank range and more than twice that distance when fired in a trajectory. Ships usually sailed in small convoys, not only for the sake of mutual protection against corsairs and foul weather, but to pool the knowledge of precious navigators.

During the first three decades of the 16th century, before sizable conquests had been made in Mexico and Peru, virtually all the shipping between Spain and the New World was directed to Hispaniola. The number of ships sailing each year depended on availability, the number of corsairs cruising in wait near the Azores and off Portugal and Spain, and the amount of exports and number of settlers bound for the New World. In 1508, for example, 66 ships sailed to the New World. In 1520 the number reached 108; in 1529, when the number of French privateers operating off the Azores was great, only 60 sailed, and of the 42 that attempted to return to Spain, 11 were captured by French privateers.

Pirates and privateers were a menace from the very beginning. Columbus was the first to have dealings with them. On his very first voyage of discovery in 1492 he sighted two French corsair vessels when approaching the Canary Islands. Because his ships were better manned, the pirates gave him a wide berth. Only foul weather saved his flagship from falling prey to a fleet of French corsairs off Cape St. Vincent at the southern tip of Portugal when he was returning from his third voyage. Although the corsairs were lucky enough to capture a few returning Indies ships each year from 1505 onward, they never took any of major importance until 1521, when two caravels loaded with treasure for the king were captured.

This disaster stimulated the formation of a special patrol fleet, maintained by a tax, the *avería,* placed on all cargoes to and from the New World. The purpose of this patrol fleet, which was named the Armada of the Ocean Sea, was to escort convoys of ships from Spain as far as the Canaries and then take up station off the Azores, where it would search out and destroy corsair vessels and meet homeward-bound convoys to escort them to Spain. Called the Royal Fleet of Spain, these warships were of major importance to Spain and existed throughout the duration of the Indies navigation.

When war with France broke out once again in 1537, the first fleet that could be called a "treasure fleet" sailed to the Indies. This fleet, comprised of six warships and 20 merchant vessels, sailed directly to Nombre de Dios on the Isthmus of Panama to collect treasures from Peru, then proceeded to Cartageña to receive gold and emeralds from the interior and pearls from the island of Margarita, off the coast of Venezuela. Then it sailed to Havana, where it met with ships arriving from Veracruz with treasures and products from Mexico as well as exotic Oriental cargoes from the Manila galleons which had been brought by mule train from Acapulco. After taking on water and provisions at Havana, the *flota* sailed through the Bahama Channel and headed for the Azores, where it united with the Armada of the Ocean Sea for its last leg to

Spain. This system of treasure fleets was kept in effect until about 1552, when galleons first came into use and a new convoy system was established.

This new system consisted of sending two separate convoys of ships each year to the New World. Other European nations referred to these convoys as treasure fleets, but the Spaniards called them *flotas*... which means just plain fleet. Each of these *flotas* consisted of four heavily armed galleons of at least 300 tons and two 80 ton *pataches,* plus from 10 to 90 merchant *naos.* One *flota* generally sailed in March and the other in September. After passing the Canaries they normally made their first landfall at either Guadeloupe or Martinique in the Caribbean. There the ships would split up.

The merchants ships bound for Mexico sailed with those for Puerto Rico, Hispañiola, Cuba, Jamaica and Honduras, The four galleons and two *pataches* would sail with those heading for Venezuela, Colombia (then called the Nuevo Reiño de Granada), and the Isthmus of Panama. The galleons called at Nombre de Dios and Cartageña and then went on to Havana to await the arrival of the ships from all the other Spanish settlements in the New World before heading back to Spain. In theory, only the four galleons were permitted to carry treasure on the voyage to Spain, but this regulation was routinely disregarded by merchants, who preferred to carry their treasure on ships they were sailing on.

The organization of this *flota* system had one big disadvantage. After the ships split up upon making their Caribbean landfall, those sailing for Mexico were left without the protection of the four galleons and two *pataches* and some fell prey to pirates and privateers. As a result of this deficiency, a much better *flota* system was put into effect in 1564 and retained for nearly a century.

There were still two *flotas* sailing to the New World each year, one called the *Tierra Firme flota* and the other the *Nueva España flota.* Each consisted of two heavily armed galleons and two *pataches*, plus the merchant *naos* sailing under their protection. The larger galleon,which was the flagship, was called the *Capitaña* and the smaller the *Almiranta*. Although the New Spain *flota* generally sailed from Spain in April, the perennial "laid back" attitude of Spaniards made it difficult to get either *flota* dispatched on time.

The voyage from Spain to Veracruz generally took from two to three months, depending on the weather and condition of the ships. The ships sailing for the Greater Antilles and Honduras would sail with this *flota*. Since so many ships had been lost in the Gulf of Mexico between October and February--when dangerous northers blow in the Gulf--it became the practice for the *flota* to winter in Veracruz. They would sail the following year in February or March, either to wait in Havana and sail jointly with the *Tierra Firme flota* or to continue on alone for Spain.

The *Tierra Firme flota* usually sailed in August, taking under its protection all the ships destined for ports along the Spanish Main. After it was laden with the treasure from Peru in Nombre de Dios, it proceeded to Cartageña to winter there just as the New Spain *flota* did in Veracruz. In January it sailed for Havana and either met with the New Spain *flota* or continued on back to Spain alone. Political unrest in Europe during this period sometimes made it necessary to increase the number of galleons in the *Tierra Firme flota* to six or eight, in which case it was called the *Armada de Tierra Firme*, or simply the galleons. During such times the New Spain *flota* either sailed back to Spain with the galleons or left the Mexican treasure in Havana to be picked up by the galleons.

Threats by the English, whose naval power was increasing, to capture homeward-bound and treasure-laden galleons forced the Indies navigation to be reorganized in 1591. The new system which continued in use until about 1650 entailed dispatching three fleets annually to the Indies. The *Tierra Firme flota* and the New Spain *flota* were still maintained. The former now sailed earlier in the year and instead of wintering in Cartageña returned to Spain in the same year, generally in convoy with the new fleet, which was called the *Armada of Tierra Firme*, the Silver Fleet, or simply the galleons. This new fleet consisted of eight to twelve galleons and two or more *pataches*. Like the *Capitaña* and *Almiranta* in the *flotas*, it was not permitted to carry cargo other than treasure to or from the New World. The average size of these galleons was about 600 tons, but the *Capitaña* and *Almiranta* were sometimes as large as 1,000 tons.

In addition to being heavily armed with bronze cannon, each carried a company of 200 marines. With the reorganization of the Indies navigation, the *Tierra Firme flota* usually sailed first in March and the galleons either sailed at the same time or a month or so later. The New Spain *flota* now sailed in May or June, in an effort to reach Veracruz before the northers started blowing in October. After the galleons picked up the treasure in Nombre de Dios, or later in Porto Bello, the *flota* proceeded to Carta-

This old drawing shows a Spanish galleon wrecking during a hurricane, a scene that was repeated countless times throughout the Caribbean and Gulf of Mexico.

geña and then sailed alone or with the *Tierra Firme flota*
to Havana, where it either met with the previous year's
New Spain *flota* or picked up the treasure this fleet had
left in Havana. Then it sailed for Spain. Only on a few
occasions between 1591 and 1650, when Spain was on the
brink of bankruptcy, did the New Spain *flota* risk carrying
the treasure back to Spain unescorted by the galleons.

Throughout the three centuries of Indies navigation,
single ships, called *sueltos,* were occasionally permitted to
sail to the New World. The number sailing each year
varied from a few to as many as 50, depending on the level
of political unrest and the shifting alliances which marked
the political climate in Europe. Most of the *sueltos* were
small ships and their destinations were out-of-the-way
ports that the larger merchant *naos* didn't visit. They were
easy prey for enemy privateers and corsairs, but the Crown
benefited from their sailing, as they afforded a year-round
communication system with the New World colonies. To
protect both the *sueltos* and the smaller poorly protected
outposts in the Caribbean. Spain maintained a squadron
of from four to eight galleons known as the *Windward
Armada.*

Departure of a fleet from Spain was always a
ceremonious occasion, drawing crowds of spectators from
far and wide. The sailing date was preceded by several days
of fiestas and religious ceremonies. Once at sea, after the
excitement of the departure had died down, the normal
routine of each ship would be set and kept throughout the
voyage. The men would be placed in different watches,
assigned sleeping areas and messmates and read the rules
that would have to be obeyed during the voyage.

Spaniards were never noted for cleanliness, especially
on ships, and most of the epidemics that broke out aboard
them came as a result of this problem. An Englishman
writing in the early 17th century said, "Their ships are kept
foul and beastly, like hog-sties and sheeps-cotes in comparison of ours; and no marvel, for there is no course taken

to correct that abuse by appointing men purposely for that office as we do in our ships."

In comparison with a crossing from Manila to Acapulco, an Atlantic crossing from Spain to the New World was like child's play. Even so, it could be a long and trying experience. Quarters were painfully restricted for all but senior officers and rich passengers, and the quantity and quality of the victuals left much to be desired. To break the voyage's monotony crewmen improvised mimic bullfights, held cockfights, celebrated as many religious holidays as possible and did a great deal of fishing. But the main pastime for most of the crew and passengers was gambling, which, although forbidden by royal decree, met with little opposition from officers and officials in charge of the ships.

Weather was a continuous source of interest. Old salts could predict its behavior fairly accurately by various means. A heavily clouded sky at night meant rain would soon fall; when extra-large rays were seen emitting from a rising or setting sun, it meant bad weather was near at hand; the brighter the moon at night, the better the weather the following day; deep red clouds on the horizon at dawn or dusk meant the approach of a tempest; a halo around the moon threatened rain, etc. Some old salts predicted bad weather when they suffered from rheumatism, and this has been proven to be true...the high humidity that precedes most storms at sea also causes discomfort to persons with rheumatism.

The most dreaded combination of factors was an exceptional calm lasting several days associated with extraordinarily clear water and an unusual number of fish playing at or near the surface, followed by huge ocean swells when there was no wind about. This was a positive sign of a hurricane approaching.

From beginning to end, voyages to and from the New World were hazardous undertakings. Shipwrecks were the greatest danger. Over the three centuries slightly more than 5% of the ships in the Indies navigation were shipwrecked, mostly by bad weather but also because of incompetent navigators. A small percentage were lost by capsizing because of overloading and to fires on board. There were also other small losses from ships being destroyed or captured by enemy or corsair ships.

Once the ships sailing for the New World passed over the dangerous sandbar at Sanlucar, very few were lost until after they reached the Caribbean. Atlantic winds in this crossing were nearly all in their favor; there was little danger of bad storms in the latitudes these ships sailed in; and, of course, there was no danger of running up on a reef in deep ocean waters.

For many reasons the return passage was always considered the most dangerous. First of all, it could take twice as long as the voyage over. By this time, too, the wooden ships were weakened from worms eating at their hulls and slowed considerably by heavy growths of barnacles and marine plants below the waterline. Plus, the voyage homeward passed many dangerous areas, such as the hostile reefs and shoals on both sides of the Bahama Channel. Another problem was that crews were smaller after desertion and deaths in the New World.

Among the most interesting aspects of these transatlantic voyages were the methods, or lack of methods, used in navigation. Spanish navigational practices have been scornfully described, and among these critics were Spaniards themselves. Shortly after the foundation of the House of Trade in Seville, a school of navigation was established there, expressly to provide competent navigators. The science of navigation came into being during the early 15th century under the Portuguese, most notably Prince Henry the Navigator. By the time Columbus sailed for the New World, navigation appeared to have reached its zenith and very few improvements were made until the 19th century.

Basically, the navigator depended on dead-reckoning,

since there were no means for establishing longitude until the 19th century. The compass was used to keep a course. Instruments such as astrolabes and quadrants were available to obtain a ship's latitude at midday and various methods helped estimate a ship's speed. Deciding a ship's drift in ocean currents or the magnetic variation of the compass involved a great deal of guesswork. Charts were generally so inaccurate that many navigators preferred to rely on their own knowledge and experience.

Rarely did two navigators in the same convoy agree on the position of the ships or even the proper compass headings to take, which resulted in many ships being wrecked. In a New Spain *flota* sailing in 1582, the captain-general summoned all navigators to his ship to determine their position after five weeks at sea. Estimates of sighting Guadeloupe ranged from two weeks to only one day. The majority placed the convoy 10 days from the island, while only one predicted they were quite close enough to reach it within 24 hours. He was laughed at, but proven right that very night when the three leading ships ran upon reefs on the island's eastern side.

Once the *flota* system was established, routes to and from the New World were followed with little variation save during times of war. They were then altered to avoid capture or destruction of ships at the hands of enemy fleets. Upon leaving Spain, all the fleets passed within sight of the Canary Islands and made landfall at either Guadeloupe or Martinique, where they spent a day or two refreshing themselves.

The New Spain *flota* then set a course for St. Croix in the Virgin Islands, passing within sight of the southern coast of the island. Dropping off various ships along its way, it continued along the south side of both Hispañiola and Cuba and, after sighting Cape San Antonio, on the western tip of Cuba, on a heading for Cape Catoche on the Yucatan peninsula. It kept in sight of land until it finally reached Veracruz. The voyage from Veracruz to Havana generally took from four to five weeks, because contrary winds forced the *flotas* to take an indirect route. After leaving Veracruz, they headed north until they sighted land in the vicinity of Pensacola, where they would turn and follow the length of Florida's west coast, with winds that were usually favorable. Not until reaching the vicinity of the Dry Tortugas in the Florida Keys could they steer a direct course for Havana.

Both the *Tierra Firme flota* and the galleons followed the same routes. After leaving Guadeloupe or Martinique, they steered for a point on the Spanish Main called Cabo de la Vela, or Cape of the Sail, so called because from a distance this cape resembled a large sail. Once in sight of this point, they stayed along the coast until reaching Cartageña.

To sail from Cartageña to Nombre de Dios or Porto Bello, which superseded Nombre de Dios near the end of the 15th century, the fleets were forced by prevailing winds to sail in a direct line, but would first have to sail northwest for several days before changing course to southwest. The voyage back to Cartageña was more direct and generally made within sight of land all the way.

In sailing between Cartageña and Havana and between Havana and Spain the Spaniards took an unorthodox route. Instead of attempting to steer a course between the treacherous reefs of Serraña and Serranilla on the west and Pedro Shoals on the east, they steered directly for one of these reefs. They believed it was more important to know they had reached a dangerous area by sighting it rather than trying to sail between the dangerous areas on both sides of their course, unaware of their position or that of the reefs. Not surprisingly, reefs ripped the bottoms out of ships that happened to reach them in the dark of night. After sighting whichever of these treacherous reefs the fleet had been steering for, the vessels would then alter course for Grand Cayman Island. Upon sighting Grand Cayman they again altered course at a point on the south-western coast of Cuba. Once in sight of the Cuban coast, they would hug it until reaching Havana.

Outbound from Havana for Spain the ships once again executed the unorthodox practice of heading directly for the Florida Keys, an area that has claimed more Spanish shipwrecks than any other in the New World. With the Bahama Channel no narrower than 50 miles at any point it is hard to understand why they didn't try to steer up its middle rather than sail so close to such a dangerous area. Navigational theory of that day and age, however, dictated establishing a ship's true position by sighting as many known points of land as possible. Not even the loss of a significant number of ships on the Florida Keys was enough to change this practice.

Once the Keys were sighted, a more northerly course was taken. Ships normally stayed within sight of the Florida coast until sighting Cape Canaveral, when they headed for Bermuda. Although the reefs of the Bermudas also claimed many Spanish ships, navigators felt it absolutely necessary to sight Bermuda to determine their true position before turning on an easterly heading toward the Azores.

The route used on the return voyages to Spain remained constant throughout the Indies navigation. When most of the islands of the Lesser Antilles began to be settled by the English and other European nations-- around 1650--both fleets sailing to Mexico and the Spanish Main had to change their routes. The New Spain *flota* would make its first Caribbean landfall in the vicinity of the Virgin Islands and then pass along the northern coast of Puerto Rico and sail south down the channel separating Puerto Rico from Hispañiola.

Once in sight of the southern coast of Hispañiola, the rest of the route was the same as before. The fleets sailing for the Spanish Main would make their first landfall at Trinidad and Tobago, passing between on the body of water that retains the name Galleon Passage. They would

23

then head directly for Cabo de la Vela and proceed along the routes established previously. The main ports visited were Nombre de Dios, Porto Bello, Cartageña, Havana and Veracruz.

A gradual decline began in the overall *flota* system began about 1600, and by 1650 the system was all but defunct. Silver production in the New World had declined substantially. In addition, there was a great increase in contraband foreign goods flooding the Indies, insufficient shipping and crews for use in the Indies navigation, poor leadership by inept rulers, bankruptcy of the Crown on several occasions and depredations on her shipping and American colonies by Spain's enemies.

As the American colonists' demand for highly taxed merchandise from Spain decreased yearly in direct proportion to increasing amounts of contraband brought over by foreigners and sold at more attractive prices, the number of ships in the *flotas* kept decreasing. So great was the amount of contraband goods reaching Porto Bello that 1648 was the last year that a Tierra Firme flota ever sailed to the Indies. Thereafter the small amount of goods carried there was embarked aboard the galleons. A few years later, with so little merchandise to carry, and the mining industry in such a poor state, the Crown seriously considered the cessation of the whole *flota* system.

From 1650 onward the New Spain *flota* and the Galleons, which previously had sailed yearly, began sailing only at irregular intervals of every four or five years, and the number of ships in these fleets was negligible. Between 1570 and 1599 an average of 110 ships had sailed annually to the Indies; between 1600 and 1610 the number dropped to 55; between 1640 and 1650 to 25; and between 1670 and

Author is shown with stacks of coins and silver bars which he brought up from the Spanish ship *Maravilla*, a galleon that was wrecked in the Bahamas in 1656.

1690 to a mere 17 ships. In 1661 the Spaniards even had to use a Dutch fleet of twenty vessels under the command of Admiral Ruiter to protect their returning treasure ships from English privateers. The Dutch were willing, since most of the returning treasures were consigned to Dutch merchants in payment for goods they had shipped over earlier in the year.

Even after 1700, when the production of gold and silver in the American mines greatly increased, the overall *flota* system showed very little improvement, mainly because Spanish-American colonists preferred buying European merchandise from the English, Dutch and French, all of whom had already established settlements throughout the West Indies. During the War of Spanish Succession, from 1700 to 1713, the French virtually took control of the *flota* system. Most ships used were French with predominantly French crews.

Small *flotas* continued to sail to Veracruz every two or three years between 1715 and 1736, but during this 21-year period only five convoys of treasure galleons sailed to Porto Bello and Cartageña. With the threat of war with England looming in 1736, the Spanish Crown suspended sailing of the New Spain *flota* and the galleons. In 1740 the Crown went a step further, ending the sailings of the Galleons permanently. Thereafter, a new system was devised to bring back Peruvian treasures. Large, solitary galleons or occasionally two sailing together went directly from Cadiz to Callao and back again.

Great improvements in the design and rigging of the galleons made the perilous voyage around Cape Horn safer. Some foreign ships, mainly French, had been making this long voyage from 1700 onward. The long war

Diver is hunting with a metal detector among the wreckage of a Spanish galleon in the Bahamas, searching for treasure such as the golden items, below, from the *Maravilla*.

with England postponed resumption of the sailings of the New Spain *Flota* until 1754, and during the long period when no *flotas* sailed to Veracruz, single registered *sueltos* made the voyage yearly. Between 1754 and 1778, the year when the last New Spain *flota* returned to Spain, only six *flotas* sailed to Veracruz, and all of them had to be escorted by large squadrons of warships, which made the expense too great to permit future sailings.

When the Spanish Crown finally declared free trade for her American colonies in 1778, the *flota* system ceased to exist. Spanish ships still sailed to the New World with European products and returned with treasure, but no longer in convoys. Two or three ships usually sailed jointly, and sometimes a solitary vessel plied the sea lanes where the once mighty *flotas* had held sway.

New World Treasure

Without the discovery of the rich mines in the New World, there would have been no treasure fleets and the whole course of American history might have taken a different turn. Columbus brought the first treasure to Spain, followed by much larger amounts from Hispañiola during the next two decades...treasure made possible only by Indian slave labor. When this source of treasure was exhausted, others emerged with the conquests of Peru and Mexico. By 1530 enterprising Spaniards and Germans with mining experience sent by the Emperor had begun serious mining by digging ore, mainly silver, from rich surface deposits. Each year larger and larger amounts were shipped to Spain.

The breakthrough came in 1545 in Peru with the discovery of the prodigious mountain of Potosi (today located in Bolivia), which contained the greatest concentration of silver found anywhere in the New World. An Inca named Hualpa discovered this mine while stalking a deer on the steep slopes of the mountain. As he grasped a shrub to pull himself up, the shrub gave way and he discovered a mass of pure silver in the cavity in the ground. Spaniards were soon working this location on a large scale. Just three years later two rich silver mines were discovered in Mexico...at Zacatecas and Guanajuato, precipitating a silver rush.

The Spanish Crown never exploited the mines totally for its own account except for the Huancavalica mercury mine in Peru, but it collected the King's Royal Fifth revenue from the all the precious metals mined. Some

Spaniards, and even Indians, worked small claims by hand, but the typical silver miner was an entrepreneur. Investment capital was needed to mine, refine and transport the gold and silver to the seaports.

Another boost in the amount of precious metals reaching Spain came in 1555 when an unknown German alchemist discovered how to refine precious metals using mercury or quicksilver. Within a year this process, called mercury amalgamation, was producing good results in the New World. The Spanish Crown, realizing that supplying the miner with a steady supply of mercury could be a lucrative source of income, shrewdly placed a Crown monopoly on the liquid element.

The mercury mine of Huancavalica, which had been discovered prior to 1555, was seized by the Crown and its owners miserably compensated. This mine served most of the needs of South American mines until the 19th century. No mercury mines were ever discovered in Mexico, and all the mercury used there had to be shipped from Peru and Spain. Mercury brought from Spain came from two sources, a mine at Almaden in southern Spain, which had been producing mercury since Roman times, supplemented by annual imports from Hungary. Interruption in delivery of mercury resulted in great financial problems to the Crown, since it meant a decrease in the amount of precious metals refined and subsequently lesser amounts of revenue paid to the Crown.

Before discovery of the silver mines, gold accounted for the greatest value in precious metals. Shipment of gold in the early years of Spanish domination of the Americas came chiefly from the plundered inheritance of New World civilizations. Tragically, almost all of the artistic treasures crafted by the artisans of the New World were melted by conquerors blinded by greed.

Increasingly, gold came from panning rivers and streams. In fact, gold was always being discovered, but was generally too expensive to mine in comparison with silver.

Between 1550 and 1700 so little gold was mined that of the total value of precious metals it accounted for less than one percent, and most of this was obtained as a by-product in mining and refining silver.

Silver production expanded continuously throughout the second half of the 16th century, reaching a peak during the last decade. Production began declining slowly between until 1630, when the decline became precipitous as surface deposits were exhausted. Not only did miners have to dig deeper and deeper, greatly increasing production costs, but these deeper levels produced lower grades of ore. For example, at the Potosi mine in 1560 a pound of ore yielded two ounces of pure silver, but by 1630 it took over one ton of ore to yield an equal amount of refined silver. A greater labor force as well as more mercury were required to mine and refine the poorer grades of ore. The supply of the mercury was never sufficient. By the middle of the 17th century over half the mines that had been in operation in 1600 were inoperative because they couldn't make a profit for one reason or another.

More Gold and Silver

By the 17th century production of both gold and silver had improved because of improvements in mining techniques. During every year of the 18th century more precious metals were mined in America than during even the peak years of the last 16th century's final decade. Many gold mines discovered centuries earlier were put into production. Throughout the 18th century the value of mined gold accounted for about 10% of the total value of precious metals production.

Individual miners refined both gold and silver, but the Crown provided assayers to test all precious metals for their fineness (purity) and also collected the King's Royal Fifth and lesser taxes. Royal mints were located in most of the major cities of the New World including Lima, Mexico City, Guatemala City, Bogota and even at Potosi. Most of the King's Royal Fifth was kept in bars or smaller wedges of silver. Some was used in the Indies to pay the salaries of royal officials and soldiers.

After private individuals had paid their Royal Fifth, they kept their gold or silver in bars or wedges or minted it into coins. Most of the coins minted in the Indies circulated there except for large amounts that changed hands at the fairs in Porto Bello or Veracruz which were carried back on ships by merchants. Gold coins were called escudos or, from about 1700 onward, doubloons. Silver coins were called reals, and both gold and silver were minted in denominations of 8, 4, 2, 1 and halves. The value of gold coins to silver in the 16th and 17th centuries was sixteen to one. During the 18th century, when gold production was greatly increased, this ratio dropped to eight to one.

Treasure Ports

Caribbean terminus for receiving Peruvian treasures was first at Nombre de Dios, the narrowest point on the isthmus. Poor health conditions of this port, which was surrounded by pestilential swamps, caused the Crown in 1584 to move the town a few miles to the southeast to Porto Bello, which was a much safer port for shipping. The actual move was delayed because a new jungle trail had to be hacked to connect Porto Bello to Venta Cruz, midway point along the trail between Porto Bello and Panama City. When Drake destroyed Nombre de Dios in 1596, however, Porto Bello finally superseded it. Never a settlement of any large size except at the time of the visit of the fleets, Porto Bello was more or less a ghost town with a small garrison of Spanish soldiers manning the forts and several hundred Negroes and mulattos.

The main Peruvian port of Callao, six miles from Lima and consisting of a natural harbor defended by a strong fort, was the home base of the *Armada of the South Seas.* This armada formed after the rich ore discoveries at Potosi usually consisted of from two to four galleons. Its role was to carry the Peruvian treasures to Panama City and return with cargoes brought from Spain. Because the Potosi mines were located high in the mountains, it took about two weeks to transport their treasure on llamas to the port of Arica. Small *pataches* took another eight days to bring the treasure to Callao. The voyage of the Armada of the South Seas from Callao to Panama City took an average of three weeks, but the return voyage was twice, sometimes three times, as long since the ships had to buck contrary currents and winds.

Usually, a few weeks before the galleons were to depart from Spain, an advice boat was sent ahead to Nombre de Dios (or Porto Bello) with news of their approach. This news was rushed to Lima to insure the treasure's arrival in Panama City about the time the galleons arrived at the Isthmus. Once the galleons reached the Isthmus, word was rushed overland to Panama City for transportation of the treasure to Nombre de Dios or Porto Bello. Treasure was brought overland on mules or carried partly by mules and partly on water.

Just south of Porto Bello is the mouth of the Chagres River, which has its head at Venta Cruz, the halfway point across the Isthmus. When water was high enough on the river, treasure would be taken off the mules at Venta Cruz and carried down the river on flat-bottomed barges. At the mouth, where there was a strong fort, treasure would be transferred to either galleys or other small vessels and taken to Porto Bello. Bars of silver were stacked like heaps of stones in the streets of Porto Bello or the main square. Since the owner of each bar had his marks stamped on it, there was no danger of loss. Gold, all coinage and the King's treasure were kept in the large Customs Warehouse.

Each year a fair was held in Nombre de Dios or Porto Bello, and the town was called upon to accommodate an enormous assemblage of traders, soldiers, sailors, prostitutes, camp followers, etc. Shelter and food were sold at outrageous prices. Merchants paid as much as a thousand pesos for a moderate shop or store to house their goods.

Porto Bello wasn't much healthier than Nombre de Dios had been, and each year many men sickened and died from dysentery and malaria.

The fair generally lasted a month, but occasionally epidemics or an urgent need for the treasure in Spain cut its duration. Once the fair ended and the ships sailed for Cartageña, the port would once again become a ghost town. Cartageña served as the port for Santa Fe de Bogota, the capital of New Granada (today the nation of Colombia). Here pearls from the various fisheries along the Spanish Main were placed aboard the galleons, along with gold and emeralds sent down from Bogota. Before the fleets left for Havana, they would obtain fresh victuals and water and make any needed repairs to the ships.

Veracruz was the most dangerous port used by the *flotas*, exposed as it was to hurricanes in the summer and violent northers during most of the fall and winter months. An open roadstead, the many sandbars and reefs at its mouth made entry into the port perilous. From the beginning, the large ships anchored at, or were tied up in the lee of, a small island named San Juan de Ulia, some 15 miles down the coast from Veracruz, and goods destined for Mexico City and elsewhere had to be carried on small boats from there to Veracruz.

In 1600 the town of Veracruz was completely transferred down the coast directly opposite San Juan de Ulia. This town, like all others visited by the fleets, was never of major importance, being nothing more than a shanty town that served as a base for the *flotas* that wintered there. The only buildings of any note were the forts, a customs house and several churches. A fair was held there, as in Porto Bello. When it was over, goods were carried on mules to Mexico City and other places, including faraway Guatemala City.

Havana was the only Indies port at which almost all ships returning from to Spain stopped. The town itself was the most impressive of any they visited, and it was here that the fleets would unite for their homeward voyage. The surrounding countryside provided plenty of victuals as well as wood for necessary ships' repairs.

Contemporary documents detail a variety of frauds committed by men entrusted with refining, assaying and minting gold and silver. Silver bars were produced with centers of lead, copper or other base metals. In minting coins, base metals were sometimes added. Ironically, platinum--valueless in those days--was sometimes used as a counterfeit for silver. Corrupt mint workers sometimes minted underweight coins which was easy before coins were round in form with milled edges.

Records Kept Carefully

Before treasure was loaded on the galleons, manifests or registers were made in triplicate of every bar, wedge and chest of coins. Various marks on bars and wedges denoted where they were mined and assayed, showed that the Royal Fifth was paid and reported the owner, assayer and fineness of the metal, plus its weight and value. The average weight of a silver bar was 70 pounds, while a wedge weighed between 10 and 20 pounds. Gold in bullion form weighed from several ounces up to 30 pounds.

Smuggling of unregistered cargoes, both to and from the Indies, was the most frustrating problem confronting the Spanish Crown throughout their Indies navigation. Recoveries by divers of treasure not listed on the manifest of wrecked Spanish ships is confirmation of the degree of smuggling. Contraband cargo sometimes even exceeded the amount or value of legitimate cargo. In 1510 an ordinance was issued specifying that any unregistered treasure brought back from the Indies was subject to confiscation with the smuggler fined four times the value of the treasure. All sorts of precautions were exercised by the officials of the Crown, but they were never totally effective.

Before an arriving fleet entered Sanlucar, all ships in port were forced to vacate to Cadiz so that no treasure from the returning Indies ships could be sneaked aboard them. Patrol boats were stationed up and down the coasts between Cape St. Vincent and Gibraltar to make sure no boats approached or left the returning Indies ships. Beaches were patrolled with wild dogs. From 1576 onward informers were paid one-third of the value of any unregistered treasure recovered. Every ship returning from the Indies was also closely inspected by royal officials of the House of Trade. Notwithstanding these precautions, about 20% of the gold and silver mined in the New World was smuggled into Spain or other European nations in return for contraband goods that had been sold in the Indies by foreigners.

Gold, more valuable than silver, was naturally the choice item to smuggle into Spain, but great amounts of silver, both specie and bullion, also were smuggled, and smugglers never seemed to tire of devising new methods to avoid detection. On one occasion a royal official became suspicious of a ship's painted anchor. He had it scraped and discovered it to be made of solid gold. The most common method used, however, was smuggling gold and silver in bales, boxes or chests of unimportant commodities like sugar, molasses or tobacco since it was almost impossible for royal officials to open every container on board.

In some cases unregistered treasure on board ships exceeded that registered. A good example was in 1555, when a ship returning from New Spain wrecked on the southern coast of Spain between Cadiz and Gibraltar. Divers salvaging the wreck recovered more than 500,000 pesos, of which less than 150,000 were registered. All the officers aboard that ship were condemned to serve as galley slaves for ten years.

Manila Galleons

Of all the Spanish ships that traversed the seas, the most magnificent were the fabled Manila Galleons, the first of which crossed the Pacific in 1565 when Philip II was king of all Spain and his arch enemy Elizabeth Tudor was queen of England. Hernando Cortez, conqueror of Mexico, had been dead but 18 years. That same year Pedro Menendez de Avilas laid the foundations of St. Augustine in Florida.

The last Manilla Galleon sailed in 1815, five years after Miguel Hidalgo had begun the revolt against Spain that was to create the Republic of Mexico. The United States had been a nation for 40 years and Andrew Jackson had just won the battle of New Orleans with the help of the French pirate Jean Lafitte.

For two and a half centuries the Manila Galleons annually made the long and lonely voyage between Manila in the Philippines and Acapulco in Mexico. No other line of ships has ever endured so long. No other regular navigation has been so trying and dangerous as this, for in that 250 years the sea claimed dozens of ships and thousands of men and billions of pesos in treasure. As the richest ships in all the oceans, the Manila Galleons were the most coveted prize of pirate and privateer alike. The English took four of them...*Santa Ana* in 1587, *Encarnacion* in 1709, *Covadonga* in 1743 and *Santissima Trinidad*, largest ship of her time, in 1762.

In Spanish America, the Manila Galleons were known as China Ships that brought cargoes of silks, spices and other precious merchandise from the East. In the Orient they were the Silver Argosies, laden with Mexican and Peruvian pesos that were to become the standard of value along the coasts of Asia. They furnished the first motive for exploration of California's coast. They served as the link that bound the Philippines and Moluccas to Spain. It was their comings and goings that gave some substance of reality to the Spanish dream of an empire in the Pacific.

The Manila Galleons were the largest vessels of any nation during the Colonial period. In the 16th century they averaged about 700 tons; in the 17th the average was 1,500 tons; and in the 18th, between 1,700 and 2,500 tons. Three or four of these ships sailed annually in each direction between Manila and Acapulco.

The voyage from Acapulco to Manila was usually pleasant enough, perhaps an occasional storm unsettling the routine sailings which lasted from eight to ten weeks with a stop for refreshments in Guam or one of the other Mariana Islands. On the other hand, the voyage from Manila to Acapulco was known as the most treacherous navigation in the world. Because winds in the Philippine latitudes are from the east, the Manila Galleons had to beat their way as far north as Japan and sometimes even the Aleutian Islands before reaching the belt of westerly winds to carry them across the Pacific. They made landfall on the coast of California and worked their way down to Acapulco where their valuable cargoes were unloaded.

For those who survived, this perilous voyage took from four to eight months, depending on luck. Of the 300 to 600 persons, including crewmen, who sailed on each voyage, an average of from 100 to 150 perished en route from exposure, starvation, thirst, scurvy or epidemics. On one of two Manila Galleons sailing jointly in 1657, all 450 persons aboard succumbed to a smallpox epidemic. About half the 400 aboard the other galleon also died.

Despite the great risks involved in this trans-Pacific navigation, financial gain to those involved in the Manila Galleons trade and to the Royal Crown seemed worth the hardships. Cargoes carried from Acapulco to Manila were basically the same as those carried on the *flotas* between Spain and the Indies ports, except that gold and silver specie and bullion from the mines of Peru and Mexico were also carried on these galleons to pay for cargo sent to Manila. An average of 3 to 5 million pesos were sent to Manila annually, and in 1597 the fantastic amount of 12 million pesos reached the Asian port.

Cargoes plying the route from Manila to Acapulco were of a more exotic and diversified nature. The main item was silk of varied types from China and Japan, but crepes, velvets, gauzes, taffetas and damasks were also included. Packed in chests were silks in every stage of manufacture, from lengths of raw material to finished apparel...robes, kimonos, skirts and stockings. Finely embroidered Chinese religious vestments, silken tapestries and bed coverings were also shipped. Fine cottons from the Mogul Empire of India comprised a good part of the cargoes during the latter part of the trade, along

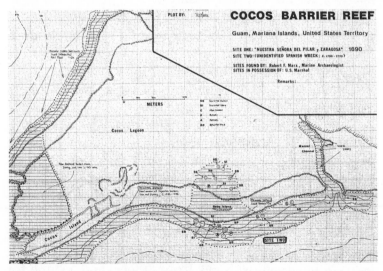

Portion of a plot chart indicates the remains of a Manila Galleon that was lost in 1690 off the island of Guam in the Pacific Ocean and later discovered by the author.

with Persian carpets imported into the Philippines through India.

The Manila Galleons also carried such exquisite jewelry as pendants, earrings, bracelets and rings. There were gem-studded sword hilts, rugs, fans, combs and a wide range of precious spices and drugs (including rhubarb, much sought after in Europe). The ships carried a great deal of beautiful Chinese porcelain, figurines made of jade and ivory, objects carved of ivory and sandalwood, gold bells, copper cuspidors and exquisite and unusual devotional pieces such as crucifixes, reliquaries, rosaries and religious sculptures in wood, ivory and gold, crafted in the Orient for Roman Catholics. From Saudi Arabia came large amounts of pearls recovered from the Indian Ocean, sent to Manila for shipment to Spain. India, the world's largest producer of precious gem stones during the Colonial period, provided vast amounts of diamonds, emeralds, rubies, sapphires and other precious stones to the island capital where they were loaded on creaking galleons for the Pacific crossing.

Considerable gold in the form of bullion and manufactured articles was exported to Mexico and Spain. Although there was a legal ban on the importation of jewelry from the Orient, in a large consignment confiscated at Acapulco in 1767 officials found hundreds of rings, many set with diamonds and rubies, bracelets, pendants, earrings, necklaces and a number of gold religious articles, including a cross set with eight diamonds. On the same occasion officials seized "a golden bird from China," some jewel-studded sword hilts, and several alligator teeth capped with gold. Many unset or uncut gems were also carried to Mexico by the Manila Galleons. Henry Hawkes, an English merchant who spent five years in Mexico in the 16th century wrote, "There was a mariner that brought a pearl as big as a dove's egg from thence, and a stone for which the Viceroy would have given 3000 duckets."

When the richly laden Manila Galleons reached

Acapulco, merchants arrived from as far away as Spain, and a fair was held at which the bulk of the goods were sold. Peruvian merchants would carry their newly acquired merchandise to Panama City and sail home on the ships of the *Armada of the South Seas*. Mexican merchants carried their goods over the mountains on mules. Agents who represented the merchants in far off Seville also used mules and traveled to Veracruz to board the New Spain *flota* back to Spain.

Over the centuries a total of 79 Manila Galleons were lost...51 in the Philippines, most around the Straits of Saint Bernardino. The majority foundered after striking treacherous reef. Others fell victim to typhoons and enemy attack. Eight were lost somewhere on the high seas, three were wrecked on the hostile shores of Japan. Eleven were lost in the Mariana Islands, five were lost on the west coast of North America, while one was lost while at anchor in Acapulco. Unlike so many of the treasure galleons lost in the New World, the majority of these Manila Galleons went down in deep water, beyond the diving depths of contemporary divers.

Until recently none had ever been found or salvaged. Of the five Manila Galleons lost off the west coast of America we know the exact location of only one of them; the *San Agustine*, lost in 1595 off Drake's Bay, CA, which I located a few years ago. Over the years storms have caused many artifacts including Ming dynasty porcelain shards to be cast upon the nearby beaches and through historical research I was able to pinpoint this galleon within a few hundred yards.

Jade carriage, fully 400 years *older* than the wreckage of a Manila galleon in the Mariana Islands from which it was recovered intact, is valued in excess of $20 million.

Other Nations' Ships

Throughout the 16th century the waters of the New World were a virtual "Spanish Lake." Almost all the ships on that lake were Spanish-built, had Spanish crews and carried cargoes and treasures between Spain and the Spanish-American colonies. Ships of other European nations made occasional voyages to the New World, many of them privateering sorties aimed at taking Spanish prizes. The Portuguese were the one exception. Soon after the founding of the early Spanish settlements, the Portuguese were granted exclusive permission by the Spanish Crown to carry limited numbers of African Negroes to be sold in the New World ports as slaves. They were in especially great demand in areas where the indigenous population was decimated, either massacred by the conquistadors or by diseases of the Spaniards.

During the period 1525-1550 an average of six to eight Portuguese slave ships a year visited ports in the New World, sometimes making additional profits by offering contraband European products to the Spanish colonists at prices far below those paid to Seville monopolists. With the acceleration in mining activity after the mid-16th century, the number of Portuguese slave ships increased to as many as 40 to 50 annually. This continued until 1640, when Portugal revolted against the Spanish Crown and even-

Author's daughter Hilary with anchor from wreck of Manila galleon recovered off Monterey, CA, the only known bronze anchor recovered in this hemisphere.

tually won total independence. The Dutch, later the English, took over the lucrative trade of supplying Spanish colonies with a steady supply of African slaves.

The first interlopers in the waters of the New World, which had been divided by the Pope between Spain (with the lion's share and Portugal (which settled for Brazil) were French pirates and privateers, who appeared during the third decade of the 16th century. Throughout the century the French made sporadic voyages to the New World, generally to attack Spanish settlements and shipping. They also made abortive attempts to establish settlements on the coast of Florida.

The English, on the other hand, initiated their voyages with the intent of peaceful trade with Spanish colonists such as those made by John Hawkins and others. The Spaniards had such complete mastery over their colonies, however, that these voyages were rarely profitable. Many years passed before the English realized that the only way to make any profit in the New World was to take what they wanted by force. During the last three decades, Francis Drake and other famous English privateers sailed to the West Indies and to other Spanish New World colonies solely to wage war on the Spaniards and accumulate plunder. Even many of these voyages were profitless, as the Spaniards were not always easy to overcome.

Dutch interest was sparked in the last decades of the 16th century, not because of greed for plunder or contraband trade but because of their great need for salt. The main industry of the Netherlands was fishing, which required prodigious amounts of salt for processing catches. Until 1580 when Portugal was annexed to Spain and discouraged trade with the Netherlands, the Dutch obtained salt from the great salt pans on the southern coast of Portugal. Spain had been at war for over 20 years with the Netherlands, and the lack of salt threatened to topple the Dutch economy. Then they discovered that vast deposits of salt available in the New World, specifically on several of the Bahama Islands, St. Martins Island and at Punta de Araya on the coast of Venezuela.

As early as 1582 there were as many as 150 Dutch ships making voyages to the Caribbean for salt. By 1600 this number increased to over 200 ships annually (actually more ships than were sailing from Spain to the New World at this time), and in the year 1616 a total of 279 Dutch ships made the voyage over and back, most of them obtaining the salt from Punta de Araya, where they had constructed permanent warehouses to store surplus salt. They continued extracting vast amounts of salt from the Caribbean until near the 17th century's close when large salt mines were discovered in Germany and elsewhere in Europe.

English Settlements

Early in the 17th century, the Elizabethan adventurer Sir Walter Raleigh founded several small English settlements near the Orinoco River on the northeastern coast of South America. Dutch and French soon followed with settlements in the same general area, but none of them amounted to much until later in the century, when the settlements were put on a firmer footing (some are still held today). Most of the ships returning from these outposts to Europe sailed directly home not up through the Bahama Channel except when a captain might take a shot at that route in hopes of capturing a small Spanish ship.

A new era in the maritime history of the New World dawned with the second quarter of the 17th century. Within a few decades the "Spanish Lake" no longer lived up to its name. English, French and Dutch ceased to be interlopers and established themselves as permanent settlers. The English settled the Island of St. Christopher (St. Kitts) in 1624, and the following year a large group of French settlers joined them. To avoid friction between the colonists, the island was divided. In 1627 the first English colonists reached Barbados, and in 628 other Englishmen settled on Nevis Island and Providencia (called Santa Catalina by the Spaniards) off the coast of Nicaragua.

Jamaica soon became England's most profitable over-seas possession...first, through privateering; then, illegal commerce with the Spanish colonies; eventually, through agriculture, mainly sugar and its by-products. The French soon followed the English capture of Jamaica with their own island of Hispañiola, the eastern half of which was finally ceded to Spain in 1697.

Thus, throughout the 17th century--particularly its second half--there were great numbers of European ships plying Caribbean waters and returning through the Bahama Channel. Most sailed singly or in small groups and carried cotton, tobacco, indigo, spices, lumber and rum, as well as gold, silver and whatever else they obtained from the Spaniards through plunder or illegal trade. Toward the end of the century the English first organized merchant fleets to be convoyed by warships. The usual practice was for the convoy to split when reaching the Caribbean with merchant ships sailing to various islands to unload goods and take on homeward-bound cargoes.

All of the ships would then sail to Kingston, Jamaica, and back to England in a large convoy, passing through the Bahama Channel. As early as 1697 one of these fleets numbered 116 merchantmen and six warships. In 1758 a fleet leaving Jamaica numbered 150 ships, and this was only one of the two fleets that sailed from there that year. As early as 1723 there were three fleets sailing from England to the Caribbean...one to Barbados and two to Jamaica, totaling over 425 ships for that year.

Not all sailed to England; many went to various ports in the American colonies. These English colonies were also sending substantial numbers of merchant ships to the Caribbean, supplying the English islands with items they could not get from the Mother Country or which they could supply at cheaper prices, such as a wide variety of foodstuffs and various types of lumber. As years passed and populations grew, maritime traffic also increased. In 1750 more than 500 ships from other Caribbean islands,

Europe, Africa, North America and the Spanish colonies entered the port of Kingston alone.

The Dutch colonies were small in comparison with the English, and they did not use convoys. Although the French colonies were not as large as those of the English, they were also soon using a convoy system. The majority of their homeward-bound traffic did not pass through the Bahama Channel. French ships from the Lesser Antilles would gather in one of the several Hispañiola ports and then sail through what was known as the "Windward Passage," passing to the east of Great and Little Inagua and Mayaguaña islands, to the west of Caicos Island out into the Atlantic Ocean. The largest French merchant fleet to leave Hispañiola sailed in 1782 and totaled 190 ships.

Not all the shipping of these nations was mercantile...throughout the 17th and 18th centuries warships escorted the merchant fleets. Since European powers seemed always to be at odds with one another, they were engaged in frequent attacks on each other's shipping and settlements. When these nations were at war with the Spaniards, warships were also utilized in attempts to capture returning Spanish *flotas*. Although at least 50 attempts were made by the English, French and Dutch between 1550 and 1750 to capture an entire *flota*, only one was taken. In 1628 a Dutch West Indies Company fleet under the brilliant command of Peit Heyn captured all 24 ships of the New Spain Flota commanded by Captain-General Juan de Benevides y Bazin and won a booty of over 14 million pesos.

Smaller vessels also sailed the waters of the Caribbean and passed through the Bahama Channel. There were packet boats that brought news from and took news back to the Mother Countries; and there were fishing vessels of various kinds, coastal and inter-island traders, salvage boats and numerous pirate and privateering vessels (about which so much has been written).

As the New World colonies grew rapidly in population,

shipping between Europe and the Western Hemisphere increased. In 1785 a total of 1,347 European ships sailed to the Western Hemisphere and to Europe. With a greater number of ships plying the seas, the number of losses increased. Between 1700 and 1850 more than 1,500 non-Spanish ships were lost just in the Bahamas alone. During this same period Florida accounted for another 350. Bermuda, tiny in comparison with Florida, managed to become the final resting place of yet another 165 ships. The dreaded reefs of Anegada in the British Virgin Islands snared nearly 100 European vessels, plus an almost equal number of American ships. These were by no means anywhere as rich as Spanish galleons, but almost every one of them carried some coinage and other valuables.

First European Settlers

When the first European settlers arrived along the present Atlantic seaboard in the early 17th century, they were faced with forest...trackless except for a few Indian trails which were difficult to use. Thus, throughout the 17th and 18th centuries sea lanes were the highways that carried an increasing volume of traffic. Like trucks and buses of today, the early vessels transported people from place to place, brought in food supplies and carried goods for sale. This was accomplished primarily by European ships during the 17th century followed by a growing number of American vessels. Most early American ships were less than 100 tons and rarely carried cannon.

Around 1700 the need for sugar and rum in the American colonies and for food and lumber in the West Indies led to the creation of a colonial merchant fleet...and, for trade not just with the West Indies but with England and other European countries as well. By 1750 no fewer than 500 American-built ships were plying the high seas, with a few used by pirates and privateers. The best areas for locating colonial shipwrecks of this period are around Charleston, Savannah, Philadelphia, New York and all along the coast of New England. Early in 1728 over 50 shipwrecks occurred off South Carolina, mostly around Charleston Harbor. In September of that same year a hurricane struck, sinking 20 large ships around Charleston. So many Colonial period American ships wrecked that it is amazing more haven't been located.

The American Revolution further increased the demand for large ships. Building them soon became the major occupation of New England. During the Revolution, more than 500 ships were lost along the east coast between Maine and Florida. Although a large number were sunk during sea battles, a greater number were lost to bad weather, faulty navigation and deliberate destruction to prevent them from falling into enemy hands. Although only a few were laden with significant amounts of treasure, they all carried countless artifacts of great historical and monetary value by today's standards.

Whether large warships or smaller merchantmen, all these ships carried weapons (cannon, swords, muskets, pistols and shot), tools of many varieties, cooking and eating utensils, ship's fittings and hardware, anchors, navigational equipment and glass bottles. Many personal items can also be found on them, including clay smoking pipes, snuff boxes, buttons, boxes, buttons, rings and some coinage. Even the ballast stones are valuable. One diver has made over $20,000 selling stone from a British warship, discovered off Savannah, for five dollars apiece. Another diver located an American privateering vessel off Rhode Island and made over twice that amount just by selling brass spikes and sheathing tacks taken from the wooden remains of the wreck.

Not all ships lost during the Revolutionary War were American. The British lost three major warships in the Battle of Sullivan's Island during their attack on Charleston on June 28, 1776, when the Americans proved victorious. Another British ship. the *Aeolus*, loaded with war materials, was set afire and sunk by the British.

The richest British ship lost during this war was the

payship *HMS Hussar*, lost at Hell's Gate in New York's East River on September 13, 1780. She was carrying a fortune in gold coins, and the British made several salvage attempts but swift river currents prevented any recovery. Several months later another British warship, the *Lexington*, also reportedly carrying a great amount of gold and silver specie, sank within a mile of the *Hussar*.

A year earlier the Americans had lost a very rich ship, the *Defense*, which was carrying a cargo of gold and silver coinage valued at $200,000, but worth ten to twenty times that amount today. This treasure was a loan from the government of South Carolina to the newly formed American government to be used to pay Washington's troops. Unfortunately, she hit rocks off Fisher's Island in Long Island Sound and was totally lost.

Not all the Revolutionary wrecks occurred at sea. During a battle in Lake Champlain during October 1776, the Americans under command of Benedict Arnold suffered badly and were forced to scuttle five of their warships. To date four of these have been located and one of them is presently displayed in the Smithsonian Institution in Washington. Last summer a side-scan sonar search for the last one, the *Providence*, was undertaken but failed to discover her remains.

The Federal Government has declared three Revolutionary War shipwreck sites off limits to divers and placed them on the National Register of Historical Places. A 30-acre area on the Penobscot River in Maine where 15 to 25 ships were lost in 1779; the privateer brigantine *Defense* also lost in 1779 in Stockton Springs Harbor, ME; and a four-mile stretch of the York river in Virginia where all of the British warships of Admiral Cornwallis were lost in 1781. Only 22 shipwreck sites have been included on this list, two of which are Spanish galleons...the 1733 *San Jose*, lost off Plantation Key in the Florida Keys, and the *El Nuevo Constante*, lost in 1766 off Louisiana.

The largest protected area is Key Biscayne Park, con-

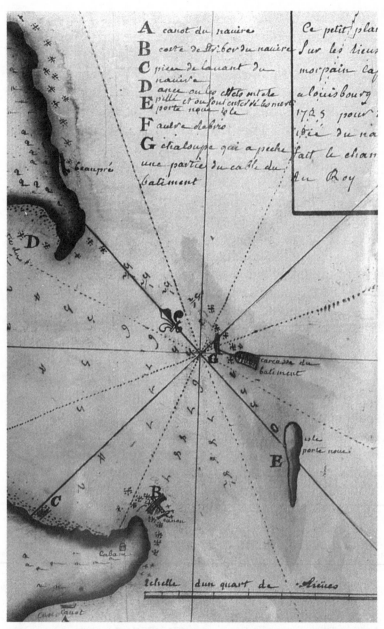

This chart shows the exact position of the French treasure ship *Chameau*, which was lost in the Atlantic Ocean in 1725 off Cape Breton, Nova Scotia, Canada.

sisting of 22,640 acres located near Miami. There are 43 known shipwrecks dating from the 18th to 20th centuries in the park. One of the protected sites is that of the *H. L. Hunley*, a hand-powered, nine-man Civil War submarine built in 1862. It was the first submarine to sink a warship, the Federal *Housatonic* in 1864. It is unusual to find it on the protected list since it has not been discovered to date.

During the Civil War over 1,000 vessels were lost, which offer interesting targets for both treasure hunters and sports divers. Shortly after Confederate artillery reduced Fort Sumter to ruin in April 1861 and her Yankee garrison was forced to surrender, President Lincoln ordered a naval blockade of all southern ports and the exciting era of the famous blockade runners began. Blockade-running became a big business in the South and at least 16,000 voyages were made by these fast and elusive ships. They served the South's lifeline by carrying cotton and other agricultural products to Europe and returning with war materials, manufactured goods and luxuries.

Some of these metal ships were 275 feet long and tripled-stacked, and carried over one thousand tons of cargo. Their remains lie scattered all along the eastern seaboard with the largest number near the shores of Georgia, South and North Carolina and Virginia. More than 50 ships of this period were also lost in Bermuda and the Bahamas. During the past 30 years more than 50 of the blockade runners and warships from this era have been located, the majority by fishermen snagging into them with nets. Some of those lost were removed from the sea floor when they constituted a danger to navigation, and others have been obliterated by modern dredging operations.

Many Civil War ships were lost in rivers and have been found in a remarkable state of preservation. One such wreck is the *Maple Leaf*, resting on the bottom of the St. Johns River near Mandarin, FL. This Union ship sank rapidly after running into a mine, carrying over 400 tons of cargo, mainly the personal belongings of thousands of

Union troops. A number of historians are trying to get this shipwreck listed on the National Register of Historical Places. The wreck was discovered several years ago by Keith Holland, a Jacksonville dentist who is taking great pains to salvage it properly. He and his volunteer divers have already recovered 1,300 pounds of artifacts, and he seeks government funding to continue this project.

The West Coast has its share of shipwrecks as well, even though little of contemporary interest happened along this area prior to the California Gold Rush in the middle of the last century. Long before the Christian era, however, shipwrecks occurred along the West Coast. Asiatic vessels are known to have been flung upon these shores by prevailing trade winds and the Japanese currents. Many Chinese and Japanese artifacts have been discovered by archaeological excavations in California and Oregon, some dating back to 2000 B.C. These artifacts are believed to have reached American shores on Asiatic ships which wrecked after long ocean crossings. Several years ago two of California's pioneer divers, Bob and Bill Meistrell, found four primitive stone anchors near Palos Verdes. Various experts have identified them as a type used in Japan between 1,000 B.C. and 1,000 A.D.

Remains of numerous ancient ships have been found over the years all along the Pacific shore from Vancouver to San Diego. Although described in scanty documents as "ancient," no knowledgeable person examined them, and their vestiges have long since disappeared. Four of the five Manila Galleons lost in California waters have not been found. Despite rumors that one was found in the Channel Islands, nothing to substantiate these claims has been offered. The Channel Islands are under the control of the National Park Service and the 90 known shipwrecks in these waters can only be explored and not salvaged.

One of the best preserved wrecks in this area is the *Winfield Scott,* lost in 1853 on Anacapa Island with a considerable amount of gold. I found my first gold coins on her in 1950, long before she became a ward of the Park Service. Two years ago the Park Service pulled off a sting operation by having two rangers clandestinely tag along on a diving charter boat. Upon returning to port they promptly arrested two of the divers who had recovered a few bronze spikes from the wreck. After costly litigation, the divers paid severe fines. Around the same time that this event was making the news, I had an unpleasant experience with the Park Service myself up in Drake's Bay. The *San Francisco Chronicle* published a photograph of me holding a ballast rock I had found on the beach. (And, after the photograph was taken, said rock was deposited right where I had found it.) After the photograph appeared, the Parks Service's top ship historian James Delgado notified the journalist who had taken my photograph that I would be arrested the next time I set foot in Point Reyes National Seashore. Delgado had to recant his words and apologize. The unfortunate moral of the story is that bureaucrats, frustrated because they are desk-bound, make life miserable for anyone who might take any glory away from them.

Wreck of the Rio

After the Manila Galleon *San Agustin*, California's best known shipwreck is the *Rio De Janeiro*. In 1901 she struck a rock and sank within minutes while attempting to enter San Francisco harbor in the fog. The amount of gold the *Rio* carried seems to double every time another article appears in the press. Even discounting gross exaggeration, she was indeed carrying a large amount of gold. There have been numerous attempts to locate her remains. During the past two decades especially, hardly a year passes without an announcement that she has been found.

It now appears that someone actually has located her remains in a spot that discourages even the hardiest salvors...right under the Golden Gate Bridge in about 300 feet of water where the tide runs over eight knots. One ROV (remote-operated vehicle) has been lost already in

56

the fierce current, but the booty hidden in *Rio's* ghostly remains is such that future attempts will probably not be deterred. The DEA has an interest in this wreck because she was carrying over a ton of opium when she went down.

California Wreck Divers, a club based in the Los Angeles area, specialize in exploring 19th and 20th-century shipwrecks. Members concentrate on recovering brass and copper objects such as portholes and instruments from the wheelhouses of shipwrecks. Most wreck diving by sports divers is done on the semi-modern and modern shipwrecks which offer good photographic possibilities and the chance of finding a souvenir or two. Such diving in metal-hulled vessels is not without peril. Every year some divers die or are injured when they run out of air, are trapped or meet with countless other types of accidents. Submarine diving is another recent craze among sports divers, even though such diving is strictly illegal. Submarines of all nationalities are protected by the International War Graves Protection Act and are off limits to all divers. Those who would ignore this law need to consider that some German submarines were reported to have used mercury as ballast and many German and Japanese submarines scuttled by their crews were booby-trapped before they were abandoned.

The Great Lakes are littered with shipwrecks, more than 5,000 of them...many containing treasures that make them worth searching for by sports divers as well as commercial salvors. The majority are of recent vintage compared with shipwrecks elsewhere in this hemisphere. Although a small number of vessels were plying the Great Lakes by the end of the 17th century to supply the needs of early settlers and to transport products of forest and field, water-borne commerce really didn't open up until the beginning of the 19th century. Lake traffic was stimulated by the discovery of iron ore in Minnesota, and locks were constructed to connect the lakes to one another and to the St. Lawrence River in 1855. Rapid expansion westward made Chicago the railhead for settlers headed for the frontier. With no connecting train lines from the East settlers, supplies, locomotives and rolling stock were transported on the Great Lakes to Chicago.

During this great push westward, many British, French and American warships were lost in these lakes. The first warship built for Great Lakes duty was the British *Halifax* in 1756. Several years later it sank in Lake Ontario. During the War of 1812 many British and Americans ships were lost in the Great Lakes. The best known are the American two-masted schooners the *Hamilton* and the *Scourge*, recently featured in *National Geographic*. First discovered in 1973 by treasure hunters using side-scan sonar and a magnetometer, the ships were identified through closed-circuit television. The two wrecks lying 275 feet deep have been explored by several ultra-sophisticated ROVs and appear remarkably well preserved. Plans are being made to raise them for preservation and permanent exhibit.

Fresh water and the absence of shipworms and other species of wood-boring creatures leave most of the Great Lakes shipwrecks relatively intact, enabling them to be located much easier than those lost in the ocean. Since they present a large target on the lake bottoms, side scan sonar can find most of them without too much difficulty. A less expensive and sometimes more efficient method is to drag a long steel cable between two vessels and snag the wrecks. The one big disadvantage of locating and salvaging wrecks in these lakes, with the exception of Lake Erie, is the great depth of many of the wrecks. Lake Huron reaches a depth of 750 feet; Lake Michigan, 923 feet; Lake Superior, 1,290 feet; and Lake Ontario, 778 feet. On the other hand Lake Erie's greatest depth is only 210 feet, easily reached by qualified scuba divers. Another disadvantage is that underwater visibility is quite poor in most of the lakes, and the chilly water is far from enjoyable. I prefer the Caribbean myself!

One of the richest wrecks in the Great Lakes is also the

oldest. In 1679 the French frigate *Griffin*, commanded by Captain Robert La Salle, carrying a considerable amount of gold specie, struck on Birch Island Reef in Lake Huron. Almost equally as rich was another French frigate named *Le Jean Florin*, that carried more than six chests of gold coins when it sank during a storm about 15 miles east of Erie, PA, in Lake Erie. Lake Ontario has its own French treasure wreck as well...*Le Blanc Henri*, wrecked in 1764 on Wold Island Spit near Kingston, Ont., with a small fortune in silver and gold bullion.

Lake Superior's richest wreck was the American yacht *Gunilda*, lost in 1911 after striking some rocks and sinking in 200 feet of water off Rossport. Because the safe of the *Gunilda* reportedly contained over half a million dollars in jewels, she has been a much sought after target in recent years. Lake Michigan's richest wreck may be the steamer *Chicora*, which sank in 1895 near South Manitou Island, carrying $85,000 in gold and silver specie in her safe, worth considerably more today, of course, and 150 barrels of whisky. Hundred-year old whisky is hard to find today...if the barrels have survived, the whisky might be worth its weight in gold.

Coursing through the heartland of America, the vast Mississippi River captures the imagination, evoking images of paddlewheel steamers, riverboat gamblers, fog-shrouded duelists and Tom Sawyer and Huck Finn. It has served as a vital artery of transport and commerce throughout history and is the theme of some of the richest American literature and folklore. Although we know that more than 6,000 steamboats were built for use on the Mississippi between 1820 and 1880 alone, no estimate exists of how many were lost and the amount of treasure that lies in their hulks. When the river fell to record low levels during the summer of 1988, remains of more than 50 vessels were spotted on dry river banks and sand bars. Other rivers have also claimed large numbers of ships over the years, some no doubt lost in later years to dredging operations and construction. These await discovery by divers who have mastered the *braille* system of finding things in murky water, which I learned during my four-year excavation of the sunken city of Port Royal in Jamaica. If you have a choice, stick to clear ocean waters which are not only much safer but more enjoyable to dive in.

If you insist on diving in rivers for something of interest and value, then I suggest those in Florida. Millions of years ago when all of Florida was covered by sea, the area was the cruising ground for the *carcaradon megaladon*, the Great Shark, a specie that reached over 100 feet in length. His distant relative is the Great White Shark, a creature that divers fear meeting in the sea. Florida's rivers contain millions of the teeth of these monstrous and extinct sharks. Some of the fossilized teeth exceed six inches in length and can net the finder a hefty sum if the right buyer is found.

After the prehistoric seas lowered, Florida was the home of many exotic animals (now extinct) such as giant mammoths and mastadons, 400-pound beavers, camels, tapirs, saber tooth tigers and others. Their bones, teeth and claws can be found in great abundance. Human remains and artifacts can also be found in rivers, streams and sinkholes of Florida, but these artifacts must be left for archaeologists to study. State archaeologists are grateful to amateurs who notify them of any finds and will work with them to everyone's benefit. Divers in America's Western states also have clear, but colder, rivers in which to search for placer gold deposits...a subject well covered in other books from Ram Publishing Co.

Diver at the bottom of the Caribbean Sea inspects the keel of a French ship that was wrecked off the island of Guadeloupe.

Divers and Salvors

No one knows who the first divers were nor can we be sure what enticed them into the water...although it was probably the lure of mollusks, crustaceans or some other food. We know that men were diving as early as 4500 B.C. in Mesopotamia where archaeologists have unearthed shells that must have come from the sea floor. A gap in the history of diving of more than a thousand years follows until around 3200 B.C in Egypt, where a vast number of carved mother-of-pearl ornaments have been unearthed at archaeological sites from the Theban 6th Dynasty, indicating that diving was widespread at that time.

Early Greek sponge divers apparently were the first to explore the depths of the sea systematically and bring back sponges...references to sponges can be found in both the *Iliad* and the *Odyssey*. Greek divers also brought back man's first knowledge of the kingdom under the sea, some of which has been distorted by contemporary writers. The divers were considered the most courageous men of their time, far more than the warriors who showed bravery in battle. "'No ordeal is more terrible than that of the sponge divers and no labor is more arduous for men," said the Greek poet Oppian in the 2nd century A.D. In a gripping

Jennifer Marx holds a gold scabbard tip, next to a British cannon on a 1755 shipwreck in the Bahamas. Below are Chinese Ming porcelain jars and a figurine found by the author on a 15th-century wreck in the China Sea.

63

description of the sufferings of the sponge divers of his day he wrote:

"The first diver to go down attaches a cord to his middle. He also takes oil into his mouth, puts oil into his auditory canals, soaks sponges in oil and places them over his ears. He has only two tools and these he holds one in each hand: a very sharp curved knife something like a bill-hook and a heavy stone. Taking a deep breath of the air which he is about to leave, he then dives. Thanks to the weight of the heavy stone, he plummets down rapidly. Despite the fact that his ears are full of oil and covered by oil-soaked sponges, they begin to pain him. At the same time his temples, his eyes and his chest are taken as though in a liquid vise.

"He hits the bottom rather than lands on it. Then he spits out a little of the oil he has in his mouth and this rises to the surface, spreading out and calming the surface agitation and lighting up the waters as a torch lights up the darkness and allows man to see in the middle of the night. He then makes for the rocks and discovers the sponges he is seeking. They grow on the underwater rocks and seem to be part of the submerged reefs. One might think they were animated with the breath of life. Without losing a moment, he darts at the sponges, vigorously wielding his knife, which is something like a sickle.

"As soon as he has severed the sponge from the rock, he pulls the cord to let his companions above know that he must now be pulled to the surface as quickly as possible. Once cut away from the rock, the sponge bleeds a nauseating liquid which spreads around the diver and is sometimes sufficient to kill him, so offensive is the smell to the nostrils of man. That is the reason why the diver is eager to depart, and now his companions draw him up to the surface as rapidly as possible. The diver is now out of the water once again, but it is impossible to look at him without sympathy. The joy of seeing him once again is mingled with sorrow at observing how exhausted and at the end of his strength he seems, so much have fear, fatigue and suffering affected his vitality. Sometimes his efforts end miserably and cruelly.

"Once he has plunged into the waves, the unfortunate often does not return. He has encountered some hidden monster of the deep and lost his life. Desperately at first he pulls the rope in order to be hoisted to safety, but the monster seizes him and then a horrible tug of war takes place. The monster holds him from below and his friends pull him from above, disputing the half-devoured corpse of the unfortunate diver between them. Then with heavy hearts his companions hasten away from the ill-fated area, abandoning a hopeless undertaking. In tears around the remains of their dead comrade, they carry him back to shore."

The earliest account of using divers to hunt for sunken treasure was written by Herodotus, a Greek historian writing in the mid-5th century B.C. Some 50 years earlier, a Greek diver named Scyllias and his daughter Cyane had been employed by Xerxes, king of Persia, to recover an immense treasure from some Persian galleys sunk during a battle with the Greek fleet. They recovered the treasure, but Xerxes refused to give them the promised reward. Instead, he kept them aboard his galley, no doubt for other diving jobs. Seething at this treachery, Scyllias and Cyane jumped overboard during a storm and cut the anchor cables of the Persian ships, causing several to collide.

As soon as order had been restored, the Persians pursued Scyllias and Cyane, but they escaped by swimming underwater to Artemisium, about nine miles away. Herodotus had some doubts about those nine miles. Such a feat was unheard of then. But later historians were impressed. They think Scyllias and Cyane may have used hollow reeds to breathe air from the surface...the forerunner of the snorkel. Such a device was first mentioned by Pliny the Elder, a Roman scholar and naturalist of the 1st century A.D., but may well have been used earlier. Diving for sunken treasure had become so common among the Greeks of the 3rd century B.C. that special laws were passed regulating the division of the finds. A diver who recovered treasure in two cubits of water (about one and a half feet) or less was entitled to a tenth of its value; treasure recovered between two and eight cubits entitled him to a third; and treasure recovered at depths of more than eight cubits entitled the diver to half of its value. The part of the treasure not given to the diver was the property of its original owner; or if the owner was dead or couldn't be found, the treasure became the property of the ruler from whose waters it was recovered.

In 169 B.C., during Rome's wars against the Greeks, Perseus, the last king of Macedonia, was defeated at the battle of Pydna. Perseus fled to Pella where he ordered all of his treasures cast into the deeps of Lake Lydias. When the Romans were no longer pursuing him, he had skilled divers raise them again. To make sure no one would be left to tell of his great panic, Perseus had the divers put to death. All of the other witnesses suffered a similar fate but not even such ruthless measures kept word from leaking out.

Nearly as famous as the free divers of the Mediterranean were the pearl divers of the Caribbean. They remained free divers long after the introduction of modern diving equipment. After scuba had made free diving virtually obsolete, as recently as the 1940s they were still plying the centuries-old trade of their ancestors. Aborigines in the New World were diving well before Columbus, and like their Mediterranean counterparts they found the sea floor an abundant source of food.

Diving was a basic hunting technique for North American Indians. Swimming underwater and breathing through reeds, they could sneak up on unwary game and capture it with nets, spears or even bare hands. Like the ancient Greeks, the Mayans of Mexico venerated a diving god. A fresco of their deity may be seen today in the

Temple of the Diving God at the archaeological site of Tulum on the Caribbean coast of Yucatan. A Peruvian pot depicting a diver illustrates diving very early in the history of the New World. When the Spanish explorers first reached Tierra del Fuego on the southernmost tip of South America, they found expert women divers among the Yahgan Indians. The women would descend to great depths in the 42° waters to gather clams, crabs and other seafood.

Arrival of Columbus

Diving for pearls didn't become a major occupation until the arrival of the white man although it had been done on a small scale in the Caribbean by the Lucayan, Carib and Arawak tribes. During Columbus' third voyage to the New World in 1498, his fleet anchored one day at the island of Cubagua, off the coast of Venezuela, to obtain fresh water and fruit. Some of his men went ashore where they noticed a Carib Indian woman wearing a necklace made of pearls. They learned that the natives of Cubagua possessed great quantities of exquisite pearls found in the waters all around the island. Columbus sent Indian divers in search of oysters which they opened to find a sufficient quantity of lustrous pearls to confirm what his men had been told by the Indians.

When he returned to Spain, Columbus reported to the king who ordered the establishment of a pearl fishery on Cubagua. During the next few years, large oyster beds were found near Cubagua and especially on Margarita Island which eventually became the center of the Caribbean pearl industry, a position it still holds today. So Columbus, already assured of a place in history, had another discovery to his credit.

Over the centuries, Caribbean pearl fisheries furnished Spain with a source of wealth surpassed only by the gold and silver that Spaniards took from the New World. Jewelers throughout Europe prized the American pearls, crafting elaborate pieces to show them off. A stroll through any gallery featuring portraits of European and English nobility in the 16th and 17th centuries reveals how popular pearl jewelry was for men and women alike.

Not long after the pearl fisheries at Cubagua and Margarita were opened, the supply of local divers was exhausted. Many died from diseases brought from Europe by the Spaniards, while others died from the exhaustion of being forced to dive as many as 16 hours a day. The Spaniards then turned to the Lucayan Indians in the Bahamas as a source of divers. The Lucayans were considered the best divers in the New World. The Spanish historian, Oviedo, writing in 1535, described a visit to the pearl fisheries at Margarita where he watched the divers. He marveled at their abilities, saying they could descend to depths of nearly a hundred feet, remain submerged as long as 15 minutes, and, unlike the Carib Indians who had less stamina, dive from sunrise to sunset seven days a week without appearing to tire. As the divers of the Old World had been doing for thousands of years, they descended by holding stone weights in their arms before jumping overboard, naked except for a net bag around their necks, in which they would deposit the oysters they found on the sea floor. So much in demand were the Lucayan Indians that within a few years, nearly all of them were enslaved and worked to death. Thus, the first natives Columbus saw on his epic voyage of discovery had vanished.

By 1550 the Spaniards were again hard pressed for divers. To solve the problem, they imported Negroes from Africa, many of whom had never seen the ocean, much less dived. Surprisingly, they adapted almost immediately, soon becoming as good at diving as their predecessors had been. Women were preferred to men probably because of the extra body fat. However, regardless of sex, their average working life was only a few years. Like the Indians before them, they succumbed to overwork and disease. As though this weren't enough, cannibalistic Carib Indians regularly descended on the pearl fisheries and carried of large numbers of divers. They were also subject to attack by sharks. Writing in 1618, the governor of Margarita Island said, "So few divers dare venture out these days without being threatened with instant punishment, for just this past year more than two dozen were devoured by sharks and during the twenty-odd years that I have resided on this island no fewer than 200 have met a like fate."

And a visitor to the island in 1693 wrote, "The divers here who number some 500 or more are among the best in the world, for these dive to depths of 15 fathoms and spend as long as 15 minutes beneath the sea. They are exposed to a great deal of danger from the large fishes, which are numerous here, called tiburones (sharks); they are of a monstrous size, very fierce and voracious and they often devour the poor divers. Another sort called manta rays, which are the size of a large blanket, are like monstrous thick thornbacks and they embrace the diver so strongly that they squeeze them to death, or else by falling on them with their whole weight they crush them to death against the bottom.

"In some measure to secure themselves from these fishes, each diver takes along with him a sharp knife, with which he wounds the fishes and puts them to flight. The Negro overseer who stays in the boat watches constantly through the clear waters and when he sees any of these fishes making towards them, gives them notice by pulling on he line which is fastened to the diver and at the same time, takes some weapon and dives to their assistance. But notwithstanding all these precautions, the Negro divers sometimes lose their lives and often a leg or arm. The pearls found here are among the most cherished in the whole world and that is the reason the kings of Spain feel no sorrow about forcing these unfortunate Negroes to risk their miserable lives in pursuit of the pearl oysters."

The most interesting feat of the Caribbean divers was their ability to stay under water so long. While Oviedo's mention of 15 minutes appears to be an exaggeration, there are at least six later accounts by travelers in the Caribbean who witnessed the Margarita pearl divers in action, and all say the same thing. Were they merely echoing Oviedo or did the Caribbean divers really possess a long-lost secret which enabled them to stay underwater that long?

The divers believed they owed their remarkable endurance to, of all things, tobacco. They were very heavy smokers. In 1617 the governor of Margarita wrote to the king of Spain, saying that when the island had run out of tobacco, the divers went on strike. The governor first tried punishing the divers to get them to go back to work but finally gave up and sent a ship to Cuba for a new supply of divers.

Whatever the Caribbean divers of three centuries past believed about the virtues of tobacco, today's would-be diver is not advised to take up smoking to build up his endurance. Medical science has proved conclusively that it has just the opposite effect. So we are left to wonder about another substance in which early divers had faith. In 1712 the Governor of Margarita wrote that during his 50 years on the island many divers had been killed by sharks "and other monsters," but that a few years earlier, divers had found a mineral which, when rubbed over their bodies before they dove, would repel sharks. Unfortunately the governor didn't identify the mineral. Divers today are still seeking an effective shark repellent.

In 1738 another European visitor to the Margarita pearl fisheries wrote a pathetic account of the dangers and hardships the divers faced:

"This business of a diver, which appears so extraordinary and full of danger to a European, becomes quite familiar to a Negro, owing to the natural suppleness of his limbs, and his habits from infancy. His chief terror and risk arrive from falling prey to the large sharks which frequent these waters. Only young Negroes who can hold their breath for a long time are suitable for the work. They fill their mouths with coconut oil which they spit out into the water and this gives them a moment of breath.

"Upon reaching depths of 20 fathoms, where more of the oysters are found, the diver spends around 15 minutes filling the net hung around his neck with the oysters. The exertion undergone during this process is so violent that upon being brought into the boat, the divers discharge water from their mouths, ears and nostrils and frequently even blood. But this does not hinder them from going down again in their turn.

"They will often make 40 or 50 plunges in one day, and at each plunge bring up about a hundred oysters. Quite often these divers will suddenly drop dead from hemorrhage or congestion. It is work that cannot be done for more than four or five years in succession. Having reached the age of 24 they cannot hold their breaths long enough anymore. A good diver does not eat much and always only dried food and never any type of seafood, for they feel that it can cause them to drown."

Shortly after Balboa crossed the Isthmus of Panama to

Contemporary salvors from Spain are shown working to salvage treasure and other goods from the wreck of a galleon that was lost in 1787 off the coast of Portugal.

71

discover the Pacific Ocean, Spanish explorers found fabulous pearl beds around the Pearl Islands south of Panama City. In an attempt to appease the bearded invaders, the Indians gave them hundreds of pounds of pearls, "some of them as big as hazel-nuts." By 1540 the Spaniards had established a pearl fishery in this area which rivaled Margarita's. Within 50 years all of the Indian divers were used up and Negroes from Africa were brought in to replace them. A visitor in 1750 wrote, "Those only are accounted compleat divers who have kept themselves under water till the blood gushes from their eyes, mouth and nose. This accident is said never to happen a second time and is not dangerous, the hemorrhage stopping itself. The divers have more fear from the sharks, manta rays and poisonous sea snakes...this latter type of sea fish accounting for more deaths than the other two. Generally after one year of diving the divers lose complete facilities of hearing and their eye sight is poor except when beneath the sea."

There is little in the stories about the Caribbean divers for us to take seriously today, but their stamina must command our respect. The Spaniards, who knew when they were onto a good thing, soon began using these talents for a task as important as pearl diving...salvage work. From 1503 on many ships sailed each year from Spain carrying supplies to settlements in the New World. On the return voyage they carried treasures and products of the New World. Poor seamanship, faulty navigation and storms caused many of the ships to be lost at sea. In such major colonial ports as Havana, Veracruz, Cartageña and Panama, teams of native divers were kept aboard salvage vessels which always remained ready to depart on short notice to attempt recovery of the treasure from a sunken ship.

From the 16th to 18th centuries, more than 100 million ducats worth of treasure was recovered from Spanish wrecks by these divers who, on more than one occasion, literally saved Spain from bankruptcy. Ironically, when the other European nations began colonizing the West Indies, the same divers were instrumental in depleting the Spanish treasury as their new employers used them to salvage Spanish wrecks. But this time, profits went into the English, French, and Dutch treasuries.

By the mid-16th century the Spaniards were forced to send their ships across the Atlantic in organized *flotas* because of the increasing number of attacks by pirates and enemy fleets. Every ship in a *flota* carried West Indian or Negro divers who proved invaluable at every stage of the voyage. Before a *flota* left port, divers would inspect the ships and make necessary underwater repairs. They were so highly regarded that just their adverse report on a ship's condition was enough to prevent it from sailing. There is no doubt they were responsible for saving many ships and their cargoes.

Once a *flota* was underway, the divers were in constant demand. Since ships were routinely overloaded and sailed in all kinds of weather, not infrequently their seams would open, causing them to leak badly. Once a leak had been located, the divers were lowered over the side where they would seal the leak with wedges of lead or nail large planks over it. Neither method was easy. A ship couldn't stop or it would fall behind and lose the protection of the convoy. An admiral of a *flota* in 1578 wrote to the king, recommending conferring a title on one of his divers who, by keeping several ships from sinking, deserved much of the credit for the safe arrival of 12 million ducats in Spain that year.

Another task assigned to divers was a kind of underwater customs patrol. When the treasure-laden *flotas* reached Spain from the New World, a great deal of smuggling ensued. To avoid high taxes, passengers and officers came up with various ways to outwit the king's customs officials. One of the most common tactics was for dishonest divers to attach part of the cargo to the underside of a ship. Another was to throw these hoards overboard before the customs officials arrived and recover them later by diving. Rarely did a year pass in which divers working for the king did not find a large treasure hoard. On one occasion a diver discovered that an enterprising captain cast the lower part of his ship's rudder in solid silver while in port in the New World. The fraud was detected when the diver noticed that the paint concealing the silver had worn off during the voyage. Presumably, he was well rewarded. Divers engaged in this work were usually well paid. Sometimes they earned enough to buy their freedom.

Settling on Bermuda in 1609, the English soon realized the importance of Negro pearl divers. Shortly after Bermuda was settled, privateers based there raided Spanish pearl fisheries where they captured a large number of divers and put them to work salvaging wrecked Spanish treasure ships. These divers fared much better under their new masters; many were given their freedom in return for salvaging valuable sunken treasure. Until the mid-17th century, when Port Royal was founded, treasure-hunting, or "wracking," as the English called it, was the major industry on Bermuda. The settlers had dozens of sloops and schooners working wrecks throughout the Caribbean.

Due to its strategic location near the middle of the Caribbean, Port Royal, Jamaica, quickly became the headquarters of the "wrackers." It was known as the most wicked and richest port in the Western Hemisphere...a nest of pirates, privateers and other shady characters. A Spanish spy who sneaked into Port Royal in 1673 reported that as many as 50 sloops and schooners were operating out of the port, hunting for treasure from Spanish shipwrecks.

The lure of sunken treasure has long drawn men to the depths of the sea. As might be expected, Spain, which lost countless ships during the 16th and 17th centuries, took the lead in recovering treasure. Despite this Spanish effort, it was an American, Sir William Phips of Boston, who with Jamaican divers effected the greatest recovery of treasure from a single vessel until the present century.

To add to the fairy-tale quality of this story, the ship involved was Spanish, a member of the *flota* of 1641, one of the richest ever to sail from the New World for Spain, consisting of eight heavily laden galleons. Six of them developed leaks even before sailing, and most of the gold and silver bullion (valued at more than 20 million ducats) had to be carried by only two galleons the flagship, *Capitaña* and the vice-admiral's ship, the *Almiranta* called the *Concepcion*. Traveling with the treasure galleons under convoy were 22 merchant ships carrying various products, including tobacco, chocolate, lumber and sugar.

Struck by Hurricane

Two days out of Havana, while passing through the Florida Straits, the *flota* was struck by a severe hurricane. Within a few hours all of the ships had sunk, except for the *Capitaña*, which later sank off the coast of Spain and the *Almiranta*, which was filled with water and barely stayed afloat, losing its mast, sails and rigging. In a frantic effort to keep the *Almiranta* from sinking, the officers, crew and passengers bailed around the clock during the hurricane and its aftermath. For nearly a week the ship was carried along by the wind and currents. At last, some 50 nautical miles north of Hispañiola, it struck a reef. Most of the 600 passengers managed to swim to a nearby sand spit where their chances of survival seemed slim. Much of the *Almiranta's* food and water had been thrown overboard in the struggle to keep her afloat. Makeshift rafts and boats were built from the wreckage that remained above water, and in them 200 survivors sailed for Santo Domingo. Only a few survived.

When the Spanish government learned of the fate of the *Concepcion*, they prepared an expedition to help survivors and to salvage the wreck, but bad weather delayed its departure. When the expedition reached the sand spit where those who didn't sail to Santo Domingo had stayed, not a soul was found alive. All 400 or so had died of thirst, hunger or exposure. The expedition sailed on to Margarita to pick up 50 pearl divers for the salvage operation, but one storm after another delayed them. They didn't reach the site until the following spring, when it was found that numerous storms had not only completely submerged the wreck but had washed away the sand spit, so that the salvors now had no idea where it was. During the next 20 years, the Spanish mounted over 60 unsuccessful expeditions to locate and salvage the wreck, finally admitting defeat. Thus, the richest known wreck in history was lost forever...or so the Spaniards thought.

Although the rest of the world may have been content to leave the treasure on the reef, now known as Silver Shoals, William Phips wasn't. As a child in Boston, Phips had been bitten by the treasure bug as he listened to sailors' tales. In 1681 he used money he had saved working as a shipwright and in his own shipping business to embark on his first treasure hunt to the Caribbean. He didn't find the vast treasure of his dreams, but he located several wrecks in the Bahamas, which more than covered his expenses. It was a promising beginning. Certain that he would hit the jackpot sooner or later, Phips decided to go after a Spanish galleon sunk near Nassau that reputedly carried gold.

For the venture Phips wanted the best possible ship, men and equipment, which required more money than he possessed. Unable to raise money in Boston, he went to London in the spring of 1682, where he sought help from King Charles II. It was 18 months before Phips was granted an audience, but he was a determined man. Eventually he persuaded Charles to back the expedition in return for a large share of the booty.

Phips spent several weeks locating the wreck which turned out to have no treasure, either because it had never carried any or someone had gotten there first. Undaunted, he decided to look for another wreck; but his crew had other ideas. Disgruntled at not having found the treasure and thus gotten their share, they mutinied, intending to take over the ship and get rich as pirates.

With only eight of the more than 100 men remaining loyal, Phips somehow managed to put down the mutiny and bring the ship into Port Royal where the mutineers were thrown in prison and a new crew signed on. While there, he heard about the *Concepcion* lost on Silver Shoals. This was enough to send him off again. Before Phips reached the vicinity of the wreck, however, his new crew mutinied. Once again, he put down a rebellion. But this time, hoping to find a more trustworthy crew, he returned to England.

During his absence Charles II had died and the new King James II showed no interest in financing treasure hunts. James had Phips' frigate repossessed and, when Phips protested, imprisoned him for several months. Captivity did little to crush Phips' spirit or his salesmanship, however. After his release Phips persuaded the Duke of Albemarle and Sir John Marlborough to back the attempt to salvage the *Almiranta*. They, in turn, persuaded the king to join the venture. The Duke and Sir John, argued so effectively that not only did James furnish a ship, but he granted Phips' salvage company the exclusive concession for treasure hunting in the Caribbean, thereby gravely offending the Spanish ambassador.

Phips sailed for Silver Shoals, detouring by Jamaica where he took on about 24 Negro pearl divers, refugees from the fisheries at Margarita. For several months he drove himself and his men nearly to the breaking point. The divers worked from sunrise to sunset. But Phips' perseverance was rewarded when in 1685 they found the wreck. As one of the divers rose to the surface with his hands full of silver coins, Phips shed his Boston reserve and burst into tears of joy. For a month they struggled to bring up treasure while fighting off pirates who had heard about their success.

Some 32 tons of silver, a vast amount of gold, chests of pearls and leather bags containing other precious gems were recovered before bad weather and exhaustion of provisions forced Phips and his men to suspend operations. Value of the treasure was put at $3 million in today's currency, of which Phips received a sixth, enough to make him one of the richest men in the New World. Each Port Royal diver received a large bonus, and those not already freemen were able to buy their freedom. Some of the now-rich divers decided to retire from the sea and invested their bonuses in taverns and other businesses in Port Royal...all of which were lost in the earthquake of 1692.

Phips was knighted and after declining a post in the British Admiralty, was named governor of the Colony of Massachusetts. But Sir William Phips was living proof of a saying that was already centuries old...*once the treasure bug has bitten a man, it never turns loose.* After a few years of performing his gubernatorial duties adequately, he abandoned the post for another treasure hunt. Although he had enough money to finance the expedition properly, he didn't get the chance to put it to use. While in London in 1694, waiting for his ship to sail, Sir William died.

At the time of the earthquake on June 7, 1692, many Port Royal divers were in the pay of the Spanish. Faulty navigation had wrecked four Spanish galleons sailing from Cartageña to Havana under the command of the Marquis de Bao a year earlier on Pedro Shoals, about 130 nautical miles south of Kingston. Several Port Royal boats were in the area at the time and helped rescue 776 persons from

Diamonds, sapphires, rubies and other precious stones were recovered from a pirate vessel of the 18th century off Antigua in the Caribbean.

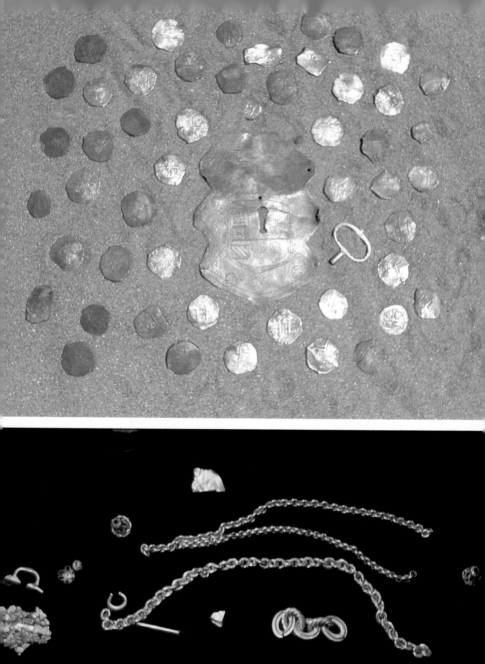

the wreck along with part of the treasure and other cargo. No sooner had the survivors reached Port Royal with news of the wreck than dozens of ships hastily sailed for its site.

Although the divers from Port Royal recovered considerable treasure, they benefited little from the venture. Spain and England were at peace, and high-ranking Spanish officials among the survivors convinced the governor of Jamaica that it would cause ill feeling between the two countries if the divers were permitted to keep the treasure they were so feverishly salvaging. As ship after ship put in at Port Royal, loaded with treasure, Admiralty officials seized everything aboard the vessels, and the salvors ended up with only a tenth of what they had salvaged. Within a month of the disaster the Spaniards had several warships stationed at the wreck site to prevent further diving. The Spaniards finally hired all available divers from Port Royal and, in addition to a reasonable salary, gave them a bonus of one-fifth of all that they recovered.

From contemporary documents, however, we know that when Port Royal was obliterated by an earthquake and tidal wave in 1692, not all the Port Royal divers were at Pedro Shoals diving for the Spaniards. Various accounts state that almost immediately after the earthquake, divers were searching submerged buildings for items of value. Some used diving bells which allowed them to remain submerged for an hour or more. Others had no diving equipment, but these free divers were a fearless breed. It was reported that they often fought with sharks around Port Royal just for the sport, and they undoubtedly recovered much of value from the submerged buildings.

Above are Spanish silver pieces of eight, a brass key plate and part of a key found by the author on the sunken city of Port Royal. Below are gold bars and other artifacts found by a sports diver fishing for lobsters in the Bahamas.

Although sections of the city sank to depths of 30 to 50 feet within two minutes of the third tremor, the section between Fort James and Fort Carlisle sank gradually, with the upper parts of buildings remaining above water for years. In July 1693 a visitor wrote, "The principal parts of Port Royal now lie four, six or eight fathoms under water.... Indeed, 'tis enough to raise melancholy thoughts in a man to see chimneys and the tops of some houses and masts of ships and sloops, which partaked of the same fate, appear above the water, now habitations for fish."

Since most of Port Royal's roofs were made of wood and slate shingles which could easily be torn off, access to the buildings must have been simple, not only for the divers but for salvors who didn't have to descend into the water. The latter used two methods, dredging and fishing. To dredge they would lower heavily weighted fishing nets and drag them across the bottom, snagging anything loose. To fish they would first spread oil on the surface of the water to calm it so they could see to the bottom better. Then they would use either long poles with hooks or spears at the end or grappling hooks attached to ropes.

The divers, dredgers and fishers overlooked little of Port Royal's treasure. Extensive salvaging continued for several decades after the earthquake, but how much treasure was lost and how much was salvaged, we can only guess. From my own excavation at the site, however, I learned several important facts about the early salvors. First, they were good at their work, missing little of value. Inside three houses we excavated, there was nothing except a grappling hook in one house and a two-pronged harpoon in another, both probably lost by the original salvors. In between standing or falling walls, rarely did we find anything valuable except such items as bottles, ceramic shards and clay smoking pipes, which the early salvors wouldn't have considered of any value.

Luckily, those salvors weren't able or didn't consider the effort worth it to remove the hundreds of fallen walls from old buildings. Otherwise, there would be little left today. During our excavation nearly every item of value in pewter, silver, gold, brass, etc. was recovered from under fallen walls. There was only one major exception...a hoard of Spanish silver coins, found in a wooden chest with a brass keyhole plate and bearing the coat of arms of the King of Spain. The only explanation of why the chest was overlooked by the first salvors is the possibility that its great weight caused it to sink immediately and deeply into the mud on the sea floor where the salvors couldn't see it.

Another Golden Opportunity

About the time the Port Royal divers had salvaged all they could from the sunken city, another golden opportunity arose. In 1715 a Spanish treasure fleet of 10 ships was wrecked on the coast of Florida between Cape Canaveral and Fort Pierce. More than a thousand people and 14 million pesos worth of treasure were lost. As soon as news of the disaster reached Havana, salvage teams were rushed to the site. Just as quickly, the news reached Port Royal, and dozens of small vessels sailed for Florida where, within sight of the Spanish salvage teams, divers began descending illegally to some of the wrecks. Contemporary accounts are contradictory and confusing. Still, it's estimated that the divers from Port Royal recovered about 500 thousand pesos before the Spaniards sent a squadron of warships to prevent further diving on wrecks the Spanish considered their property alone.

Salvage operations were halted in 1719, even though the Spaniards had recovered only about half the estimated treasure aboard the ships. The remainder, the Spanish believed, had probably been covered over by shifting sands, making it impossible to find. Once again the Port Royal salvors were presented with a fine opportunity. Each year between 1720 and 1728 ships from Port Royal searched for treasure at this wreck site.

In 1538 two Greeks designed and built a diving bell which they demonstrated for Emperor Charles V and some 10,000 spectators in Toledo, Spain. Larger than de Lorena's bell, this one accommodated both inventors who sat inside on planks. They carried a lighted candle inside the bell with them. To the astonishment of the king and spectators, the candle was still burning when they returned to the surface. The candle was good showmanship, but it also provided underwater illumination and though the inventors probably didn't know this, it served as a safety gauge. If the flame went out while the divers were below, it would mean that their oxygen supply had been exhausted. The same danger that threatened Leonardo da Vinci's "Scuba"--carbon dioxide--threatened divers who used the bell.

News of the Toledo diving bell spread like wildfire throughout Europe, and many similar bells were built. Practical use of the bell sometimes differed from the demonstration in one important respect. When they discovered that remaining inside the bell like the Greeks kept them from doing the work for which they had been hired, the divers used it as a kind of air bank, swimming outside to work and returning to it from time to time for air. However the bells were used, they seemed to serve the purpose. On the other hand, some of them, such as the two inventions of an Italian named Niccoli Tartaglia, apparently served no purpose. Designed in 1551, though never built, one of them consisted of a wooden frame shaped like an hourglass on which the diver stood. A glass bowl enclosed his head, thus assuring him of good vision but no breathing to speak of, because it provided the diver with no more than a few minutes of air. The other invention featured the same hourglass frame but differed from the first, in that the diver's entire body was enclosed in the bowl, which seemed to have no opening (how the diver was supposed to get in and out wasn't explained).

The first appearance of a diving bell in the New World was in 1612, when an Englishman, Richard Norwood, decided his regular line of piracy, wasn't lucrative enough and used a diving bell to search for treasure-laden wrecks in the vicinity of Bermuda. His diving bell was made from a wine cask with attached weights to carry him to the bottom. When Norwood didn't find much Bermuda treasure, he went on to look for wrecks in the West Indies. We don't know what success, if any, he had; but it's doubtful he struck it rich because a man who couldn't make a go of it as a pirate in an age when piracy flourished was unlikely to succeed in a more challenging line of work.

In 1677 a wooden bell 13 feet high and 9 feet from rim to rim was built in Spain and used to salvage two rich shipwrecks at the port of Cadaques. The volume of the bell provided two Moorish divers with enough air to remain submerged for over an hour at a time. They said they could have stayed below longer, but the terrific heat created in the bell by their breathing forced them to surface. When they wanted to come up, they tugged at a line attached to the rim of the bell, and their assistants on the surface pulled them up. The divers did all their work inside the bell which was lowered directly to the wrecks. The venture was a huge success. Several million Spanish pieces of eight were recovered. The divers were paid in an unusual way...each time they surfaced with chests or bags of money, they were allowed to keep as much as they could hold in their mouths and hands.

The Race for Quick Riches

Halley's diving bell, coupled with the recovery of the bulk of the treasure from the *Almiranta* by Phips in 1641, led to the formation of numerous salvage companies in Europe. The race for quick riches was on. But the only truly effective salvors were the Spanish who usually recovered treasure from their own ships just after they had gone down at sea...while they were still visible above water. The fact that others had only limited success was attested to by the English scientist, Sir Hans Sloane, in 1707:

"I remember an African ship, wrecked on the coast of

85

Sussex, loaded with elephant teeth [ivory tusks], which Mr. Halley told me was in a very short time almost covered with sand and mud, so that the project of recovering the teeth was frustrated, though by the help of the diving bell, contrived by his extraordinary skill, they had gone to the bottom of the sea and salvaged all aboard the hulk. Though the money brought into England from the Spanish wreck salvaged by Phips was very considerable, yet much more was lost on projects of the same nature. For every silly story of a rich ship lost, a patent was taken out, divers, who are used to pearl fishing and can stay under water some minutes, bought or hired at great rates, and a ship set out for bringing home the silver. There was one ship lost amongst the reefs of Bermuda which was very rich. It is said to be in the possession of the devil and I have heard many stories how he kept it. I do not find the people who spend their money on this or any of these projects, excepting the first Phips, got anything by them."

The London *Annual Register* of August 29, 1775, gives another account of the use of Halley's bell in an unsuccessful treasure hunt:

"By letters from Rome of this day, they had ended their third trial of searching in the Tiber for antiquities and with the same bad success of not having a halfpenny profit, though they had this year an English chain pump, that did for its part wonders, in throwing out the water, but it seems that all the pumps in the navy would not answer the purpose, as the water leaked in as fast as it was thrown out. Thus, if they make any more trials, it must be in the manner they should have begun by, that is by scooping up the dirt, as done in rivers and harbours, to keep them clear; but it was presumed that they would want a new subscription for it and few would contribute after so many unsuccessful trials. We cannot, however, forbear recommending the trial of Dr. Halley's diving bell on the occasion. The leakage, which has hitherto proved so fatal, is in all probability from the bottom. Now Dr. Halley's diving bell may be cleared of water within a very small way of its lower rim, and this lower rim brought so close to the bottom, if any way even, as to afford the workmen the same opportunity of digging, which they would have in a piece of ground overflowed with water to a small depth. Nay, the bell might be lowered, with the same advantages, in pursuit of treasure, into the hole itself, let it be ever so deep, if made large enough to the purpose."

That same year, a Scottish grocer from Edinburgh, Charles Spaulding, invented a means for divers to raise or lower a bell at will, independent of any help from the surface. This eliminated the danger of the bell being snagged on underwater obstructions and enabled the divers to maneuver their bell for close-up work on shipwrecks. Spaulding demonstrated the practicality of his bell by salvaging treasure from various shipwrecks in Scotland and England. But in 1783 while working on a shipwreck in Dublin Bay, he and his son lost their lives. Strong underwater currents prevented casks of fresh air from being lowered to them. Instead of coming up for air when their supply became foul, Spaulding and his son pressed their luck and were suffocated by the accumulation of carbon dioxide in their bell.

There is a ghoulish story about an incident that took place in 1790. A team of divers using a Halley diving bell were sent to Seraglio Point in the Bosporus to salvage a shipwreck. Minutes after starting their descent, they signaled frantically to be brought back to the surface. When they were pulled up, the horror-stricken divers refused to go down again. At the bottom they had come on an amazing spectacle...hundreds of life-size "dolls" in the shape of bowling pins, with skulls for heads. Most of them had been toppled over, but there were rows jammed upright among the rocks or stuck in the mud and slime, slightly swaying to and fro in unison whenever the current moved them and, of course, grinning "with a lipless grin," as though beckoning the divers to approach.

They had stumbled on the spot where generations of concubines from the seraglio had been ritually murdered by being sewn up alive in sacks weighted with stones with only their heads protruding, and then thrown into the sea at night from boats. The women had either fallen victim to court intrigue or somehow offended the Grand Signor (some of the sultans had as many as 2,000 concubines at one time). Sultan Ibrahim I, who reigned from 1640 to 1648, was said to have drowned his entire harem of 1,200 concubines. The eerie Loreleis that had frightened the divers were skeletal remains of these unfortunate women.

The first important recovery of sunken treasure in the New World by anyone other than the Spanish wasn't made for nearly a century and a half after Phips discovery of the *Concepcion*. In December of 1830 the English frigate, *Thetis*, sailing from Rio de Janeiro to England with $810,000 in gold and silver bars aboard, was driven against the rocks off the coast of Brazil in a storm and sank in 70 feet of water, drowning half the crew. When the survivors reached Rio and reported the disaster, it was assumed that the treasure was lost forever because huge waves and a current of six knots at the site of the wreck made salvage seem impossible.

Thomas Dickinson, captain of a British sloop in Rio at the time, decided to go after the treasure despite the risk. He had to contend with more than turbulent waters, though. There was no such thing as a diving bell in Rio. Worse still, there were no divers. Dickinson rigged a crude diving bell from two iron water storage tanks and converted a fire fighting pump into a compressor to provide the bell with air. Arriving at the site, he saw at a glance that the huge seas and strong currents made anchoring within a mile of the wreck out of the question. So he set up camp onshore and began building a boom on a cliff to raise and lower his bell. Using masts and spars from the *Thetis*, Dickinson took four months to construct a boom 158 feet long and weighing about 40 tons.

Fifty seamen from Dickinson's sloop received on-the-spot marine salvage training. Most of them had never dived. Fortunately, the water was clear, and during the first month, they gleaned $120,000 in treasure. Then a fierce gale sent the boom crashing into the sea. It took months to build another one. Battered by 20-foot waves, several bells went the way of the first or were smashed against the rocky cliffs. Dickinson, about as ready to yield to defeat as William Phips had been, had his carpenters build others from anything that came to hand. Sometimes they even used wooden barrels. After 18 months of labor and the loss of three divers, the salvors returned to London, expecting to receive large shares of the $750,000 they had recovered. But they were bitterly disappointed when litigation over the division of the treasure dragged on for years in the admiralty courts. Eventually the salvors were given a one-eighth share to split among themselves, apportioned according to the amount of work each had done.

Lethbridge's 'Diving Machine'

In 1715 another Englishman, John Lethbridge, received a patent for his "diving machine." The name isn't very descriptive, but what else could he have called his invention? Looking like a cross between the old diving chamber and an armored diving suit, it consisted of an irregular metal cylinder six feet long with diameters of two and a half feet at the head and 18 inches at the foot. Armholes in the sides enabled the diver to work with his hands, and a glass window gave him visibility. While the diving machine had no air supply other than the air trapped inside before the chamber was closed, it did have two valves on the top, which could be opened so that air could be pumped in with a bellows whenever the diver had to surface.

The device was raised and lowered with cables, but Lethbridge, obviously a man of considerable ingenuity, provided the diver with the means of discarding the extra ballast weights on the outside of the chamber in an emergency to allow him to ascend unaided. Lethbridge hoped to reach great depths. When he tested his machine, however, he discovered that pressures below 50 feet of water caused leaks around the armholes, window and entrance hatch. Lethbridge's diving machine thus failed to extend the depths to which divers could descend or the amount of time they could remain below, and the public lost interest in it.

Lethbridge still put his machine to good use in the waters of the British Isles and elsewhere in the Atlantic, managing to salvage several valuable cargoes from shipwrecks. In 1724 the Dutch East India Company ship *SlotterHooge*, en route to Java from Holland, sank during a gale off Porto Santo, on Madeira Island. Of 254 people aboard only 33 survived. In the flooded hold 60 feet below were three tons of silver ingots and three massive chests of coins. Lethbridge, who was considered a technical genius and one of the best salvage divers of his day, was hired by the company to salvage the wreck. His contract specified that he would be paid 10 pounds sterling a month, plus his expenses, with bonuses to be left to the "generosity of the Company directors."

In his first attempt, Lethbridge recovered 349 silver ingots, many coins and two cannon before bad weather forced him to stop. The following summer he recovered over half of the total listed on the manifest. But after the second salvage season, the amount recovered diminished every year until 1734 when he "came back with less than one could have hoped for, but still with reasonable success." The rest of the treasure was buried in the sand where it would remain for more than two centuries until discovered by a 20th-century treasure hunter.

By 1860 the helmet diving rig had replaced the diving bell and even many of the caissons used in submarine architectural work such as laying the foundations of piers, seawalls and breakwaters. Companies sprang up in every major port, where helmet divers were employed to clean and repair ship bottoms. About this time there was a resurgence of interest in salvaging old shipwrecks. Many treasures once thought lost forever were recovered. In just one year of salvaging, a diver received over £20,000 in bonuses and retired. Another diver told of the melancholy scene that confronted him when he was sent down to explore the wreck of the *Dalhousie,* a ship that had sunk off the coast of Scotland. When he entered the main cabin, he "found a mother on her knees in an attitude of prayer and clasping her two little ones in her arms, whilst the other dead bodies were clinging on by their finger nails to the beams of the ceiling." Another helmet diver exploring a wreck off Ireland found a beautiful young woman lying peaceably in one of the berths, her long, disheveled blond hair floated about like seaweed with the movement of the water. "I took good care," he said, "not to disturb her in her sleep. Where could she have found a more peaceful tomb?"

Malabar sank in the English Channel, and for many months in 1860 she lay untouched in 100 feet of water...a depth thought impossible to tackle. After Lloyd's of London wrote off the ship, a team of divers from Plymouth used Heinke's diving rig to take on what newspapers described as a "suicidal project, full of sheer folly and extreme recklessness." But within three days the divers salvaged the entire treasure worth £280,000...at a steep price, though, since two of them died from the bends.

Another major treasure was recovered in 1885 from the Spanish ship, *Alfonso XII,* which had sunk off Point Grando on Grand Canary on her way to Cuba. The *Alfonso XII,* carrying a half-million dollars in gold coin, lay under 162 feet of water and, like the *Thetis,* was believed lost for good. To add to the difficulty the treasure was stored in a strong room on a lower deck with three iron decks between it and the top deck. The insurance company was so sure that salvaging her was hopeless that they paid the owners $500,000.

No one had reckoned with Alexander Lambert who had already distinguished himself by twice closing the iron door of the flooded Severn Tunnel against formidable odds. Because no other diver would descend almost twice as far as it was considered safe for helmet divers to go, Lambert went down alone. In just two days he recovered the entire treasure by blasting his way through the three iron decks and breaking into the strong room. Lambert, however, paid a penalty that was becoming only too common. He suffered a severe case of the bends and was forced to retire from diving permanently.

Salvaging the Laurentic

One of the greatest treasure recoveries in history and probably the most difficult ever undertaken was sponsored by the British government. Early in 1917 the converted White Star liner *Laurentic*, now an armed cruiser, sailed from Liverpool for Nova Scotia, carrying in its second-class baggage room gold bars valued at $25 million. While still within sight of the Irish coast, she hit a German mine, exploded and sank in 132 feet of water with a loss of 300 lives. Although treasure had been recovered from greater depths and diving techniques had been improved considerably since Lambert's achievement in 1885, salvage still appeared formidable. There was also the danger that a salvage vessel would be sunk by a German U-boat or a floating mine. Nevertheless, the attempt had to be made. The loss of so much gold would deal a serious blow to a British economy already weakened by the war. Plus, sinking of the *Laurentic* had to be kept secret from the Germans, who almost surely would have tried to block recovery efforts. For reasons of security, the British public wasn't informed either.

Captain G.C.C. Damant, a naval salvage expert, was put in charge. His salvage vessel, disguised as a fishing trawler, appeared on the scene a few weeks after the disaster, carrying some of Britain's best helmet divers. The divers found that because of the 60-degree angle at which the wreck lay, walking on or inside it would be impossible. They would have to crawl, pulling themselves along by grasping whatever projections they could find. The route to the second-class baggage room, where the gold bullion lay, was blocked by a watertight door halfway down the ship's side, which had to be blasted open.

After they accomplished this and removed the debris, the divers discovered that the passage beyond was filled with floating wreckage which also had to be cleared away. This job alone took hundreds of diving hours. The next obstacle was another door which was also blasted open. At last they reached the door to the baggage room, and a diver opened it with hammer and chisel. Damant carried out one of the boxes of gold, which weighed 140 pounds and was worth $40,000. The weight wasn't as great as it would have been on land, but owing to the difficulty of crawling along the slanted passage, he could retrieve only one box that first day. The next day they took out three more.

In good weather the operation might have proceeded well, but the salvage site was battered by a succession of winter gales. Rough seas made it difficult for the salvage vessel to maintain its position over the wreck, and the divers' hoses were in constant danger of snapping. After the fourth box of gold had been raised, a gale of such force sprang up that Captain Damant was forced to seek shelter in the nearest port.

When they returned to the site after the storm had moderated, the first divers to go down brought back discouraging news...the *Laurentic* had collapsed like an accordion, and settled even deeper into the sediment on the sea floor. The entry port on the side, which had been at a depth of 62 feet before, was now 103 feet below the surface. Worst of all, the passage beyond the door, originally nine feet high, had been compressed to a mere 18 inches, too narrow for the divers to get through. Difficult enough before, the job had taken on monumental proportions. Even if they could get through the constricted passage, each diver would now be able to spend only 30 minutes below (and 30 more decompressing) because of the greater depth.

The work was fatiguing. No diver could make more than one descent a day, and only two could work at the same time. Otherwise, air lines might become entangled. Not surprisingly, salvaging progressed at a snail's pace. Explosives were used to blast a path through the wreckage. Finally, after the dangerous job of clearing the debris was completed, the divers once again reached the baggage room. It was a shambles. The floor was full of holes, and there was no gold to be seen. The boxes containing it had disintegrated along with everything else. Apparently the gold bars had slid through the holes, deeper into the wreck.

Captain Damant needed a new plan and time was critical because the wreck was crumbling with every passing hour. For instance, the decks above the baggage room were supported only by water. Damant decided to cut straight down through the decks to the spot where he judged that the gold had fallen. As usual, "cutting" meant more demolition. After some two months of blasting, gold bars were sighted in that part of the wreck which had sunk into the sea floor, and divers then groped for the bars. This slow, grinding work went on day after day until September when bad weather again forced Captain Damant to suspend the operation for the year. They had recovered $4 million in gold so far.

Because Captain Damant and his team were needed for another highly secret salvage job, there was no work at the *Laurentic* site in 1918. When the salvors returned to the in the spring of 1919, they found only a pile of wreckage which bore little resemblance to a ship. Again divers cleared a path to the spot where they had previously found gold. This time they found more, a total of $2,350,000. But then came a period during which they found nothing more. Damant concluded that the remainder must have fallen into a depression deep within the tons of wreckage. Until this debris was cleared away, the divers couldn't continue salvaging. Throughout the summers of 1920 and 1921 the divers cleared away debris, using large centrifugal pumps to pump tons of mud to the surface. Only 50 bars of gold turned up during these two years, but Captain Damant and his men were determined to continue looking.

Finally, their luck changed in 1922. The first diver down that spring sighted several gold bars sticking out of the mud on the sea floor. For once the winter storms had worked in their favor, washing away silt that had been covering the bottom. Between April and October, when work stopped for that year, they found about $7,500,000. The most that was found in a single trip was $750,000. The salvors did even better in 1923, recovering nearly $10 million. Only 154 bars, valued at $1,200,000, remained below and during 1924, 129 of those were recovered. By this time, it had become unprofitable to continue the effort, and the operation was abandoned. It had been a highly successful venture for the British government, since the salvors were members of the British navy and received no share of what was recovered. Ninety-nine percent of the bullion aboard the *Laurentic* had been recovered, at a cost of only 2 percent of its value.

Salvage Firm Founded

Because of the large number of vessels sunk during the American Civil War, the Merritt, Chapman & Scott Company of New York was founded. The company soon became the largest and most prestigious salvage firm in the world. Their divers were involved in salvaging, repairing and refloating hundreds of ships. One of the company's major salvage operations took place in 1918 when the 13,000-ton liner *St. Paul* sank in New York Harbor in 54 feet of water. The *St. Paul* had been converted into an armed cruiser during World War I, which meant that the first thing the divers had to do was remove her munitions. More time was spent removing other movable objects.

To lighten the ship as much as possible, the superstructure was blasted away. Cofferdams were built along the deck, and all of the openings were sealed off before air was pumped into the wreck. In addition, the divers had the dangerous task of digging tunnels beneath the ship, in order to sling cables and put lifting pontoons in place. Six months later, the 22 divers had done their work well. With the wreck posing a hazard to navigation in New York Harbor, it was refloated and towed away to be cut up for scrap.

During the Second World War Merritt, Chapman & Scott had over two dozen salvage vessels operating around the world. Serving as a civilian arm of the U.S. Navy Salvage Service, the firm received 498 major assignments. All told, their helmet divers reclaimed ships and cargoes valued at approximately $675 million, which is a dry statistic that doesn't begin to tell the whole story. The Official History of the Navy Salvage Service said it better: "No mere figures in dollars and cents can adequately measure the value of the recovered hulls and cargoes to the successful prosecution of the war."

The author and assistant, Louise Judge, examine ceramic shards from one of two ships lost by Christopher Columbus in St. Anne's Bay, Jamaica, in 1504.

Modern Salvors

The image of underwater treasure hunters as romantic crackpots chasing some pot of gold at the end of the rainbow has changed in recent years. My discovery of the 1656 *Nuestra Senora de las Maravillas* galleon in the Bahamas in 1972, followed by Burt Webber's discovery of the 1641 *Concepcion* on Silver Shoals, followed by the enormous amount of gold raised from the *HMS Edinburgh* in the North Sea soon attracted the attention of Wall Street. Prior to these discoveries investors were content to participate in a small way, more for the opportunity of living out a Walter Mitty fantasy than in hopes of getting a return for their money. Thanks to "big bucks" now available from investors, Mel Fisher was able to finance finding of the *Margarita* and *Atocha* and bring up their fantastic treasures.

Most of today's professional treasure hunters launched their careers in the days when scientific methods played a small part. Typically, a treasure hunt began when a diver's imagination was fired by a waterfront chat with a fisherman who knew of a place where "cannon lie strewn on the bottom." It wasn't unusual for the fisherman to offer to show the location for a fee...paid in advance of course. Sometime these leads paid off. Often they didn't.

Those were the Glory Days...for us all!

Famed salvor Teddy Tucker of Bermuda, who sometimes wishes that he could have been a pirate, is shown smoking an English clay pipe from the 17th century.

There were no bureaucrats and very few, if any, laws to hinder our work. It was all so simple. Go out and find the shipwreck and bring up the treasure! Museums throughout the world benefited from our underwater salvage efforts. We were generous with knowledge and artifacts and most of us excavated with great care and attention to preservation.

When today's treasure hunters were still wearing diapers, the late Art McKee was already a veteran. Until his death five years ago he was the oldest and most experienced treasure hunter in the business. McKee's first contact with the sea was as a lifeguard at New Jersey resorts during his summer school vacations. As a young boy he read books on sunken treasure and after graduating from high school decided to become a deep sea diver. He got a job as a diving tender for an old helmet diver who was repairing a bridge that had been destroyed by a hurricane.

One day when the old diver was too drunk to dive, McKee talked a friend into tending the lines and made his first dive in a helmet diving suit. With no training he was, of course, afraid; but, within a few minutes he had fallen in love with diving. His employer then put McKee to work as a full-time diver, and he quickly became a good one. After the bridge job was finished, he was hired to search for a large anchor lost by a tanker in the murky waters of Delaware Bay. By accident he discovered the remains of an early 18th-century English merchant ship. Although he found only pieces of broken rum bottles and ceramic shards, he developed a full blown case of treasure fever and decided then and there to go after a real treasure wreck someday.

Longing for clearer, warmer waters in which to continue his diving career, McKee moved to Florida in 1934 and took a job as recreation director for the city of Homestead. On weekends he prowled around the many reefs of the Florida Keys, searching for brass and other metals from modern shipwrecks, a pastime that proved profitable since there were few other professional divers. McKee was sought out for so much diving work that he was able to quit his regular job and work full time as a diver. Most people who came to him asking if he would help them find sunken treasure were crackpots. There were exceptions, however.

"I was approached by a man who really had a good lead from an old chart pin-pointing a treasure wreck. He offered me diver's wages for a 10-day job, and I accepted. When we got to the wreck site, in shallow water, I went down and discovered several cannons on the coral reef. Never having seen a wreck in clear water before, I just figured that the cannon had been jettisoned by a ship which had run aground on the reef...to lighten itself and get off again. But, was I ever fooled! I spent the whole day probing around the reef without finding anything. Just when I was about to quit for the day, I noticed that down in deeper water there were more cannon.

"The next morning I dropped over the edge of the reef into 80 feet of water and landed on a sandy bottom. There were a lot of cannon strewn about. Noticing what appeared to be a large coral growth, I walked over and hit it with my pick. After knocking off a piece of coral, I saw a hollow place where there had been barrel staves, long since rotted away. I hit the coral a couple of whacks, and this exposed some hard pitch or tar with several shiny gold coins sticking to it. I broke off a larger piece of the stuff and sent it topside. They told me over the phone that they had found eighteen doubloons in it. Man, was I excited! I had only dreamed about gold. I'd never actually seen it on the ocean floor. After several hours of working, I broke the mass apart, and we found over 1,600 gold doubloons altogether. Unfortunately for me, since I was only on a diver's salary, my employer just gave me a few of the coins as souvenirs. I've been back to that same wreck at least 50 times since then but haven't found any more treasure."

It was a common practice in the 16th, 17th and 18th

centuries for treasure to be concealed in this manner, when it was being smuggled into Spain to avoid paying the exorbitant import taxes and also as a precaution in case the ship was boarded by pirates.

While working on a pipeline job in 1937, McKee was approached by an old fisherman who told him about a "pile of stones with corroded pipes on top." On his first dive McKee saw that it was an old wreck. He brought up several coral-encrusted iron cannonballs and four heavily sulfated silver pieces of eight. Not sure what the coins were, he took them to a marine biologist at the University of Miami who told him they were worthless pieces of lead. Unsatisfied with this answer, McKee took them to a jeweler who said they were silver.

During his next dive on the wreck, McKee discovered a Spanish gold escudo stamped 1721, indicating that the wreck had occurred after that. Exhausting every source in the United States and unable to learn the identity and history of this ship, he wrote to the director of the Archives of the Indies in Spain. Months went by. Finally McKee received a large package from Spain, containing hundreds of pages of old documents concerning this wreck. In addition, there was a photograph of an old chart, showing the locations of 20 shipwrecks, one of them McKee's.

In July 1733 a hurricane struck a homeward-bound Spanish treasure fleet in the Florida Keys. All 20 ships in the fleet were wrecked on the reefs and shoals. Intensive salvage operations followed almost immediately, and most treasure the ships were carrying was recovered. McKee's wreck was the most important ship in the fleet. Her name was *El Rubi*, but since she was the flagship under the command of Admiral Don Rodrigo de Tarres, she was also called the *Capitaña*. Her original cargo consisted of treasure worth five million pesos. According to the ship's manifest, it had all been salvaged.

For months McKee worked alone on the wreck. Anchoring over the site, he would start his air compressor, don his shallow water helmet, and go down a line to the wreck. There he would spend as many as 10 hours a day, moving massive ballast stones and fanning away sand by hand. He made interesting finds almost every day.

During the summer of 1938 McKee found partners who enabled him to step up the tempo of his operation. After 250 tons-plus of ballast stones had been moved to one side, he realized that much of the cargo must be hidden deep in the sand. Since they could fan down only a few feet by hand, McKee looked for a new tool to remove sand. When he heard that Navy divers were deepen muddy harbors with a device called an "airlift," he built own...the first time ever used on old shipwrecks. It remains one of the most important tools for underwater excavation.

During the next 10 years McKee and his partners searched the Florida Keys from one end to the other. They located and explored 75 shipwrecks, including some 30 old cannon wrecks. During World War II, when there was a great demand for scrap iron, commercial salvage divers scoured the sea floor around Florida and the Bahamas raising thousands of cannon, as well as anchors and anything else of value. Realizing the historical and archaeological importance of the items, McKee tried in vain to stop them.

By 1949 McKee had a warehouse full of artifacts and treasure from dozens of shipwrecks. On Plantation Key, only a few miles from the sunken *Capitaña*, he built and opened the first museum in the world devoted entirely to sunken treasure and artifacts. The year before, Charles Brookfield, an old Florida "conch" who had begun to treasure hunt shortly after McKee, told him that he had heard rumors that Bahamian fishermen had been finding large numbers of Spanish silver coins on the beaches of Gorda Cay between Abaco Island and Nassau. Brookfield and McKee got up an expedition and verified the story by buying some of the coins from local fishermen. But, they couldn't find the shipwreck.

103

The men went back in 1949. While McKee walked the sea floor looking for the wreck, Brookfield tended his lines and searched with a glass-bottom bucket. Brookfield was luckier, finding two small ballast piles. He signaled McKee to come over, and McKee spotted a long dark bar which he hooked with a long pole and inspected. It appeared to be iron and he sent it topside with a line, following it up himself. A few blows with a hammer revealed the bar to be silver with numerous markings on it. Brookfield asked his partner, "Are there any more down there?" and McKee replied, "Yes, one."

"Well, get the hell down and send it up!" Brookfield shouted.

Before sending it up, though, McKee shot some movie footage, the first of an authentic treasure find. Then Brookfield went down and photographed McKee prying the bar loose from the ballast rocks, where it was cemented by coral. Both ballast piles were resting on a limestone bottom with no sand to conceal any more treasure. They decided that any remaining treasure would be hidden in the ballast rock. Later that day McKee found a third silver bar weighing 75 pounds. In the days that followed, the two men didn't find any more silver bars, they did find many artifacts, as well as about 50 silver coins.

Teddy Tucker

Of all the underwater explorers I've known over the years, few have even come close to leading as exciting and interesting a life as Teddy Tucker, who claims that he would prefer to have lived several centuries ago as a pirate. Even today, he looks the part. In addition to being one of the best known residents of Bermuda, Teddy is a knowledgeable and successful underwater treasure-hunter.

At the age of 12 in 1938 he convinced a helmet diver working in Hamilton Harbor to teach him to dive. Tucker became so fascinated with the underwater environment that he fashioned a diving helmet from a small boiler tank

104

by connecting a garden hose to a hand-operated air pump on the surface. With some of his school chums he explored miles and miles of the reefs surrounding Bermuda. They earned spending money by selling coral, sea fans and shells to tourists. Tucker loved the sea and hated school so much that his parents had to physically take him each day.

At 15 he stowed away on a merchant ship to England where he lied about his age and joined the Royal Navy for the duration of World War II. Tucker claims to have spent most of his navy years in brigs and jails. While stationed at Plymouth, England, he was ordered to clean up the base's mascot, a jackass. Given methylated spirits to clean the animal's hooves, he mixed the spirits with beer instead and drank the mixture, ending up in the brig for several weeks. Tucker supported himself after the war by working as a commercial diver, salvaging modern shipwrecks among other jobs. This gave him a chance to see the underwater world in such exotic places as the Malacca Straits, Gulf of Siam, Bay of Bengal and elsewhere in the Indian Ocean.

American salvage crew in 1858 with gold and silver bars and chest of gold dust recovered from a Gold Rush shipwreck off Panama, using a grab bucket as their primary tool.

Returning to Bermuda in 1948, Tucker decided to forsake his reckless past and become a respectable citizen. He even gave up drinking, which he blames for many of his past problems. In 1949 with diver Bob Canton, who became his brother-in-law, Tucker started a commercial salvage firm They recovered brass, lead and other metals from modern shipwrecks. When the salvage business was slow, Canton and Tucker worked as commercial fishermen. While searching for one of his fish traps with a glass-bottom bucket in 1950, Tucker spotted two iron cannon on the bottom. A few days later he returned to the spot about 10 miles outside Hamilton Harbor and raised the cannon as well as a large copper kettle full of lead musket balls. He and Canton planned to sell the cannon for scrap, but some members of the Bermuda Monuments Trust Commission heard of his discovery and bought the cannon for more than he would have gotten by selling them as scrap. They went back to the wreck site and recovered four more cannon, an anchor and a pewter plate. While the wreck was interesting, Tucker and Canton decided to stick to their normal salvage work.

After a storm in the summer of 1955, the two men stopped at the wreck site, and Tucker jumped in with a face mask. With excellent underwater visibility he noticed that the storm had removed a great deal of sand. On the bottom he pulled out a piece of metal...a beautifully decorated bronze apothecary's mortar, bearing the date 1561. Excited by this find, Tucker returned to the boat, started the air compressor, and jumped back in, wearing his shallow water diving mask. With a small board he began fanning the sand away in the area where he had found the mortar and in five minutes had a handful of blackened silver coins. He dug a trench about 18 inches deep. Soon a bright object fell out. It was a gold cube weighing about two ounces. Tucker was so excited that he bumped his head on the bottom of the boat while surfacing. Right then and there, he and his brother-in-law decided to forget about their salvage company and become full-time treasure-hunters.

They had about a week before bad weather would set in and force them to quit for the season. It was during that week that they struck it rich, finding more gold cubes and larger gold bars in addition to gold buttons studded with pearls and other gold jewelry. Then on the last day, Tucker discovered one of the most valuable single items of treasure ever recovered from an old shipwreck. It was a magnificent emerald-studded gold cross, subsequently valued at $200,000. Of course, this find hooked them for good. They became two of the most successful treasure hunters in the business, continuing into their fifties and sixties, considered advanced ages for a diver.

Kip Wagner

Kip Wagner got started as a professional treasure hunter rather late, but this had little effect on his success. In fact, Wagner was the only treasure hunter who became a millionaire by recovering sunken treasure. He retired in the early seventies and died not long after that.

Wagner was born and spent most of his life in Ohio and had absolutely no interest in treasure or shipwrecks until he moved to Florida after World War I to start a construction business. He heard stories of people finding gold and silver coins on the beaches, usually after storms, but scoffed at them as idle tales. Yet when one of his employees showed up for work drunk, Wagner took the man to the beach where fresh salt air could sober him up. As they walked along, the man bent down and picked up what appeared to be a piece of rusty metal. It was a silver coin. During the next half hour, he found six more and told Wagner he had found hundreds over the years.

His interest aroused, Wagner learned through research about the fleet of 12 Spanish treasure galleons that had been wrecked in the area in the hurricane of 1715. He learned too that millions of dollars in treasure still lay in their remains. With local divers he formed the Real Eight

Company. Although all were amateurs, never having seen a shipwreck, Wagner and his divers learned the ropes by trial and error. He located sites of most of the shipwrecks from the 1715 disaster by finding coins on nearby beaches.

After exploratory dives in the spring of 1960, Real Eight's salvage project got underway. The task that immediately concerned them on their first target was to move tons of ballast stones by hand before they could reach the treasure. At first everyone worked enthusiastically, but after spending several weekends at the back-breaking labor, they grew skeptical. Just as they approached the point of calling off the effort, a diver found a large wedge of silver...the beginning of one of the major treasure finds of this century. During the next decade the Real Eight Company recovered over $10 million in treasure and artifacts.

Mel Fisher

It may sound preposterous that a man who has recovered millions in treasure from the sea has had the electricity in his house turned off because he lacked money to pay the bill...or that his wife was forced to use pieces of eight instead of dollars to buy groceries.

But, that's what really happened to Mel Fisher, whose name became familiar to most Americans after his long search for the richly laden *Atocha* paid off. And, after a lifetime of successful treasure hunting, he's still trying to get rich. When asked what he did with all the millions he and his partners found, he answers quietly, "Man, most of it went to the State of Florida, my backers and to Uncle Sam for income taxes." Actually, a lot of it was invested in expeditions to find shipwrecks.

Fisher's favorite expression, which he repeats a dozen times a day, is, "There's a pot full of gold below; let's go get it."

Mel began diving at the age of 10, when he made his own diving helmet from a five-gallon paint can. To sink it, he melted his toy soldiers, but the helmet still had no window or air supply. His earliest dives were in a clear-water gravel pit. By looking down, he could stay under water for about five minutes at a time. On a few occasions he stepped off a ledge and tipped the helmet, thus losing his air and had to make a quick ascent to the surface.

After a near-fatal accident in which he lost consciousness and almost drowned from breathing stale air too long, Fisher drastically revised his helmet. He put a window in and fitted the valve stem from a bicycle tire on top. The helmet was connected to a bicycle hand pump via 15 feet of hose. A friend worked the pump while sitting on an inflated inner tube on the surface. On his first dive with the new helmet in a lake near Gary, IN, Fisher wore too much weight and mired himself waist deep in silt on the bottom. To make matters worse, his buddy was pumping so hard that the glass window blew out, nearly drowning him before he could reach the surface. Again, he modified the helmet by putting metal bars over the window, and it worked well for many years.

Fisher got his first salvage job when he was 12. He and a friend raised a speedboat that had sunk in a lake. They bought it, minus the engine, for a dollar, added a sail and oars, and used it as a diving boat. When they were 14, they caught treasure fever from reading books on the subject and decided to run off to Florida via the Mississippi River. They had covered about a hundred miles when someone stole their boat and everything in it as they slept on a river bank. So, they gave up and came home.

Fisher encountered skin diving during World War II when he was on furlough on the French Riviera. With no equipment he had to be content to watch others spear fish and lobsters. After the war he spent a few years in the construction business in Chicago and Denver, yet never forgot that his aim was to become a diver. He moved to Tampa in 1948 and started his own construction business.

The sport of skin diving was then so new that it was months before he saw anyone engaging in it. Fishing from a bridge one day, he encountered a man with snorkeling equipment and a spear gun. Right where Fisher was catching one and two-pound fish, the spear fisherman bagged a 60-pound grouper and a 35-pound snook. Fisher was so frustrated that he broke his fishing rod and threw it in the water. The next day he returned with his own equipment and a homemade spear gun. Until the diver who had been there the day before taught him the rudiments, however, it appeared that skin diving was harder than it looked. Yet within a few days he was free-diving to 50 feet and spearing fish with ease.

Fisher later moved to Los Angeles where he discovered what appeared to be an old cannon. As it turned out, this discovery caused him much embarrassment since news of the find created a lot of interest. It was the first cannon to be found in California waters, and NBC television covered it nationwide. The cannon was placed on exhibition at a pier in Redondo Beach where thousands paid a dollar apiece to see it...until Fisher removed the coral encrustation and discovered that it was a sewage pipe!

When he failed to find treasure on shipwrecks, Fisher tried diving for gold in California's rivers and streams. It began as a hobby, but when he made his first "strike" (actually, a few small nuggets), thousands of divers got gold fever, and Fisher turned to developing and marketing an underwater vacuum dredge that featured a venturi jet. To teach potential buyers how to use it, he began taking small groups to the rivers on weekends. The groups got larger and larger. One weekend he had some 500 families out in the mountains with him. Fisher says he was too busy selling dredges and other equipment to find much gold himself...though some divers did. One of them made $75,000 in a few weeks.

Some time later, Fisher's treasure fever led him to a number of unsuccessful expeditions to the Caribbean and coast of Panama. In late 1962 he was approached by one of Kip Wagner's divers and talked into joining the Real

Eight Company team. With some close friends he formed the Treasure Salvors Company, and they headed for Florida. While the Real Eight team was picking up treasure hand over fist, Wagner had Fisher's team hunting for new wrecks. After a year of finding nothing, Fisher and his disgruntled associates were ready to go back to California. They had been digging on a shipwreck for weeks without success.

Then it happened...one of Fisher's divers discovered two seven-and-a-half-pound gold discs.

The next morning Fisher said he had a feeling that if they moved about 500 feet to seaward, they would make a big find. Everyone thought it crazy to leave the area where they had found the gold discs, but the salvage boat was moved. The blaster, an excavation tool used to remove sand covering a wreck site, exposed a hole 15 feet in diameter between two large coral heads, and divers went down to check The bottom of the hole was such a veritable carpet of gold they were almost blinded by the glow. The three divers stuffed coins into their gloves. When they

This old print shows a scene from the 16th or 17th century, more imaginary than real, as one Spanish galleon sinks and another stands by to rescue survivors who are scurrying away.

dumped them in glistening cascades on the deck of the boat, the total came to 1,073. Mel Fisher's hunch had resulted in the most valuable treasure recovery of the century up to that time.

They returned to the area the next day, along with most of the Real Eight divers, and recovered another 900 coins. During the next five days another 600 were recovered, bringing the total to 2,573. For a few days, no more were found before the dry spell ended, and they began finding coins again.

During those days, Fisher says, he dreamed that the ocean floor was paved with gold, He even feared the world gold market would be ruined if word got out about their discovery. They adopted elaborate security measures, putting the treasure in various banks. But the news was too spectacular not to leak. Subsequently, they had great difficulty keeping pirate divers away, especially at night when they weren't at the site.

By the end of the summer more than 3,500 gold and 6,000 silver coins had been recovered, along with numerous gold chains, medallions, rings and other pieces of jewelry. Total value exceeded a million dollars. To raise working capital for the next season they sold 107 of the gold coins at auction for $50,000. Since bad weather caused that diving season was the worst they had ever experienced, only Fisher's dedication kept the season from being a complete failure.

The 1715 shipwrecks are still producing. During the summer of 1989, for example, more than 20 different diving groups spent the summer working these sites...some with more success than others. Even as I write this book, Mel Fisher is only six miles away dragging a magnetometer in an area where a large number of gold and silver coins were flung upon the beach during a winter storm a few months ago. Five of the shipwrecks of this fleet have never been located, and Fisher feels that these coins are from one of them. Now 68 years old, Fisher has little difficulty in paying his light bill. But, the lure of finding more treasure is just too strong to overcome.

Other Treasure Hunters

Fisher isn't the only treasure hunter who has spent years fighting the bureaucrats. Two brothers from Gary, IN, named Paul and Max Zinica suffered years of anguish and frustration, but, like Fisher, won in the end. In 1967 they located one of the galleons of the 1553 fleet which wrecked on Padre Island, off the coast of South Texas. After they recovered over a million dollars in treasure and artifacts, the State of Texas moved in to confiscate the booty, leaving the brothers nothing more than a single piece of eight. After a battle in the courts which lasted over 10 years, not only did they win their case and have their treasure returned, but they were also awarded costs of legal fees and other remuneration.

In recent years fantasy became reality for quite a few people with countless accidental finds of sunken treasures. For obvious reasons not all have been publicized. Two teenage divers searching for lobsters on a shallow reef near Vero Beach, FL, in 1963 discovered more than $200,000 in American double eagle gold coins. They lay exposed on the sandy bottom as shiny as the day they were made. It took the boys less than two hours to harvest all the treasure, using no more than snorkeling equipment.

Even more startling was the fortuitous find a vacationing couple from Georgia made in Grand Cayman in 1969. While wandering along the shore in search of seashells they came across a gold cross inlaid with diamonds in water three feet deep. Keeping the discovery mum, the man came back to the site with an underwater detector and scuba equipment and proceeded, literally, to strike it rich. Under a thin layer of sand he found a fantastic cache which included a large bar of platinum dated 1521, about 45 pounds of small silver bars, a three pound gold disk, a gold bracelet in the form of an emerald-studded serpent and almost 300 pounds of gold artifacts. Subsequent re-

113

search showed that his find came from a small ship returning to Spain with loot seized by conquistadors in Mexico.

Not all treasure hunts have good endings and one such case is that of the British warship *De Braak*, which went down in 1798 in 100 feet of water off the coast of Delaware. Many attempts had been made to locate her based on legends of a great treasure aboard that had circulated for years after her loss. She was pinpointed by Harvey Harrington in 1984, a discovery that received considerable press coverage when he and others soon began bringing up gold and silver coins. One of the most interesting finds was a gold ring belonging to the ship's captain James Drew.

Unfortunately, the salvors were a bit hasty in their recovery work and decided to lift a substantial portion of the ship's wooden hull. During this attempt most of the artifacts and treasure still on top of the wooden remains fell off and were lost again. Bureaucrats jumped at the chance to use this as an example of how treasure hunters destroyed archaeological sites, and it became a cause celebre around the world.

With stories of successful recoveries to spur them on, many people have spent years and untold sums of money pursuing sunken treasure that never existed. A wild goose chase lasting for centuries involved the *Florencia*, a ship of the Spanish Armada, which supposedly went down in 1588. According to legend, the *Florencia* was carrying $5 million in treasure, when forced by bad weather and lack of fresh water to put into Tobermory Bay in Scotland. There the Spaniards took a hostage, a Highland chieftain named Donald McLean, who in retaliation set fire to the

Mel Fisher, whose name became a legend in treasure hunting when he discovered the *Atocha*, is shown with a clump of pieces of eight and a gold disk from a shipwreck.

Spaniards' ship. The fire and resulting explosion killed everyone aboard, including McLean.

Within just a few months treasure hunters descended on the wreck with diving bells. Although they found nothing, for most of the next four centuries, hardly a decade passed when a search for the *Florencia* wasn't undertaken. Total money spent in these endeavors must by now far exceed the value of the treasure allegedly lying in the wreck. Ironically, it was confirmed a few years ago that not only was this wreck not carrying treasure...it wasn't even the *Florencia*, which turned out to be one of the few Armada ships that survived the battle and returned to Spain. Experts are fairly sure that the wreck at the bottom of Tobermory Bay is that of another ship in the Armada.

Another wild-goose chase focused on Vigo Bay, Spain. In 1702, during the War of the Spanish Succession, a homeward-bound Spanish treasure fleet of 20 galleons and its escort of 23 French warships fought a combined fleet of English and Dutch warships. Legend has it that most of the Spanish ships, laden with treasure worth more than $50 million in modern currency, sank in Vigo Bay, paving it with riches for those courageous enough to seize the treasure. Many have been daring enough to try. At least 75 treasure-salvaging expeditions to the site have been mounted, but only a few silver coins--of value only to collectors--have been recovered.

Like the stories about Tobermory, those about Vigo are largely myth...for records tell a different story. Yes, when the Spanish treasure fleet sighted the English and Dutch, it hurried into Vigo Bay. But, the Spaniards immediately began unloading the treasure (amounting only to

Kip Wagner, whose salvaging of the 12 galleons in the 1715 fleet off Florida was a landmark in treasure hunting, fits together silver wedges from one of the wrecks.

a fifth of what the legend claims, incidentally) and it was taken overland to Madrid. Before the transfer had been completed, the Anglo-Dutch fleet entered the harbor and the battle began with 11 Spanish ships captured and the rest burned to prevent their falling into enemy hands. Documents in the Spanish archives confirm beyond a doubt that no appreciable amount of treasure was on the ships set afire by the Spaniards. What wasn't taken to Madrid was captured by the English and Dutch.

The only treasure at the bottom of Vigo Bay was on an English ship, the *Monmouth*. Leaving ahead of the main fleet with the English share of the Spanish treasure in 1702, it struck a rock and sank in 150 feet of water. Because of the depth, no attempt to reach it was made until this century. In 1955 some American divers formed a company, raised $100,000 and went after it. After four years of continuous effort they found what they believed to be the *Monmouth*, but there was no treasure. Did they have the wrong wreck? Or, had the English managed to unload their treasure from the *Monmouth* before she sank? We don't know. Whatever happened, it's just the tale of one more fruitless treasure hunt to add to the many about Vigo Bay.

Through the centuries there have been innumerable quests for sunken treasure on "phantom" wrecks...ships that never existed or never sank. Even today, when people are allegedly more realistic, there's a thriving business in maps, articles and books on fantasy treasures and their locations. Each year, thousands of gullible souls use them to hunt for sunken treasure in hopes of becoming rich overnight. I sincerely hope that you will not be among them.

After reading this book, you should find *yourself* on the road to learning how to locate and recover genuine sunken treasure.

Archaeology

All over the world objects are lying on the bottom of the sea...objects that belonged to civilizations long since vanished. Like relics painstakingly unearthed by land archaeologists, those found underwater can be valuable clues to the past.

In 1928 Salomon Reinarch, a leading Hellenist, wrote, "The richest museum of antiquities in the world is still inaccessible to us. It lies at the bottom of the eastern Mediterranean. We are able to explore the land and air without much difficulty, but we are very far from rivaling the fish in their element, which in the words of St. Augustus, 'have their being in the secret ways of the Abyss.' Those ways remain closed to us." Dr. Reinarch made this statement before the wonderful technological developments that have enabled man to explore the great treasures of the living undersea museum.

First to show interest in underwater archaeology were a group of English antiquarians who in 1775 sponsored an expedition to recover historical artifacts from the Tiber River near Rome. Using a diving bell, Greek divers worked for three years under their direction with little success. They had no way of removing the river mud, accumulating for centuries, that covered wrecks they wanted to excavate for artifacts. Interest in underwater archaeology then declined, and it wasn't until early in this century when Greek and Turkish fishermen and sponge divers brought up interesting ancient artifacts that the interest of archaeologists was again aroused. Recognizing both the beauty of these items and their value as clues to antiquity, archaeologists hired divers to search for more. Most of the magnificent bronzes on display in the National Museum in Athens were recovered by sponge divers.

Fishermen have been finding unique hand-crafted antiquities for centuries. Many finds made of metal were melted down for scrap. Early in the 18th century fishermen near Livorno, Italy, recovered bronze statues of Homer and Sophocles. Shortly afterwards, fishermen in the Gulf of Corinth snagged a bronze statue of the "Zeus of Livadhostro." In 1832 off the coast of Tuscany, near the site of the ancient city of Populonium, fishermen hauled up a bronze statue of Apollo. This exquisite work is today one of the Louvre's major exhibits. Until the mid-1960s, when a dredging operation at Piraeus uncovered many spectacular bronze statues, this statue of Apollo was the only bronze original from the Greek Archaic period (before 480 B.C.).

In 1900 Greek sponge divers reported finding a large cache of statuary at a depth of 30 fathoms off the island of Antikythera. A salvage operation was then sponsored by the Greek Ministry of Education. At this depth, however, divers had only about five minutes bottom time. This was emphasized when one diver exceeded the time and died from the bends. Also, it could not be considered a proper archaeological excavation. The uneducated divers had no idea what was worth saving and what wasn't. Several large marble statues which they mistook for boulders were mistakenly picked up by cranes and thrown into deeper water. Because the site was not worked systematically, many valuable objects still remained on the bottom when the exhausted divers stopped working.

This wreck proved to be a Roman argosy laden with works of art looted from Grecian temples. Amphoras and other ceramic objects found at the site date the wreck at about 75 B.C. In addition to a number of priceless bronze statues, including the well-known "Antikythera Youth," 36 marble statues and a bronze bed decorated with animal

120

heads were raised. Smaller objects such as a gold earring in the form of Eros playing a lyre, some exquisite glass vessels and the gears from a unique astronomical computer were also brought up. This discovery provided magnificent examples of original works by master sculptors of the Argive and Athenian schools. French divers who briefly revisited the site in 1953 claim that the wreck itself is buried deep in the sand and that many more works of art await recovery.

Another Roman argosy dating from the 1st century B.C. was found by Greek sponge divers in 1907, three miles off Mahdia on the coast of Tunisia. The bulk of this ship's cargo consisted of stone bases, capitals and 60 columns, each weighing about 200 tons. Between 1908 and 1913 divers under the direction of the Tunisian Department of Antiquities worked on the site in 150 feet of water. They recovered most of the cargo which included well-preserved busts, dancing dwarfs, a heron and a large statue of Agon, all in bronze.

In 1948 a team of French divers led by Jacques Cousteau used scuba equipment for the first time on an underwater archaeological project at the same site. They removed the overburden of mud covering the wreck with water jets and raised more of the ship's cargo to the surface. The site was again worked in 1954 and 1955 by amateur divers from the Tunisian Club of Underwater Studies, but much still remains there to be accomplished. In 1928 sponge divers made still another accidental discovery off Cape Artemision in Greece...a Roman shipwreck dating from about the time of Christ. Employing helmet divers, the Greek navy conducted a salvage operation which ended abruptly when a diver died from the bends. The famous statue of Zeus (or Poseidon, god of the sea), a bronze jockey and parts of a galloping horse of the Hellenist period were among the objects found. Although the wreck lies in sand only 130 feet down, no more excavation has ever been done.

The first disciplined archaeological work on an underwater site came in Lake Nemi near Rome in 1928. Area residents had long repeated tales passed down from antiquity about two Roman ships that sank there during the 1st century A.D. Both were enormous and sumptuous. Over 230 feet in length with decks paved in mosaics and colored marbles, the vessels had heated baths, marble columns and other luxurious features. The ships were probably pleasure craft for Roman nobility.

Feeble attempts to salvage them were made in 1446 and again in 1535, but the equipment used was too primitive. Twice during the 19th century divers recovered artifacts from the site, but the last operation was halted by the Italian government in 1895 when divers were discovered removing large quantities of wood planking from the wrecks.

In 1928 the dictator Benito Mussolini decided that the government of Italy should salvage the ships, and over a period of four years the lake was drained. When the ships were exposed, and before they were disassembled and taken to a warehouse in Rome, archaeologists had a unique opportunity to study the two well-preserved hulls. Tragically, the ships were burned by the Germans in 1944, and today we have only detailed drawings and scale models to study.

The first major excavation of an underwater site in the Western Hemisphere was led by Edward Thompson, the American consul at Merida, Yucatan, early in this century. Passionately interested in archaeology, Thompson purchased some land containing the ruins of Chichen Itza, one of the most important cities of Mayan civilization. Under the auspices of the American Antiquarian Society and Harvard University's Peabody Museum, he began a systematic exploration of the site.

Near one of the temples, he found a large cenote. These holes formed in the limestone when the roof of a subterranean cave collapses are filled with rain water.

Thompson's cenote was 190 feet in diameter, and the water in it was 65 feet deep with walls rising 60 feet above the water's surface. Local Mayans told him that the cenote was called the "Well of Sacrifice." According to legend, it contained an immense treasure. Thompson's research confirmed the Indians' story. For centuries before the Spaniards invaded Mexico, the Maya had worshiped Yum Chac, the rain god believed to inhabit the cenote. Dependent on the maize crop for food, the Maya made offerings to Yum Chac, especially during times of drought. These offerings included gold and jade and, occasionally, young maidens.

Returning from the United States in 1909, where he had raised money from the Peabody Museum and learned to dive in a helmet suit, Thompson began work. A derrick was built for lowering and raising him, as well as holding a suction dredge to be used to remove the mud from the bottom of the cenote. Thompson's early dives revealed that much of the mud on the bottom was 10 feet deep and that the water was inky black. For months he relied solely on the suction dredge, which was manipulated from the surface.

Tons and tons of mud were pumped up, but the ooze didn't yield even one artifact. Just as he was about ready to admit defeat, the dredge brought up the first object...a round ball of resinous incense. Thompson then switched to a steel-jawed grab bucket. Hardly a day passed thereafter without a relic coming to light. Working by touch alone, Thompson dived into the gloomy depths and found more incense balls, ceramic incense burners, vases, bowls, plates, axes, lance points, arrowheads, copper chisels, discs of beaten copper...even human bones.

Among the artifacts were about $800,000 worth of gold bells, figurines and discs, as well as pendants, beads and earrings of jade. Like the pioneers of land archaeology, most of whom were highly educated, well-to-do gentlemen, Thompson was in love with ancient history.

Also like them, he wasn't particularly interested in making money. He was an amateur archaeologist pursuing a passion. This priceless collection, like many others in the early days of archaeology, was thus shipped to the Peabody Museum where it was put on display until 1960 when it was given to the Mexican government.

During the Revolutionary War, several British warships were sunk in the York River, just off Yorktown, VA. In 1934 oystermen discovered the hulks of some of them, which the Colonial National Historical Park Service and the Mariner's Museum of Newport News joined in salvaging. U.S. Navy divers used water jets to blow the mud off two of them and found they were too poorly preserved to be raised. A grab bucket operated from a barge was therefore used to recover a fairly representative collection of late 18th-century armament and equipment...cannon, anchors, weapons, ship's fittings, tools, bottles, crockery and pewterware. During the summer of 1976 Dr. George Bass, who had recently formed the American Institute of Nautical Archaeology, spent six weeks surveying the shipwrecks. After locating 12 possible sites with a magnetometer, he dug test holes at some of them and found many interesting and important artifacts. Lack of money has prevented him from continuing this project, but he hopes to raise the capital necessary to continue the excavation.

Grab buckets such as those used by Thompson in Mexico were still being employed in 1950. Techniques and standards of underwater archaeology had progressed little in 40 years when Nino Lamboglia, director of the Institute of Ligurian Studies, initiated a project which pointed up the destructive capabilities of the grab bucket. In 1925 fishermen snagged amphoras in 140 feet of water off Albenga, Italy, from what proved to be a 1st-century B.C. Roman shipwreck. Unable to get government funds for a salvage project or to arouse any interest among amateur divers, Lamboglia accepted assistance from a commercial salvage firm. Under his direction, helmet divers removed a few of the amphoras by hand. Then a large grab bucket was used, directed by an observer in a diving chamber who was in telephone communication with the surface. Giant steel claws smashed into the wreck, wrenching up amphoras, wood and other objects. The excavation went on for 10 days, during which 1,200 amphoras were raised. All but 110 of them were broken. Such destruction of an archaeological site proved a catalyst for development of scientific techniques for underwater archaeology. Lamboglia was the first to admit that he had made a serious mistake in not making drawings of the site or making better plans for the excavation.

The next major underwater excavation of an ancient wreck took place in 1952. Divers working on the construction of the great Marseilles sewer outlet off the small island of Grand Congloure come upon the remains of a 2nd-century B.C. Roman ship in 150 feet of water. Excavation of this wreck was the proving ground for many of the

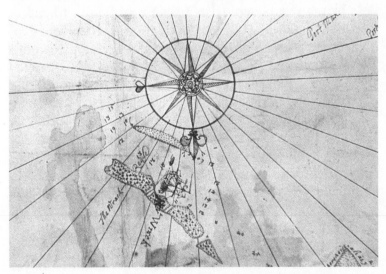

Treasure chart showing the position of the Spanish galleon *Concepcion,* lost in 1641 on Silver Shoals and later salvaged by Sir William Phips and in recent times by Bert Weber.

tools and techniques still used today. Captain Cousteau joined forces with Fernand Benoit, an archaeologist, for the project. To clear away the layer of mud and sand that covered most of the site, Cousteau used a kind of underwater vacuum cleaner. Called an "airlift," they had been used by treasure hunters in the Florida Keys during the 1930s, but never before had they been used on an archaeological dig.

Benoit and the other non-diving archaeologists watched the operation over closed-circuit television. They were frustrated because they couldn't communicate with the divers and exercise better control over their activities. Divers were similarly frustrated at being limited to three dives a day, or a total of 45 minutes of bottom time by the depth of the water. Fortunately, while several thousand dives were made during the project, only one diver lost his life.

Although many unusual and priceless artifacts were recovered, the excavation wasn't considered a total success by many archaeologists because of failure to gather pertinent data while the artifacts were still on the sea floor. There was no plan of the site, and neither Cousteau nor Benoit provided information on how they had reached their conclusions about the wreck site. An accepted rule of archaeology demands that archaeologists record and publish their findings, for what may seem unimportant at the time can prove significant in the future. However, like Henrich Schliemann, the excavator of Troy and Mycenae, these men were pioneering a new field. Their mistakes should be judged accordingly. Other commitments following the project at Marseilles prevented Cousteau and his team from devoting themselves to underwater archaeology for many years.

In 1968 Cousteau made a brief expedition to Silver Shoals, off the coast of Haiti, in search of the *Concepcion,* the Spanish galleon that sank in 1641 with a large treasure in gold, silver and gems. He didn't find it but photographed the wreck of a Dutch merchantman that sank during the 18th century and had been thoroughly worked by treasure hunters over the years. Then in the summer of 1975 the Greek government hired Cousteau to make an archaeological survey in the Aegean Sea. When he and his team didn't find any interesting shipwrecks, they decided to explore a wreck off the island of Antikythera...the Roman wreck found and salvaged by helmet divers at the turn of the century. They recovered three gold bars, a large number of gold coins and an engraved jewel-studded necklace.

The first complete and successful excavation of an ancient shipwreck to be directed by a professional archaeologist working under water took place at Cape Gelidonya on the coast of Turkey. The project was the idea of an enthusiastic young American named Peter Throckmorton, an erstwhile student of archaeology and a diver in the throes of a wanderlust that had brought him to Turkey after roaming all over the world. Sharing countless bottles of raki with garrulous Turkish sponge divers led Throckmorton in 1959 to the location where the divers saw "old pots in the sea"...amphorae, the ceramic containers used to store everything from wine to grain and oil in ancient times.

Nearly every sponge diver in the Mediterranean knows of a wreck site or two, and in the course of the next year, Throckmorton checked out about 35 areas that divers had mentioned. Most of them were heavily traveled lanes where ships had sunk over a period two centuries. One of these wrecks, lying in 90 feet of water off Cape Gelidonya, turned out to be the second oldest shipwreck ever found, a Bronze Age wreck dating from 1300 B.C. Throckmorton realized its importance on his first exploratory dive. He convinced sponge divers who had planned to dynamite the site and sell the cargo of copper and bronze for scrap to leave it alone for the moment. Then he reported his find to the University of Pennsylvania's Department of Archaeology. Dr. Rodney Young, director of the university's Institute of Classical Archaeology, offered to find the money and personnel to mount a major expedition to the site.

In the summer of 1960 20 specialists in various aspects of underwater archaeology joined Throckmorton at Cape Gelidonya. The team included Frederic Dumas, who was experienced in underwater projects off the French Riviera, and Dr. George Bass. Because of the wreck's depth, a diver was limited to 68 minutes working time per day. But since each man's task was carefully planned, the team was able to make the most of the brief bottom time. When the area had been cleared of seaweed, drawings and plans of the wreck were made. Then they made a photographic mosaic of the site. On the bottom the area resembled a conventional land site, with meter poles staked about and numbered plastic tags marking the objects that were visible. Each item was drawn, photographed, triangulated and plotted before being raised to the surface.

A thick deposit of lime as hard as concrete covered most of the cargo, with only an occasional piece protruding through the hard sea floor. Fragility of many of the artifacts made trying to extract individual pieces underwater too time-consuming and risky. Working with hammers and chisels, the divers broke off large clumps of conglomerate, some weighing 400 pounds, and sent them to the surface in lifting baskets to be broken apart. Some of the larger masses had to be separated with automotive jacks. Until each day's recovery could be processed in this fashion, it was stored in a freshwater pond on the beach.

When the clumps were separated, a fascinating array of artifacts was revealed...bronze chisels, axes, picks, hoes, adzes, plowshares, knives, spades, a spit and many copper ingots. An airlift used in the few sand pockets at the site yielded other artifacts, including four Egyptian scarabs, oil lamps, polished stone mace-heads, apothecary weights, pieces of crystal, mirrors, awls, a cooking spit, whetstones, olive pits and the bones of animals and fish.

Although little of the hull had been preserved, distribution of cargo suggests that the ship was approximately 12 meters long. Brushwood dunnage like that described in the *Odyssey* still lay over fragments of planks. The cargo and personal possessions that were found indicated that the ship was a Syrian merchant vessel that had picked up a cargo of metal on Cyprus. The wreck shed new light on seafaring during the Bronze Age and furnished a wealth of information on early metallurgy and trade.

Additional Projects Now Possible

The expedition opened the way for future underwater archaeological projects in the Mediterranean. Dr. Bass, convinced of the importance of this fledgling science, decided to make it his life's work. Before he left for Turkey, he had consulted several land archaeologists who were discouraging in their assessment of a future for underwater archaeology. Most of them believed that underwater archaeology could never become an exact science. "Nothing could be preserved under water," they said and "It's impossible to make proper plans under water." Some called it was too dangerous and far too expensive for the amount of knowledge that could be gained.

During excavation of the wreck, Dr. Bass and the others had been able to dispel these concerns. They were elated to discover that a surprisingly large part of the cargo was in an excellent state of preservation despite having lain under water for some 3,300 years. They made accurate plans and drawings under water...more professional, in fact, than many produced for land excavations. Also, although most of the expedition's members had little previous diving experience, there were no diving accidents. Finally, to the surprise of the skeptics, the whole project, including expenses of air transportation for all those involved, had amounted to less than $25,000. The only disappointment Bass and Throckmorton felt was that so that little wood from the original ship had been preserved, making it difficult to determine details of the ship's construction.

In September of 1975 Throckmorton found a shipwreck even older than the one from the Bronze Age. At a depth of 75 feet, near the entrance to a secluded harbor near Hydra, an island south of Athens, he found remains of a wreck dating from 2700 to 2200 B.C. Fragments of storage jars and other ceramicware indicated the ship was a trading vessel. Unfortunately, the Greek government refused to grant Throckmorton a permit to excavate, and he has since returned to the United States where he plans to continue his work on American shipwrecks.

Within a year of the completion of the excavation by Bass and Throckmorton, the most important and challenging underwater archaeological project ever undertaken in Europe was completed after five years of work. On April 24, 1961, the 64-gun Swedish warship *Vasa* was raised. The ship had sunk in Stockholm harbor in 1628 in full view of the king and thousands of spectators shortly after being launched with 50 passengers and crew aboard. The deepest part of the wreck lay in 100 feet of water, too deep for early divers working out of bells to accomplish much. Salvaging a wooden ship is usually impossible after 50 years because the wood has generally been eaten away by shipworms. Since Stockholm harbor is one of the few places in the world where there are no shipworms, the *Vasa* had remained intact all that time.

In 1956 Swedish petroleum engineer Anders Franzen became interested in the *Vasa* and narrowed down her location after several years of research. Using a core sampler (a device that permits geologists to obtain samples of sediment from the sea floor) operated from a small boat, he found the wreck. Divers from the Swedish navy were sent down to identify and investigate its condition. As Franzen had anticipated, they found it intact. With encouragement from the Swedish government and money from private sources, Franzen began the tedious job of raising the ship. He used helmet divers, but the job was far from simple. The *Vasa*, large for her time, displaced 1,400 tons (four times the size of the *Mayflower*) and was buried deep in the mud of the harbor.

Divers first had to remove all loose objects aboard. Tunnels were then blasted under the wreck with a water jet to permit insertion of steel lifting cables under the hull...a perilous undertaking because the ship could easily have slipped deeper into the mud and crushed them.

Constructing these tunnels alone took three years while other divers removed the masts, spars and rigging. Finally, in a thrilling climax to all this preparation, cables were strung through the tunnels and pontoons were used to lift the *Vasa*.

She was then towed into dry dock and placed on a specially built concrete barge equipped with a sprinkler system to keep her wet until she could be properly preserved. The moment *Vasa* broke the surface, Franzen was very busy. With scores of archaeologists and historians, he entered every accessible part of the vessel. They found themselves in a fantastic time capsule. Everything lay as it had fallen nearly three and a half centuries earlier...sea chests, leather boots, weapons, carpenter's tools, beer steins, cooking implements, money, powder kegs. More than 1,000 artifacts were found. Franzen even discovered the remains of some of the victims of the disaster, lying among the cannon carriages. Twelve partially clad skeletons were dug out of the mud inside the ship. The sheath knife and a leather money pouch containing 20 coins were still attached to the belt of a seaman. *Vasa* was a veritable underwater Pompeii. Here, mud and cold water had taken the place of volcanic lava and ashes.

Since 1973 underwater archaeologists have been exploring the remains of the U.S. brig *Defense*, a 16-gun vessel lost in Penobscot Bay, ME, during a battle with the British in 1779. She was one of 38 ships that entered the bay to attack the British-held Fort George. So far, divers have been occupied with mapping the site, and few artifacts have been recovered. Meanwhile, in Rhode Island a group of 18 cadets from West Point are assisting archaeologists in exploring two other Revolutionary War shipwrecks, the British frigates *Cerberus* and *Orpheus*. The frigates were scuttled off Aquidneck Island in August 1778 to prevent their falling into the hands of the French. Archaeologists and cadets have recovered many valuable artifacts, and more excavation is planned.

Equally as important and thrilling as the *Vasa* project was the raising of a portion of the *Mary Rose*, King Henry VIII's flagship, from the depths of Portsmouth Harbor, England, in 1982, culminating 11 years of work and tens of thousands of hours spent on the bottom...thanks to the perseverance of Dr. Margaret Rule and her volunteer sports divers. After spending 437 years buried in the mud, the ship's starboard side is now on display for all to see along with more than 19,000 priceless Tudor artifacts, many of which have been displayed in tours of the United States and other countries.

Above
Diver searches floor of the Red Sea as part of an 1988 project that traced route of the Hebrews during their Biblical exodus from Egypt.

Below
Famous gold-emerald cross and other pieces of jewelry recovered by Teddy Tucker from a late 16th-century Spanish shipwreck off Bermuda.

Research

Research is the key to success in finding shipwrecks and sunken treasure. Sitting in a musty archive or library may not be as exciting as diving or dragging a magnetometer, but if you want to be successful and save a lot of time and money, it is critical that you start with good research.

During the first half of this century very few attempts were made to recover sunken treasure or to salvage any type of shipwrecks. Most "hard hat" helmet diving was confined to underwater construction and work in seaports. Many fictional books and articles were written, however, and gobbled up by the gullible public...all telling of brave divers finding Spanish galleons intact with skeletons at the wheel and holds crammed with chests of treasure. Usually, a giant octopus or schools of voracious sharks prevented the recovery of the treasure. Such was the case in the 1948 John Wayne movie *Wake of the Red Witch.*

It was such literature and movies that got me and other old-time divers started in the sunken treasure business. One author in the 1930's spun a compelling yarn about exploring the sunken city of Port Royal in Jamaica in water 19 times deeper than it actually is. And, he convincingly described (at least to my 10-year-old self) walking the submerged streets of this pirate port in helmet diving gear.

Front and back of Spanish silver pieces of eight, Pillar dollars, dated 1732 and 1733, each worth around $10,000 because of their rarity.

He told of standing before a cathedral filled with golden relics and guarded by a 12-foot crab. He described taverns full of skeletons at tables with tankards in their bony hands, and chests of gold and precious stones everywhere...just for the taking. What a surprise I was in for when I eventually dived on this same sunken city !

These tales with their accounts of intact galleons set many of us early treasure hunters back for years as we kept searching for such sunken ships. I was *really* thrown off since I found my first gold coins on a nearly intact California Gold Rush ship, a ship made of iron. During my first two years in the Caribbean I kept making the same mistake over and over again. I would find a reef covered with ballast rock--with cannon and anchors strewn about--each time believing that a ship had merely run aground here and cast these materials overboard to lighten itself. One day while extracting a lobster from a ballast pile, I accidentally found silver and gold coins and suddenly realized that *this* was an actual shipwreck. Like many of my friends in the business, I had to learn the hard way.

And, there were the "Authentic Treasure Charts" allegedly pinpointing locations of fabulous shipwrecks loaded with millions in treasure. In the late 1950's I spent three exciting years living on Cozumel, off the coast of Yucatan, then a sleepy undeveloped island. I spent a lot of time exploring the surrounding waters and found quite a number of interesting wrecks and some treasure without the assistance of any books or articles.

In 1959 I made the mistake of falling for the "Authentic Treasure Chart" business. I was eager to return to the eastern side of the Caribbean where I had made several interesting discoveries before settling on Cozumel. So I reasoned, why spend weeks and months snorkeling over reefs and combing the sea floor for shipwrecks when all I had to do was make use of the information I had already accumulated from my collection of treasure charts. From more than a dozen or so of these charts I compiled a list of 100 wrecks scattered all over the Caribbean and set off to track them down.

Fifteen months later, after exploring from the Gulf of Honduras to the San Blas Islands off Panama and from Trinidad to the Bahamas, diving off almost every island and on every reef and rock in between, I had found only two of the 100 wrecks on my list, neither of which had yielded anything of interest. Subsequently, after years of research in European and American archives and libraries, I came to understood why this lack of success should not have been surprising.

Most Were Imaginary!

Of those 100 "authentic" wrecks, 74 never existed! They were simply the creation of highly imaginative writers. Of those 26 others that actually existed 18 had, in fact, sunk with real treasure on board. They sank, however, not in the shallow coastal waters where writers had conveniently placed them, but far away...in very deep water...on the high seas...where there was almost no chance of recovery. Four others had indeed sunk in shallow waters, but hundreds of miles from the locations given in the books and charts. The remaining four were real, and I had found two of them.

Professional treasure hunters and underwater archaeologists have long since realized that most of the information in such books is fictional. They label those wrecks "ghost wrecks," and have a hearty laugh when they hear of a newly organized expedition setting out after one of them. Even the assistance of so-called experts on maritime history cannot always be relied upon. An example of this is what happened to the late Kip Wagner, considered one of the most successful treasure hunters in the world. In his early days, before realizing the only place to get reliable information was from original documentation in archives, he sought assistance from an expert at the Smithsonian Institution and was told that the 11 ships of the Spanish treasure fleet lost in 1715 were all wrecked in the Florida Keys. If Wagner had researched no further, he would never have recovered the more than $10 million in treasure and artifacts from those shipwrecks which he located...not in the Florida keys at all, but where they actually sank more than 200 miles to the north.

Numerous important underwater discoveries have been made by men who never did a bit of archival research, yet paid no attention to information of the "ghost wreck" variety. Teddy Tucker of Bermuda has worked closely with underwater archaeologists from the Smithsonian Institution on many shipwrecks in Bermuda waters for several decades. Tucker started off by searching the reefs surrounding Bermuda using a glass-bottomed bucket. When he sighted something that didn't appear to be a natural formation, he dived to check it. This led to significant discoveries. But he is one of the few who have been successful with this method. For every one who has found a good shipwreck, there are hundreds who have searched unsuccessfully. Most professionals would agree it is best to have the odds in one's favor. This means a commitment to patient and undertake scrupulous research on a shipwreck before setting out after it.

There are two approaches to research:

— To explore areas of probable sites and then concentrate research on a particularly promising site you have located. Identify and learn everything possible about it;

— To select a particularly promising site or sites as objectives and undertake research in depth before any attempt is made to locate or excavate. Although this approach calls for research before you even get your feet (or fins) wet, it has proven more reliable for me and many others in the field.

This book will recount how my research has born fruit. Many treasure hunters believe that only a limited amount of research is necessary to find shipwrecks. They tend to rely too much on magnetometers and intuition and wonder why they end up failing to locate their targets.

Even archaeologists have suffered the same fate. Ten years ago a team of archaeologists attempted to locate the sunken city of Charlestown, which sank in 1687 off the island of Nevis in the Caribbean. Relying on secondary sources they searched on the wrong side of the island and ended up in failure.

Even commercial salvors with sufficient funding have repeatedly made this same mistake. The first three groups seeking the Spanish galleon *San Jose*, which was wrecked in deep water in 1708 and is considered the richest galleon ever lost, spent over $10 million and five years in vain. The secondary source literature they used gave the shipwreck location as being more than 10 miles from where the ship actually went down. With 22 million pesos at stake on that wreck the groups that followed were smarter and at least got into the ballpark by hiring competent researchers who specialize in ferreting out information from primary documentary material in archives, libraries and repositories around the world.

Good research means more than approximating or, with luck, being able merely to pinpoint the area where a particular ship was lost. It means finding out about the ship itself and the voyage. You need to know what kind of ship it was, to whom it belonged, where it embarked from, where it was headed and, most importantly, what it was carrying. After a disappointing experience relying on secondary sources the Belgian Robert Stenuit understood the importance of thorough research when he found a number of shipwrecks by systematically pursuing them in archives before he began diving. Even today articles appear that perpetuate stories about the great treasures reportedly aboard many Spanish galleons sunk in Vigo Bay, Spain, by an Anglo-Dutch fleet in 1702. Stenuit went after and found several of the galleons but found no treasure because they had previously been completely salvaged by contemporary salvors.

Research would have told him this and saved a great

deal of time and money. About 20 years ago he proved the importance of research with his discovery of the *Girona*, one of the many Spanish ships lost after the ill-fated invasion attempt by the Spanish Armada in 1588. Because the *Girona* was carrying survivors and treasure from four other Spanish ships when she was dashed to pieces on the rocks of Northern Ireland, it was like finding five shipwrecks in one. After spending 650 hours in the archives just to pinpoint her location, Steniut's tedious work paid off. He was able to find the wreck in less than a hour. Within minutes of entering the water he was bringing up gold coins and jewelry. He went one step further than archival research several years later with his discovery of the Dutch East Indiaman *Slot Ter Hoge,* lost in 1724 off Porto Santo, Madeira. He had the exact location from the archival documents but decided to do further research.

He contacted the ancestors of Lethbridge, the English diver and inventor of the "diving machine," who had salvaged some of the ship's treasures soon after it went down. He turned up a pewter mug, actually engraved with a scene showing Lethbridge's salvage vessel working the wreck and showing various features of the surrounding landscape. Armed with a photograph of this scene Stenuit found the *Slot Ter Hoge* in less than 10 minutes. He has performed similar near-miracles with discoveries off Madagascar, Santa Helena Island and elsewhere. In the business it's now called "doing a Stenuit" when we go after a shipwreck backed by excellent archival research.

One of my associates, a Frenchman named Jean Yves Blot, used the system with a twist to find a rich Spanish galleon, the *San Pedro Alcantara,* lost in 1787 off Peniche, Portugal. He found a series of paintings depicting contemporary salvage efforts with the surrounding landscape shown in full detail. By matching topographical and landscape features, he placed his survey vessel in the exact spot where the Spanish salvage ship was depicted and located the wreck in a matter of minutes.

Studying historical accounts by contemporary salvors has led to the discovery of numerous treasure wrecks in recent years, the most notable being the 1641 *Concepcion,* lost on Silver Shoals north of Hispañiola, a target of salvors for centuries. Before Burt Webber discovered this fantastic wreck in 1980, more than 20 major expeditions went after her. One of the first in the 20th century was led by Mel Fisher who ended up finding a Dutch merchantman instead, the same Dutch wreck Jacques Costeau and his team had come upon during their fruitless search for the elusive *Concepcion* in 1969.

Burt Webber spent the summer of 1977 and up a quarter of a million dollars with negative results. When he decided to spend the money for research in England, he was finally able to find the wreck that so many had hunted. His researcher fortuitously located the logbook of the "Henry" Phip's salvage vessel, which gave the precise location of the *Concepcion.* Just $10,000 spent on this bit of research netted the salvors over $100 million!

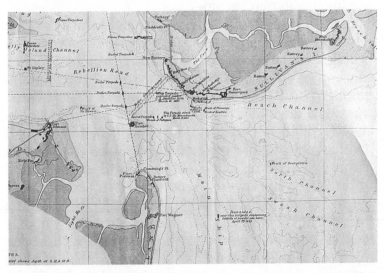

This chart showing the precise location of six blockade runners that were lost in Charleston Bay, SC, during the Civil War is typical of the results that are ordinarily sought from research.

After my wild goose chase of the "ghost wrecks" in the Caribbean I realized that almost everything published up until that time had been fictitious. It was clear that if I wanted success, I would have to undertake *original* archive and library research on both sides of the Atlantic.

This quest for information from primary sources has taken me to more than 25 countries and into more than 100 libraries and archives. In fact, I discovered that I love to pore over dusty documents and 16th-century manuscripts for clues about a wreck...just as much as I love plunging into the depths to work on the shipwreck itself. In Spain alone I have spent a total of four years reading old manuscripts and since 1961 I have had at least one full-time researcher employed in the Archives of the Indies in Seville where there is an unsurpassed wealth of information about Spanish Colonial maritime affairs. As a by-product of this research, I have learned to read five languages and have written more than 30 books and hundreds of articles on maritime history, treasure hunting and underwater archaeology.

My shipwreck files contain pertinent data on more than 75,000 wrecks dating from the time of the Phoenicians and ending with the American Civil War, the point when my concern with shipwrecks ends. As a byproduct of my consuming interest in shipwrecks and maritime history, I have amassed a large library which includes over 7,500 books at last count--not to mention over 45,000 slides and photographs of old charts and maps, as well as an equal number of slides of shipwrecks and artifacts recovered from them. When I wrote *Shipwrecks of the Western Hemisphere 1492-1825* back in 1971, space limitations kept me from including more than a small percentage of the sites that I had data on at that time. Although this book has been reprinted numerous times, most recently in 1988, it has not been expanded with the new wreck data that I have acquired. However, it is still the most comprehensive work on the subject.

I followed with three other books, *Shipwrecks in the Waters of Mexico, Shipwrecks of the Virgin Islands and Puerto Rico* and *Spanish Treasures in Florida Waters.* Although many of the shipwrecks in these three books are covered in my first book, they have information on additional shipwrecks as well as the sources for information about each shipwreck, which were not included in my first book. Even anyone interested in shipwrecks prior to 1825, the cutoff date for each of these books, should consult them first. The locations for each wreck, however, are given only to the extent that I have documentation.

In some cases I may have found only a mention of the shipwreck in an old newspaper article, in which its location may only be general. In other instances I may have had hundreds of pages of original documentation to consult. Keep in mind that it generally takes many, many hours of sharply focused research on each shipwreck's history to find the relevant information one should have before initiating a physical search. To do this for each of the shipwrecks covered in my books would have taken several lifetimes. My purpose in writing these books was to provide a guide to aid wreck divers simply to select a particular target which then requires further and more extensive research. These books also serve as a good source for identifying shipwrecks found by accident.

There are myriad sources for researching ship losses after 1825. This is particularly true of ships wrecked in United States waters. The most reliable book is the *Encyclopedia of American Shipwrecks* by Bruce D. Berman, published in 1972. The author spent eight years collecting data on more than 50,000 wrecks in American waters. He wrote about over 13,000 of these, excluding all vessels of less than 50 gross tons. A small number of these wrecks are pre-Revolutionary, and his list includes ships lost up to 1971. Included in the information about each wreck is the name and tonnage of the vessel, the year of construction, the date and cause of loss and the location.

Another excellent reference work is *A Guide to Sunken Ships in American Waters* by Adrian L. Lonsdale and H. R. Kaplan, which lists 11,000 wrecks off the coasts of the United States as well as many in rivers and the Great Lakes. Although most of the wrecks mentioned in this book are also listed in Berman's, they are covered in somewhat greater detail here. Dozens of other books deal with shipwrecks in particular areas or with ships lost during specific eras. For the Great Lakes I recommend reading *Memories of the Lakes* and *Shipwrecks of the Lakes,* both by Dana Thomas Bowen. New England area wrecks are dealt with in *Wrecks Around Nantucket* by Arthur H. Gardner and *Shipwrecks of Cape Cod* by Isaac M. Small, both especially interesting. A good book on West Coast shipwrecks is *Shipwrecks of the Pacific Coast* by James A. Gibbs, Jr. An excellent book about river wrecks is *Steamboat Disasters and Railroad Accidents* by S. A. Howland. For information on almost every military and merchant ship lost during the Civil War there is a 42-volume work entitled *Records of the Navies of the Civil War,* published by the U.S. Government Printing Office in Washington, D.C.

Numerous pamphlets published by various government agencies also contain wreck information postdating 1825. The best source is the Treasury Section of the National Archives in Washington, D.C., which will furnish the following reports for a small fee: "Marine Disasters North of San Francisco from January, 1870 to August 1886," "Marine Casualties on the Great Lakes from 1862 to 1873," "Wreck Reports of the Great Lakes 1886-1891" and "List of Wrecks and Casualties: Coast of Rhode Island and Fisher's Island, 1752-1907." This last report gives the location of 600 vessels lost in the area.

Over the years the Public Information Division of the United States Coast Guard has also published (free of charge) lists of ship losses including "Principal Marine Disasters, 1831-1932" (with data on more than 600 vessels lost on rivers, lakes and at sea), "Life Saving Annual Reports, 1878-1914" and "United States Merchant Ship Losses: December 1941-August 1945." Other good sources for information are the U.S. Naval Hydrographic Office and the U.S. Maritime Commission, both located in Washington, D.C.

The most comprehensive general book on shipwrecks throughout the world is *The Treasure Diver's Guide* by John S. Potter, Jr. Many books have been published in various countries dealing with their own ship losses. For Spanish ships there are two major works: *La Armada Española* in nine volumes, and the six volume *Disquisiciones Nauticas,* both by Fernandez Cesareo de Duro. For French ship losses consult *Histoire des Naufrages* in three volumes by Jean L. Desperthes. British ship losses are covered in dozens of books by various authors. The best work on British warships is *The Royal Navy* in three volumes, by William L. Clowes.

Although books published in recent years can be quite helpful in selecting and locating a site, it is wise to go back to the *primary source* whenever possible. Every state in this country has many books written about its history, and it is a good idea to consult these, especially when doing research on a specific wreck. Start with the oldest or those written soon after the time of a particular ship loss.

Although books published before 1800 are generally difficult to find, they can often be borrowed from large libraries or through inter-library loans. As a guide in determining which older books might be helpful I suggest consulting *Incunabula and Americana 1450-1800* by Margaret B. Stillwell. This volume lists over 11,000 titles and gives the libraries which have them. Another source, international in scope, is the *Subject Index of Books Published Before 1800,* a four-volume work by Robert A. Peddie. It has an alphabetically arranged subject list of more than 50,000 books written in various languages. Through it I have located hundreds of useful books.

Old newspaper accounts are also a valuable source of information on shipwrecks after the mid-17th century. More than once I have been able to identify or learn more about a shipwreck or other type of site through newspapers. Some of the best descriptions of the 1692 earthquake which destroyed Port Royal can be found in newspapers.

In 1959 I found and salvaged a Spanish merchant ship off the coast of Yucatan. In researching its identity I discovered a newspaper item which resolved all mystery. This wreck was located off a place called Matanzeros Point, and I surmised that the point took its name from the wreck. Because dating the artifacts I had found on the wreck had already convinced me that it sank between 1730 and 1740, I began searching through all newspapers and periodicals covering those years. I eventually came across an item regarding the wreck in a February 1736 issue of *La Gaceta de Mexico*, a daily newspaper published in Mexico City. My hunch was right. The ship had been named *El Matanzero*, and from that paper and subsequent research in the Spanish archives I had the pleasure of learning her whole history.

First American Newspapers

Newspapers were first printed in the American colonies in 1690 and for some time were the only general medium for dissemination of news of all descriptions. In addition to listing the movements of all ships in and out of ports and their cargoes, the papers printed a great deal of information on shipwrecks, not only in America but throughout the world. To determine which newspapers were being published or were published nearest to the site of a wreck or a site one is researching, it is helpful to consult the following exhaustive works: *History and Bibliography of American Newspapers, 1690-1820,* two volumes, by Clarence S. Brigham; and the *Dictionary of Newspapers and Periodicals* by N. W. Ayer and Sons, which covers the period until 1880. The *New York Times* was founded in 1851 and is a comprehensive source of information on later shipwrecks.

Original research undertaken in archives is by far the most rewarding--as well as the most challenging and time consuming--method of learning about underwater archaeological sites. But, it isn't always possible to track down every objective in primary sources. Original documentation simply no longer exists for many ships that were lost and for many of the towns and settlements that were inundated. In these cases you must rely on secondary sources for information.

For example, a Portuguese fleet of 20 ships heading from Brazil to Lisbon in 1746 was struck by a storm and forced to run before it. The fleet was still intact when it entered the Caribbean and passed within sight of Barbados. Shortly afterward the storm matured into a full hurricane, and the ships were widely dispersed with 13 lost without a trace. Consequently, there is no documentation on these wrecks other than the fact they disappeared. During the third decade of the 16th century the town of Nueva Cadiz on Margarita Island off the coast of Venezuela sank during an earthquake, yet not a single surviving document tells of this event. All that is known comes from a brief paragraph in a book written in 1558

Documents concerning various shipwrecks or other disasters were often lost when the ships that were carrying them back to the Old World sank. Unfortunately, we can never hope to know about many rich sites because thousands upon thousands of historical records have been destroyed by man and nature. Moreover, countless other manuscripts and documents dealing with ship losses are stacked in unknown depositories in a number of countries. Until they are cataloged, which may take years, they are inaccessible to researchers.

Climate, fire, war and natural disasters have taken their toll on historical documents. All of the documents predating 1670 that were kept in Panama City were destroyed by fire when the pirate Henry Morgan and his men burned the city to the ground. In addition many documents postdating 1670 have been destroyed by Panama's humid and corrosive climate. Complete archives in Cartageña and Bogota, Colombia, were destroyed during that nation's War of Independence. Similarly, a great wealth of records was destroyed in Veracruz and Mexico City during the Mexican War of Independence.

When Cuba revolted against Spain near the end of the 19th century, its Colonial archives fortunately survived. After the war the Cubans turned over the archives to the Spanish, who took them to Seville. Almost a century later these thousands of bundles of priceless historical material remain stacked as they were when they arrived, unopened in an old building in Seville, collecting dust and ravaged by mice and insects.

The main archive in Lima, Peru, was twice destroyed by earthquake in the 18th century. Even in Spain, vast numbers of documents have been destroyed, particularly in 1551 when the House of Trade building burned to the ground, and in 1962 when many documents were destroyed in a flood. Spanish Colonial history is not alone in suffering destruction of its records. Documents of other European nations have shared a similar fate. Portugal had the great misfortune of having its main depository of historical documents, the Casa da India, sink into the Tagus River in an earthquake in 1763. Firestorms from World War II bombing destroyed untold amounts of irreplaceable documents in London, Paris, Rotterdam and Amsterdam.

In many documents the precise location of shipwrecks is vague. When most of the Spanish ships were lost, there were few fixed place names on charts used by navigators. In Florida, for example, only two places are named on most 16th-century charts...Martires (spelled a number of ways) in the Florida Keys and Cabo de Canaveral or Cape Canaveral. By the mid-17th century a few more place names had been added, including Las Tortugas (the Dry Tortugas), Vivoras and Matacumbe (two islands in the Florida Keys), Rio de Ais (Fort Pierce Inlet on the east coast) and La Florida (St. Augustine). By the beginning of the 18th century many more names on charts rendered them more accurate. One reason Spanish documents are often vague on shipwreck locations is because little effort was made to pinpoint a wreck. When writing to Spain to tell of a disaster, officials in Seville were interested only in *what* had been lost and in knowing *how much* had been--or could be--recovered.

Another important factor to keep in mind when doing research on primary source material is that there was no standardized calendar system followed by all countries. In 1582 Pope Gregory XIII ordered that 10 days of the year be omitted to bring the calendar and the sun once again into correspondence, thus creating the Gregorian calendar which we use today. For many years afterward, however, all of the Protestant countries in Europe continued to use the old calendar. Until England adopted the Gregorian calender in 1752, her new year began on March 25. The date of February 11, 1733, to the English, therefore, was February 21, 1734, to Catholic nations.

Although the Dutch were very active on the maritime scene in the Western Hemisphere, very few documents have survived in Holland concerning Dutch shipwrecks in the New World. Information on Dutch shipping can be found in Spanish and British depositories. References to Dutch ship losses elsewhere in the world can be found in the Netherlands Royal Archives in the Hague and the Netherlands Historical Ship Museum in Amsterdam.

Portugal has very little documentation concerning shipwrecks predating 1763 when the Casa da India was lost, but for information after that time there are three important depositories, the Museu da Marinha, the Arquivo Nacional da Torre and the Arquivo Historico da Ultramar, all in Lisbon.

Although a great deal of documentation on French maritime history has survived the centuries, French depositories are so badly cataloged that it is most frustrating to work in them. The three main sources of information on French ship losses throughout the world are all in Paris: the Musee de la Marine, the Bibliotheque Nationale, and the Service Historique de la Marine. Other archives in the remaining nations of Europe are generally well cataloged, but most of their shipwreck documentation deals with losses in areas other than the New World.

A researcher finds England the least taxing place to work with depositories well cataloged and staffs generally helpful. The main places in England to research shipwrecks are the British Museum, the Public Records Office, the Admiralty Library, the National Maritime Museum and the Archives of Lloyd's of London, all of which are in or near London. Because of the Great Fire of London in 1666, there are virtually no extant documents on British shipwrecks in the New World before the mid-17th century; but then again, there was not much British shipping to the New World before then.

For the years between 1666 and 1740 a limited amount of original documentation exists on British ship losses in New World waters. All of the ships built and used by the American colonies until the War of Independence were under British registry. Even after the war the vast majority were insured by Lloyd's of London, established in 1688. It is a great shame that a fire in 1838 wiped out Lloyd's archives, which contained all insurance records and reports of tens of thousands of shipwrecks throughout the world.

Discovering the location of offshore shipwrecks through research can prove valuable to the beach hunter who finds treasure from these locations that has washed ashore.

In 1740 a newspaper called "Lloyd's List" was founded. It is still published today to report the movement of British shipping around the world. Past issues give brief accounts of ship losses and the movements of important foreign shipping such as the Spanish fleets or ships engaged in the East Indies trade. "Lloyd's List" has also published information regarding the salvaging of ships. Until recently it was necessary to go to England to consult these "lists," invaluable in gathering information on ships lost after 1740. Now, however, all the "lists" dating from 1740 to 1900 have been republished in a multi-volume work which can be found in a number of large United States libraries, including the Library of Congress in Washington and the New York Public Library.

Research in the Public Records Office, Britain's most important depository of shipwreck information, can begin in the United States by consulting the following reference works which deal with these documents in the Public Records Office: the *Calendar of State Papers, Colonial Series, America and West Indies,* in 42 volumes, and the *Journal of the Commissioners for Trade and Plantations from 1704 to 1872* in 14 volumes. These books contain brief extracts of tens of thousands of documents concerning the New World, many pertaining to ship losses. Complete documents are available from the Public Records Office for a small fee.

In gathering information on British warships lost anywhere in the world, you first should consult lists of *Admiralty Records* preserved in the Public Records Office.

Above
Author comes ashore with encrusted musket from late 17th-century shipwreck.

Below
Three gold rings from the Spanish galleon *San Jose,* lost in 1733 in the Florida Keys.

If you know the name of a ship, this index book makes it easy to learn what documents about it exist. Another good source for locating shipwreck documents in other British collections is *A Guide to Manuscripts Relating to American History in British Depositories* by Grace Gardner Griffin.

Before doing any research in United States depositories, either on American or foreign ship losses, you should consult the *Guide to Archives and Manuscripts in the United States* by Philip M. Hamer to determine which archive or library has relevant material. The National Archives in Washington is the most important source of shipwreck data postdating the American Revolution, but there are many others with original documents. Each state has archives which should be investigated, especially when you're interested in a wreck off the coast or in a river or lake of a particular state. In some cases many of the most important documents in state archives have been published, as have indexes of what the archives contain. If you are interested in ships wrecked off Virginia, for instance, your first step in research would be to consult the *Calendar of Virginia State Papers and other Manuscripts Preserved in the Capitol at Richmond* in 11 volumes, edited by Kraus Reprint Corp. of New York.

In addition to the state archives, many state and private universities have large manuscript collections. Some libraries can boast of a wealth of information from foreign archives. At the University of Florida there is a rich collection of microfilmed documents dealing with early Florida history, obtained from the Archivo de las Indias and other depositories abroad. Thus, when seeking primary source material about Spanish shipwrecks off the coast of Florida, you may first consult this source and quite possibly find everything needed, making a trip to Spain unnecessary. The Bancroft Library of the University of California at Berkeley has a good collection of documents and microfilm from many archives which deal with ships lost off the California coast and throughout the Pacific.

Old maps and charts are often valuable sources for locating underwater sites. In my research I have come upon hundreds of maps showing shipwreck locations...with astonishing accuracy in some cases and an equally astonishing lack of accuracy in others. Three old maps by three cartographers pinpoint the positions of all 21 ships of the 1733 Spanish Fleet which sunk in the Florida Keys in 1733. On the other hand, a chart showing the locations of a number of galleons lost in 1622 in the same area was so badly drawn that it has proved useless. The most accurate maps or charts pinpointing shipwrecks were generally those drawn by contemporary salvors.

A number of important factors should be considered in referring to old maps and charts. Over the centuries shorelines have receded in some places and extended farther into the sea in others. Of particular concern to today's underwater archaeologists are those areas that have built out, since many sites have been covered by land. Port Royal presents a good example with approximately 60% of the 2,000 buildings that sank into the sea now covered by land. Near Port Royal, but on the other side of the harbor, the shoreline has been built out by sediment brought down from rivers. Recently three 18th-century shipwrecks were found buried on land in this area. This has occurred in many other places. Many small islands or cays that existed years ago have disappeared. Others have built up and some have been made by man.

Many old charts show numerous small islands that no longer exist. North of Memory Rock on the Little Bahama Bank, I discovered that the islands here were by no means imaginary. While searching for shipwrecks in that area and digging test holes in zones where a magnetometer had indicated the possible presence of wrecks, we found the lower portions of large tree trunks...right where they had been rooted centuries ago when those areas were still islands. They were still firmly attached to the limestone sea floor.

The mouths of rivers and streams have in some cases meandered considerable distances. Several inlets on Florida's Atlantic coast have closed up over the centuries and others have opened, some due to natural forces and others to manmade causes. The present Fort Pierce inlet on Florida's east coast is now two miles south of where it was about 1750.

Because positions of latitude taken from a rocking ship were often inaccurate it was the practice, when possible, to establish the latitude of a shipwreck from the nearest *terra firma*. I have found that on the whole these reckonings, even those from the earliest days of New World exploration, are accurate to within a few miles. The distance or measurement of a mile and a league was not universal in the old days. From the end of the 15th century and well into the 19th the Spanish and Portuguese divided a degree of latitude into 70 miles of 5,000 feet each, or into 17 1/2 leagues of four miles each. The English and French divided it, as we know it today, into 60 nautical miles or 20 leagues of three miles each. The Dutch also divided it into 60 nautical miles, but used 15 leagues of four miles each.

All nations used the fathom as the unit to measure the depth of the water, but its true length or depth was not uniform. The fathom varied between five and six and one-half feet, depending on the size of the seaman making the measurement. A fathom was considered the distance between the outstretched arms of a man hauling in a sounding lead line. In areas where there is a considerable variation in tide levels, care must be exercised when relying on depths given in historical documents, charts and maps, since they rarely mention tidal conditions when water depth was reckoned.

Most depositories of primary source material have good collections of maps and charts. The most extensive collection that covers the entire world is the Map Room of the British Museum. In the United States the two best sources are the New York Public Library and the Library of Congress. The Map Division of the NYPL houses a magnificent collection of maps and atlases from the 16th century to the present. With 12,500 atlases, 4,900 monographs and over 400,000 maps and charts, it is one of the world's most frequently consulted public map collections. Unlike most archives and libraries, the Map Division permits photography.

Book of 'Treasure Maps'

Several years ago the Library of Congress published *Treasure Maps in the Library of Congress* by Hill and Ladd. Approximately half of the 65 maps listed deal with land treasures. The rest are of shipwreck locations, mostly of "ye olde sunken treasure" variety, pinpointing nonexistent "ghost wrecks." Many books of fine reproductions of old maps are available. An excellent guide to colonial maps and charts of Florida and several adjacent states is the *Southeast in Early Maps* by William Cummings. It locates hundreds of old maps and charts covering these areas.

A number of charts showing locations of ships lost during the last 20 years of the 19th century are available. In 1893 the U.S. Hydrographic Office produced a "Wreck Chart of the North Atlantic Coast of America," covering the area from Newfoundland in Canada to the mouth of the Orinoco River in South America. It shows the locations and gives pertinent information about 965 vessels lost between 1887 and 1891.

The U.S. Weather Bureau published two charts about the same time, the "Wreck Chart of the Great Lakes," which lists 147 ship losses between 1886 and 1891, and the "Wreck and Casualty Chart of the Great Lakes," listing all ships lost in 1894. In 1945 the U.S. Coast and Geodetic Survey published nine large "Wreck Charts" that cover the area from Newfoundland to the Gulf of Mexico. Almost every wreck listed on these charts occurred after 1900 and is of no archaeological interest at the present.

Modern navigation charts are sometimes useful in locating shipwreck sites. Many bear place names associated with wrecked ships. There is a Man of War Cay in the Bahamas and a Man of War Bay on the island of Tobago, both named after British warships lost In those areas. Rose Key near Nassau was so called because the *HMS Rose* wrecked there in the 18th century. Spanish Cay in the northern Bahamas is so named because of three Spanish ships wrecked off it with survivors coming ashore on the cay to await rescue. Golden Rock near Freeport on Grand Bahama Island got its name after two Dutch ships carrying a fantastic amount of gold plundered from the Spaniards were lost there in 1628.

Throughout the world there are countless places named "Wreck Point" or "Wreck Bar" or bearing other names indicative of shipwrecks. In the Caribbean there are at least two dozen places with such evocative names as Money Cay or Treasure Cay, implying ships sank nearby with treasure or that treasure was hidden ashore there. On the southern coast of Spain between Cadiz and Gibraltar there is a headland, Silver Point, which owes its name to a number of treasure-laden Spanish ships wrecked there in 1553. In the British Isles alone more than 200 place names can be traced to shipwrecks. On the northeast coast of Malta there is a St. Paul's Bay, which has been called that for almost 2,000 years to commemorate the apostle's shipwreck.

In a book of this length it is not possible to list every available research source. The following example, demonstrating how much material is available for one random area, illustrates a proper approach to shipwreck research:

Assume you have either found a shipwreck off the North Carolina coast and want to identify it, or you want to research first before actually going in the water. After thoroughly studying all relevant sources already mentioned in this chapter, you would first refer to two excellent books by David Stick listing hundreds of shipwrecks off North Carolina: *Graveyard of the Atlantic* and *The Outer Banks of North Carolina.* If the wreck appears from the evidence to have sunk after 1749, or if you are searching for a wreck postdating that year, when the first newspapers were printed in North Carolina, you would consult *North Carolina Newspapers on Microfilm* by Jones and Avant and their *Union List of North Carolina Newspapers 1751-1900.* Before researching any original documents, you could refer to the *Index to the Colonial and State Records of North Carolina* in four volumes by Stephen Weeks, *The Colonial Records of North Carolina* in 10 volumes by William Saunders and the *Guide to the Manuscript Collections in the Duke University Library* by Tilley and Goodwin. The best source for old maps of the state in addition to those already mentioned is the Mariner's Museum in Newport News, VA, which has published a helpful guide: *Catalogue of Maps, Ship's Papers and Logbooks.* Three years ago the Duke University Marine Laboratory published *An Oceanographic Atlas of the Carolina Continental Margin* containing a number of charts that show hundreds of shipwrecks in North Carolina waters, some dating back more than 200 years.

Lloyds of London

From humble beginnings in a coffee house over 300 years ago, Lloyd's of London has grown into an international market where almost anything afloat can be insured...from the world's largest shipping fleets to waterskiing elephants. Marine insurance, the first type of insurance ever initiated, was introduced to British in the 16th century and soon spread throughout Europe. It was sometimes ironic that Spanish merchant ships insured by Lloyd's or other British insurance firms ended up being captured or sunk by British-owned and operated ships, with the poor British insurers taking a bath.

Today, following tradition, each time a marine disaster occurs a bell is rung twice in the main underwriting room at Lloyd's. This bell was recovered from the frigate *La Lutine,* which wrecked off Holland in 1799 with an enormous treasure that has never been salvaged. Most of the early records of Lloyd's have been lost over the years, but they are excellent for all 19th and 20th centuries shipwrecks worldwide, even including those not insured by Lloyd's.

As discussed elsewhere in this book in relation to problems facing the salvors of the *Central America,* there have also been marine insurers in the United States for many years. Some firms have shipwreck information dating back to the Revolutionary War. One of the most complete sources for 19th and 20th-century marine disasters is the Atlantic Mutual Insurance Company archives, located on Wall Street in New York. Years ago there were many marine insurance firms which are now defunct, but good detective work sometimes turns up their old records. In the famed "Blizzard of (18)88," more than 200 large ships lost along the Atlantic seaboard and were covered by 63 different American and European insurers. Some of the records from these old firms may be in university or local libraries located where the firms once did business. Others may have been turned over to maritime museums such as Peabody outside of Boston or the Mystic Maritime Museum in Connecticut.

Whatever kind of ship you are interested in finding...remember that shipwrecks are generally found first in the archives and then in the sea. Keep in mind as well that researching a wreck can be every bit as exciting as salvaging it. In addition, reading about the historical period of the wreck you are interested in adds a rich dimension to your project and may lead you down unexpected avenues that will offer new and greater opportunities.

Galleon Research

Since Spanish galleons are the most sought-after objective of wreck divers, this entire chapter is devoted to these rich prizes...and how they can best be located. Archival research is the answer, but this can be costly and very time consuming. Even if you know the modern Spanish language, you will not be able to make much sense of old documents written prior to 1750 in archaic Spanish mixed with other languages and dialects spoken by those who wrote them. Luckily, qualified researchers both in the United States and in Spain can be hired for this task. They can be located through the cultural attache of the Spanish Embassy in Washington or through historians in major universities.

I already had a grasp of modern Spanish from having studied it and Latin in school. But, I learned to master archaic Spanish by poring over thousand of microfilm pages of old documents from various historical periods. I isolated myself for several months far from the sea in an old wooden cabin in the wilds of Canada and studied the documents until I could read them as if they were in English. Following are but two examples of how this knowledge paid off.

In 1503 on his fourth and last voyage to the New World Columbus purposely ran two of his badly leaking ships aground in St. Anne's Bay on the north coast of Jamaica to keep them from sinking. He and his men were rescued by another vessel, and the two ships were left to settle beneath the bay's muddy bottom...where they lay forgotten for centuries. From historical documents I unearthed in the Spanish archives, I found sufficient clues to enable me to locate the wrecks without difficulty.

In his diary Columbus mentioned he had run both ships aground "about a bow shot distance from the shore (usually about 100 yards) and close to two fresh water streams and an Indian village," from which he had received supplies of victuals to feed his men before they were rescued. Although the streams no longer exist, old maps of the area showed their courses and it wasn't difficult to find traces of the Indian village near the shore. With this information I was able to narrow the probable location of the wreck site to an area about the size of a football field. I had the help of the late Dr. Harold Edgerton of Massachusetts Institute of Technology, who developed sub-bottom profiling sonar. Using his sonar we located both wrecks in a matter of minutes after laying out a grid search pattern system with buoys.

In 1656 the Spanish galleon *Nuestra Señora de las Maravillas,* carrying a prodigious treasure, was lost on the Little Bahama Bank. Contemporary salvors were able to recover only a small portion of her wealth before the wreck was covered over by shifting sands. For centuries repeated attempts were made to locate this wreck, but all failed. In recent years it intrigued many treasure hunters who spent more than a million dollars searching for her. A book on sunken ship locations came out in 1960 giving the *Maravilla's* location in the Florida Keys. A stampede, reminiscent of the Gold Rush, ensued and almost everyone in the treasure-hunting business searched here in the wrong area.

I, too, was fascinated with the *Maravilla,* the second richest ship to sink in the Western Hemisphere. My intense research effort on here was concentrated in Seville's Archivo General de las Indias and in other manuscript collections in Spain. After culling more than 12,000 pages of documents dealing with this ship, including a copy of her original manifest that listed and described every item of registered cargo she carried when lost, I came upon a 144-page book published in Madrid in 1657 by one of the few survivors of the wreck. Doctor Don Diego Portichuelo de Ribadenyra wrote an exciting and vivid account of everything he had observed from the time he boarded the ship in Porto Bello, Panama, until his rescue, including an excellent narrative of the ship's loss. I was unusually fortunate in locating three different contemporary charts showing the location of the *Maravilla*. Armed with all this research, I was able to find this ship in the summer of 1972 and recover a substantial amount of treasure and artifacts from her. The three charts had placed her location in 27 degrees and 15 minutes of latitude, and she lay only a half mile south of this spot.

Documents that reported news of various shipwrecks never reached destinations in Europe or elsewhere because the ships they were carried on sank or were captured by pirates or privateers. In addition, many documents that did survive are not available to researchers because they

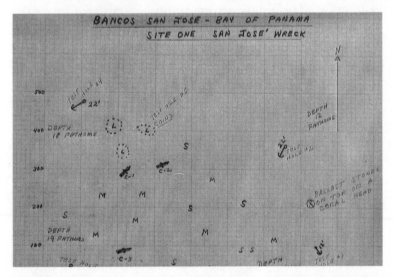

Plot chart showing disposition of the major objects on the Spanish galleon *San Jose*, which was lost in 1631 off the Pearl Islands in the Bay of Panama.

are in private libraries, are not cataloged properly or lie in depositories closed for one reason or another. Plus, catastrophes of man and nature have destroyed unknown quantities of information about shipwrecks.

Prior to undertaking any historical research on Spanish maritime history and shipwrecks, you should consult the most comprehensive guide book to the various depositories on both sides of the Atlantic which covers this topic. The two-volume work is entitled *Los Archivos de la Historia de America,* by Lino Gomez Canedo, (Mexico, D.F., 1961). Unfortunately, only 500 copies of this work were published and it is very difficult to find. Sr. Canedo, who spent a lifetime in the depositories he describes, gives the researcher a good idea of the best sources for the various types of historical data he may be seeking.

While, the greatest collection of Spanish colonial records is stored in the Archivo General de las Indias in Seville, a wealth of material on the subject exists on this side of the Atlantic as well. The most comprehensive collection of original documentation and microfilm on the Spanish colonial records is in the Hispanic Room of the Library of Congress in Washington. The best guide to this collection is the *Handbook of Manuscripts in the Library of Congress* (Government Printing Office, Washington, D.C., 1918). There are also other more recent and updated printed source books of the various collections in this depository. Among the most interesting collections are the Lowery, Harkness, Stevens, Del Monte and Las de Force collections. The National Archives is another good source in Washington. You should first consult *Guide to Materials on Latin America* in the National Archives, by George S. Ulibarri and John P. Harrison (Washington, D.C.1974).

New York City has a number of good places to pursue shipwrecks. The most important is the New York Public Library where the most interesting collection of material about Spanish shipwrecks is the Rich Collection. Consult

A Guide to the Reference Collections of the New York Public Library by Earl Brown (New York, 1941). The New York Library's cartographical collection is second only to that of the Library of Congress and has many maps and charts covering the New World. A less frequented but most interesting depository is the library of the Hispanic Society of America on upper Broadway. Valuable collections of the Pierpont Morgan Library and the small but important collection in the library of the New York Historical Society are also worth consulting.

In New England there are collections of documents in the Libraries of Harvard University's Peabody Museum and the main library of Yale University. Since the 1920's the University of Florida has been collecting microfilm and a original documents which not only deal with the Spanish colonial period of Florida history but also the history of the rest of the Spanish world. Recently the university received a grant to have the entire collection indexed and a catalog published. In the Midwest there are several important collections. During the past three decades researchers in Spain have transferred to microfilm several million pages of documents in various Spanish archives. At present no guide has been published of this collection. Chicago's Newberry Library has good material. Consult *A Check list of Manuscripts in the Edward E. Ayer Collection,* Chicago, 1937). Another source is the Hispanic American Collection at Northwestern University, near Chicago.

Other important collections include the Middle American Research Institute of Tulane University in New Orleans, the University of Texas in Austin, the Archives of New Mexico in Santa Fe, the Bancroft Library of the University of California at Berkeley, the Henry E. Huntington Library in San Marino, CA, and the William Andrew Clark Memorial Library in Los Angeles.

Of all the Latin American nations Mexico has by far the most comprehensive archives concerning Spanish shipwrecks. A good source book is *Guide to the Materials in the Principal Archives of Mexico,* by Herbert E, Bolton, Washington D.C., 1913). The bulk of material is in the Archivo General de la Nación in Mexico City. Other important depositories in Mexico City are the Biblioteca Nacional, the library of the Instituto Nacional de Antropologia y Historia, the Archivo del Cabildo and the Archivo Histórico de Hacienda.

All of the Latin American nations possess similar archives, but the majority are poorly cataloged and are not as extensive as those in Mexico. In the National Archives of Mexico, for example, are almost 26,000 bundles and volumes of documents. In contrast the archives in Honduras has less than 3,500 bundles (called *legajos*) and the National Archives of El Salvador, which was destroyed by fire in 1899, was left with only a few hundred original documents predating the period of the disaster. Although the Spaniards carted away their entire archives when they were expelled from Cuba, the Archivo General de la Isla de Cuba houses a vast collection of original documents dating back to the earliest settlement of the island. This archives was established in 1906 when documents found in civil and religious archives around the island were brought together. Most of Puerto Rico's colonial documents are in the National Archives in Washington.

The original state archives of Spain was the Archivo de Simancas, located near Valladolid. It became so jammed with documents that in 1784 the King ordered all documents dealing with the New World shipped to Seville, thus creating the Archives of the Indies in the old House of Trade building. In recent years it has been discovered that between 600 and 700 *legajos* were never transferred and must still be consulted in Simancas. In addition, in various sections of the Simancas Archives countless documents deal with New World shipwrecks. For example, in the section called "Papeles de Inglaterra" (Papers of England) I located data on over 100 Spanish shipwrecks in the New

World. In another section dealing with the Royal Armadas of Spain I discovered documents concerning wrecks of more than 250 additional Spanish ships.

The Royal Armada (*Armada de Mar Oceano*) had the task of meeting the returning New World fleets each year in the vicinity of the Azores. Each time this happened the Capitan General of the Armada would dispatch an advice boat to Spain with written notification for the king, detailing the condition the fleets were in and, most important, the amounts of treasure they were carrying. The various leaders of the New World fleets also sent long reports describing what had occurred during the course of their voyage both out and back. Usually they included all ship disasters. In theory, copies of these reports were also sent to the House of Trade in Seville and should exist today in the Archives of the Indies. However, many are missing and some can be found only in Simancas.

When I first began historical research in the Archives of the Indies in 1959, I was told by the director that one should never seek specific documents relating to a particular subject since the archives was so poorly cataloged. He advised me, rather, just to start reading documents. It was further suggested that when I found something of interest, I should not only copy it but eventually publish what I had found. The documents are somewhat better organized today, but even if you can read old Spanish, you can't expect to find the complete history of a particular shipwreck in a few days. After working there for a few months, however, a researcher can generally get the feel of things and manage effectively.

The archives is divided into 14 sections, and there can be pertinent information in every one of them. Each of the sections has been indexed or cataloged to different degrees of effectiveness. In most cases individual *legajos* are only described under vague terms such as "Papeles de Peru, año 1678."

In such a *legajo* you may have to labor through 2,000

pages of documents dealing with such mundane topics as construction of public buildings, local tax records, a census of an Indian settlement or local agricultural production. With luck you might happen upon a group of documents concerning a shipwreck. During the years I have worked in the archives there have been instances where I was able to find exactly the information I was seeking just by consulting the various indexes. But, this is not the norm. Until a few years ago, one section, the "Papeles de Cadiz," containing 1,260 *legajos* and 750 ledger books, was not available for research while it was being cataloged...a process which took over 10 years. When I was finally able to consult the Cadiz papers, I found a wealth of information on the 1715 *flota* disaster which I had failed to find in other sections of the archives.

I have a few suggestions for those setting out to research in the Archives of the Indies for the first time. Over the years its staff has been deluged by letters from divers requesting research aid on shipwrecks. They have also been swamped by people with a limited knowledge of Spanish who turn up at the archives asking for help because they want to do research on shipwrecks but have no idea of how to get started. As a result, the staff is not particularly happy to hear questions about shipwrecks and treasure. When applying for admission, it is best to indicate that your interest is in maritime or nautical history. Understand also that while the staff of the archives cannot undertake any research for individuals, they can recommend private researchers. Photocopying small numbers of documents can be done overnight but any orders for large

Sorting silver coins and bars that were part of the treasure recovery from the 1656 wreck of the Spanish galleon *Maravilla* in the Bahamas.

amounts of microfilming or photography generally take from one to three months. A new guide to the archives is in preparation and should be out soon.

Madrid has quite a few sources to explore for documents you may not be able to find in Seville. Those in which I have found sufficient documentation to warrant investigating are the Archivo Historical Nacional, the Biblioteca Nacional, the Biblioteca del Palacio Real, the Real Academia de la Historia, la Biblioteca de Academia de Historia, Archivo General Militar, Biblioteca del Servicio Historico Militar, Museo Naval, Archivo General de la Marina and the Archivo del Ministero de Asuntos Exteriores. Local municipal archives in Cadiz, Puerto de Santa Maria, Jerez de la Frontera and San Lucar de Barrameda can also yield valuable information. Private family archives, too numerous to list here, are also worth investigating in certain instances. That of the Dukes and Duchesses of Medina Sidonia in San Lucar de Barrameda, for example, contains tens of thousands of documents concerning New World shipping and ship losses.

The archives is in the ancient Castillo de Medina Sidonia, overlooking the mouth of the Guadalquiver River, which was the main debarkation point for shipping bound to the Indies, as well as where returning ships docked. The Medina Sidonia family played a very important role as the King's personal representative in this lucrative traffic. All dispatches arriving from the New World were delivered to these nobles, and copies were

Above
Gold coins and other objects recovered from one of the 1715 shipwrecks just off Florida's Atlantic coast.

Below
Coral-encrusted pistols and sword handles from a French wreck of 1754 found off Haiti.

made and filed in their private archive before they were sent on to Seville and Madrid.

After Spain, Rome is probably the most important center for documentation on Spanish New World shipping. In a number of cases I have found better documentation on particular fleets in the Vatican's Secret Archives than in Spain. Another fact to remember is that one of the chief objectives of the conquest of the New World was to Christianize the Indians, giving the Catholic Church a vested interest in the maritime commerce of the Spanish Indies. Many of the missionaries were well educated, unlike most of the officers and seamen on the ships. Where a ship captain might engage a scribe to describe the loss of a particular ship in a few succinct sentences, a member of the clergy might do so in many pages and in far more detail. Ship losses were old hat to the sea dogs, but to a landlubbing missionary on his first ocean crossing it was a spectacular event. The best description of the loss of the 1715 flota off the coast of Florida came from a 16-page account by a Jesuit who was present for the hurricane and several weeks of the subsequent salvage efforts. In addition to the Secret Archives (which are not really secret) there are numerous other archives in the Vatican which can be consulted.

Each of the religious orders that sent missionaries to America, including the Jesuits, Dominicans, Franciscans and Carmelites, has archives in Rome with interesting material on shipwrecks. Copies of most of the documents sent to the archives of the various religious orders can also be consulted in the Archives of the Propagation of the Faith in Rome.

The most difficult archives in Europe to investigate are those in Portugal because they are very poorly cataloged. Although by Papal decree the Portuguese were prohibited from trespassing in Spanish America, (Brazil was their sphere) they often did so on a big scale. Sometimes they had more vessels in Spanish America engaged in the slave and contraband trades than the Spaniards had in their *flota* systems. Many of the navigators on Spanish ships were Portuguese. The most important depositories in Lisbon are the Archivo de Torre do Tombo, Archivo Historico Ultramar, Biblioteca Nacional and Archivo del Ministerio de Negocios Extranjeros.

Involved All Europe

All of Europe was involved in one way or another with Spanish New World commerce. During the era of Spain's domination of the New World, she didn't understand the critical importance of developing manufacturing. Spain continued to depend on other nations to supply the goods needed to maintain the New World colonies. As a result, a great deal of the returning treasure left Spain immediately to be paid out to other European nations that had built economies on a system of goods and services. Representatives of these countries closely monitored the activities of the *flotas* and reported on them.

Seagoing European nations also had pirates and privateers operating in American waters, and reports filtered back from these sea wolves about the movements and ship losses of the *flotas*. When ships were lost in the New World, it affected most of Europe...everyone seemed to have a piece of the action. Of all the nations over the centuries, France had the most at stake in relation to the *flota* system. The French archives are so well organized that on many occasions when researching a Spanish shipwreck I have found it easier to first consult the French archives listed earlier in this book.

England also played an important role in regard to Spanish New World shipping, It is difficult to determine if the British benefited more from capturing Spanish ships, trading slaves, selling contraband to the colonists or through legitimate trade with Spain. England had a special interest in Spanish shipwrecks and made many attempts to salvage cargo and treasure from wrecked Spanish ships. English records on Spanish ship losses can be found in the

173

Public Records Office Archives, the Manuscript Division of the British Library (in the British Museum) and the National Maritime Museum Library in Greenwich.

Two facts should be kept in mind when carrying out research on shipwrecks of Spain or any other nation. First, a wreck might have been salvaged over the years with no records to indicate how much was recovered. Second, treasure was smuggled on Spanish ships on such a large scale that sometimes a ship might carry as much as four or five times the amount registered on a its manifest. For example, when British warships captured a Spanish galleon named *San Antonio* in 1743, the manifest stated that she was carrying slightly more than 800,000 pesos in treasure. Instead, the British discovered over four million pesos .

Locating Shipwrecks

While historical and archival research are crucial in locating most shipwrecks (the only way to flesh out the bare bones of a wreck is by filling in historical detail) it often pays to reconnoiter the coastal area where a wreck was reported lost. Of course, this inspection is important for assessing conditions to plan logistics for your eventual expedition. But, it can sometimes lead to a shortcut in finding the wreck you are after. Three times during the many years in which I been engaged in shipwreck exploration I put a lot of time and effort into archival research before going to the area of the actual wrecks. I discovered to my chagrin that I could have saved a lot of time and money. In each case there were locals who knew exactly where the wrecks lay.

Failing to investigate locally before mounting an expedition led one treasure hunting group to spend a small fortune with no reward other than egg on their faces. Back in 1968 when the Jamaica Playboy Club opened in Ocho Rios the island's Tourist Board decided that waters off the new hotel needed an attraction that would interest divers. An old British warship with cannon, anchors and ballast pile was removed from another area and placed right in front of the resort. To make it more exciting tens of thousands of ceramic shards and other items from my Port Royal excavation were then dumped on the site for tourists to find.

A group from Texas learned of the wreck, but not of its origin. They raised a great deal of money for a boat and equipment and then set sail after their "treasure galleon."

To their chagrin, they were stopped from digging on this site and told the true nature of the wreck.

A similar event occurred some years ago in the Bahamas. Concerned that a great deal of illegal treasure hunting was going on to the north of Grand Bahama Island, the Government chose a drastic and ill-advised course of action by deploying a large salvage vessel and crew to the area. For a period of three months divers scoured the bottom and removed every vestige of wrecks. They brought up more than 200 cannon, 75 anchors and other metal wreckage from numerous shipwrecks in an effort to prevent other divers from finding these sites. They also may have made it impossible for future licensed treasure hunters ever to find these shipwreck sites again.

Then to make matters worse the cannon, anchors and other materials were dumped in shallow waters off the south coast of Grand Bahama Island. Soon afterwards I heard rumors about a group outfitting in Miami to go after "a fleet of treasure ships in a secret location in the Bahamas." You guessed it! Their target was this junk pile...the dumped cannon, anchors and other wreckage.

Fishermen have been responsible for "making shipwrecks" as well. Generally when they snag cannon, anchors or other wreckage in their nets they bring the objects on board and then later jettison these objects in areas where they don't drag nets. Wrecks are even sometimes "made" by museum personnel as I have seen in several countries. When artifacts are turned into museums by fishermen and divers and the museum people decide they either don't have room or don't care to go through the expense of preserving the objects, they throw materials back into the sea...naturally, not where they were originally located.

Divers themselves are sometimes inadvertent "wreck-makers." During salvage operations objects are picked up which divers later consider to be of little value. They might, for example, be items from which coral growth was removed to see if coins or other valuables were attached. On the way back to port divers throw such debris overboard. The entrance to Sebastian Inlet near several of the 1715 wrecks is such a dumping site. Debris here has deluded more than one treasure hunter who is convinced that he has found one of the missing 1715 galleons or another shipwreck. Contemporary salvors during the Colonial period did the same thing. In trying to get at treasure on a shipwreck they had to remove a great deal of rigging and other impediments which they would jettison away from the shipwreck location.

Another problem the modern-day wreck hunters face is debris from the land...which in rare cases can even turn out to be treasure. There are examples in which such occurrences have confused many a wreck hunter *including me.* Once off the Island of Guadeloupe in the Caribbean I was searching for a wreck site and began finding buckles, buttons, jewelry and even a pair of eyeglasses. They turned out to have come from an old cemetery onshore which had been eroded during a recent hurricane and washed into the sea. Fortunately, I didn't find any human bones there. Recently off the Philippines, however, I did find a human skull with several gold teeth in it along with a large amount of Ming dynasty porcelain which turned out to be from another burial ground that had washed into the sea. Many cultures bury their dead with ceramics, jewelry, weapons and tools of their trade.

There are numerous accounts of old houses and other structures being swept into the sea during hurricanes along with varied objects that can easily be mistaken for artifacts from a shipwreck. And last but not least, the sea has been a dumping ground for unwanted objects by man since the earliest of times. What may have been trash to them may be treasure to us, but these artifacts can also be misleading clues to a shipwreck hunter.

Just because a ship was lost in the sea, in a lake, a harbor or a river doesn't mean that it still exists or that there are any traces of it. Some wrecks may be impossible to find. As I mentioned earlier, all metal--often the only sign of a wreck after the wooden structure has disappeared--has been removed from many wreck sites for sale as scrap.

Rivers change course over the years and a shipwreck may now be covered by farmland or under a wharf. Countless shipwrecks in rivers, harbors and at the entrance of seaports have been raised, starting as early as the Civil War, while others were obliterated by explosives because they were hazards to navigation. Entrances to ports and inlets have been changed by both man and nature over the years. Dredging operations and landfill as well as beach replenishment have also taken a great toll of shipwrecks.

In many areas the coastline has moved far seaward, and old ships are now covered over by beach homes and condominiums. This is what occurred along most of the east coast of Florida for the past three centuries. However, in recent years things have changed for the better or worse...depending upon whether you own beach-front property or search for shipwrecks. The shoreline is now receding at a rate of two to three feet per year! Thus, many shipwrecks long hidden under land are now returning to the sea where they belong. The most severe erosion is taking place in the Panhandle at Cape San Blas which has been losing ground at the rate of 27 feet a year since 1868 when a lighthouse was built there. This factor should be taken into account in going after a ship wreck which, according to contemporary reports "was lost in the breakers." Such a site may be a half mile offshore today.

The best Colonial period shipwrecks found in New York state were not in the water. During construction of skyscrapers in the Wall Street area of New York City during the past 15 years, three well-preserved Dutch shipwrecks from the early 17th century were found buried in the ground. This same occurrence is widespread throughout the world. The *Golden Hind* which carried Sir Francis Drake on his famed circumnavigation of the globe in 1578 is now covered by a warehouse on the banks of the Thames River in London. Try to make certain that your shipwreck target still exists in the water before going after her.

Finding Your Shipwreck

From experience I have found local shrimpers and fishermen to be excellent sources on shipwreck locations. They usually know the surrounding sea bottom as well as they know the palms of their hands, since they often snag objects from wrecks in their nets. They also know that fish abound around wreck sites and many have their own "wreck charts," so permit either returning to choice fishing grounds or avoiding areas where they would lose valuable nets. During a 10-year period one shrimper I talked to near Charleston, SC, had snagged his nets on more than 30 shipwrecks dating from 1650 to 1865 and was happy to share the locations with me.

In 1906 a fisherman from Grand Cayman Island was working in the area of Pedro Shoals about 130 miles south of Kingston, Jamaica. While rowing over a shallow reef he sighted something bright. He had no diving equipment of course but jumped right into the sea and brought up a gleaming Spanish gold bar. On subsequent dives he brought up six more gold bars and several handfuls of gold coins. He sold all the treasure for its gold value alone, unaware of its true historical value. News of his find spread and several expeditions went to the area but found nothing further. The *rest* of the treasure and the cargo of this shipwreck was probably concealed under coral growth or sand. In recent years over a dozen expeditions have set out to find this particular wreck. The exact location is no longer known, and no one has ever relocated the site.

I have heard a lot of tales about sunken treasures found in Florida and the Bahamas by Greek helmet divers from Tarpon Springs who dive for sponges, but I've never been able to verify any of them. During the summers of 1934 and 1935, the Mariner's Museum in Newport News, VA, conducted salvage operations on two British warships that were sunk in the York River in 40 feet of water during the siege of Yorktown in 1781. The wrecks were found by oystermen who accidentally snagged their nets on them. Helmet divers were employed to remove the mud overburden covering the wrecks with water-jets. A great number of interesting artifacts were recovered, including cannon, cannonballs, swords, axes, tools of various types, many pieces of rigging, a brass ship's bell, sounding leads, glass bottles of many descriptions and personal items belonging to the ships' crew. Most of these artifacts are on display in the Mariner's Museum.

In December 1938, fishermen sighted a number of coral-encrusted cannons on a reef off Key Largo, FL. They reported their find to Charles Brookfield, a man who had long dreamed of sunken treasure. With the help of a young diver, Brookfield relocated the cannons and brought up many cannonballs, lead musketballs, bits of rope, anchors, a silver porringer and numerous silver and brass coins. Their most interesting recovery was fragments of a prayer book found beneath a cannon. Since the cannon were identified as British from their markings, Brookfield enlisted the help of the British Admiralty in identifying the wreck which turned out to be the *H.M.S. Winchester,* a ship of 933 tons carrying 60 cannon, which was lost on September 24, 1695.

The richest treasure ship ever discovered off the coast of Louisiana was located by a shrimper in 1973 when he brought up in his nets a chest filled with 300 pounds of Spanish silver coins dated between 1779 and 1783, the year the ship went down. A group of treasure hunters followed up this accidental find with the recovery of more than $2 million worth of treasure, from what turned out to be the Spanish galleon *El Nuevo Constante.*

In Brazil and several other countries there are special fishermen who are called *marcadores* (markers) because they know the exact locations of shipwrecks which in the main areas for bottom fishing in these countries. I once went out with an old *marcador* off Recife on his small balsa raft after hearing a tale that an astrolabe had been brought up in a net. When we were about 12 miles off shore, with the coastline appearing only as a low-lying ribbon, he suddenly dropped anchor and said matter of factly, "Here is the wreck." I was incredulous that he would take me for such a patsy. There was no way he could find a wreck this far offshore, or so I thought. He refused to budge until I made a dive. Much to my complete astonishment, after swimming 120 feet down through shimmering schools of fish, I found an enormous ballast pile from a Dutch warship which, I later researched and learned, had gone down during a battle with a Portuguese fleet in 1641.

I was unable to find the fisherman who brought up the astrolabe, a navigational device for establishing latitude, but later located another fishermen who had four of them tied together and was using them as an anchor from his dugout canoe. Since two had recently sold in a Christie's

Chart showing the exact location of the British warship *Chesterfield*, which was lost in 1748 on the south side of the island of Tobago in the Caribbean Sea.

181

auction for $250,000 each, here was a ragged fisherman with a million-dollar anchor. Once off an island in the Bahamas I ran into a fisherman who was using Spanish silver Pillar dollar coins as weights on his throw net. He called them "zulu money" (probably because they had been traded as common currency during slave days). He told me he knew they were valueless because he was unable to buy anything with them in a local store!

The only rock in the Bahamas is limestone which is not nearly as good ballast material as the round river rocks from Spanish shipwrecks which fishermen pick off the bottom for this purpose. Most of the old Bahamian fishermen, therefore, know of several places where such rocks have been found. I have also been led to Spanish wrecks by finding out where Spanish rocks used in walls and other construction in the Bahamas and the Caribbean came from.

Marine laboratories and oceanographic institutions are also another good source for shipwreck locations because they accidentally find many shipwrecks while collecting marine specimens or surveying the sea floor with cameras. During one month-long survey south of St. Augustine, FL, a survey vessel in search of new scallop beds located eight old and several dozen modern shipwrecks. Off Cape Canaveral during the search for the remains of the space shuttle *Challenger*, oceanographic and navy search vessels located several dozen shipwrecks, two of which are believed to be Spanish. Not only did they provide me with the locations, but in most cases they even had video records which were made by ROV's and the navy divers. Just last year during a survey in conjunction with laying a petroleum pipeline between the coast of southern Spain and Morocco, video cameras picked up the remains of 11 old shipwrecks, and I was able to get these locations from the oil company who paid for the survey.

In Spain's Cadiz Bay I learned the locations of more than 50 shipwrecks from captains of the same dredge boats that have been destroying shipwrecks in this area for many years. They know when they hit a wreck not only by seeing what is discharging from their spill pipes, but also because cutting into an old cannon or anchor damages dredging equipment. Just this past March a boat working in Florida's Pensacola Bay dredged up a small 18th century bronze cannon.

Because good seamen can generally spot places where shipwrecks are likely to occur, they should be consulted before starting any search in a new area. Jacques Cousteau believes in consulting modern navigation charts to pick the most likely places where ships might wreck. He proved this on an expedition in 1953 about which he wrote, "To find Aegean wrecks we followed the old trade routes. Any reef or cape that looked treacherous to us may have been fatal to the ancients, so we dived there. At every spot we found the litter of an old ship and, on several, signs of two or more."

Throughout the Bahamas and Caribbean thousands of divers who spearfish, grab lobsters or dive for conch can be good sources of information. Never just ask them if they know where an "old wreck" is located. They'll most likely tell you of intact modern shipwrecks which to them certainly are wrecks. If you are truly after old wrecks, you ask them where the "river stones and guns" are to be found. Usually when they find anchors they pick them up and sell them for use by fishing boats or inter-island freight boats. In the Bay of All Saints, Brazil, more than 500 divers prowl the sea floor picking up anything of value from scrap metal to marine life. To them anything from an old shipwreck is worth only its scrap value. By the time I came upon one old Portuguese shipwreck which had carried 80 bronze cannon, worth between $25,000 and $50,000 each, these divers had cut up about half of them for scrap. By following in their wakes for several months I managed to find over 30 old shipwrecks. Their cooperation soon changed after I began working a few of these sites and started bringing up treasure. Not only did they cease to be friendly and show me other wrecks, on several occasions they threw sticks of dynamite into the water while I working.

Sport and commercial divers in United States waters are generally reluctant to assist you with information, since every diver who locates a wreck of any kind dreams of the day when he will get a chance to find out if it contains something of value. Sometimes they will make an exception if you promise to share the find or let them participate in the venture. A sports diver searching for golf balls off Rio Mar Country Club in Vero Beach, FL, found one of the 1715 galleons by accident about 20 years ago. As a reward for revealing the location he only asked for the first gold coin we brought up, which he got from us, and there were many more that we brought up and split with the State of Florida.

Kip Wagner found several of the 1715 shipwrecks by finding coins on the beach, and dozens of other shipwrecks have been found in the same manner. Consult local people living in the area of your search for such information, particularly those who scan the beaches with metal detectors. You should also consult local newspapers, historical societies and museums. Check around if any cannon or anchors are on display in the local seafood restaurants or in front of the city hall. Local museums might also have objects on display which washed ashore or were donated by fishermen or divers. One of the treasure chests from the *De Braak* has been on display in a museum at Lewes, DE, for as long as anyone can remember.

Antique dealers or collectors are also worth consulting. Contact some of the oldest residents of an area and ask them to recount old legends of marine disasters. In Ireland tales of the sinkings of many of the 1588 Armada ships have been handed down for generations, and some old people there still talk about them as if they occurred yesterday. Several years ago I had an old fisherman near Sligo take me to a high rock and pointing to an offshore shoal say, "Yonder reef be the resting place of the bones of many a Spaniard from the days of the great Armada." It sounded like something they tell all tourists, but in this case I dove the site and found one of the Armada wrecks!

Land metal detector enthusiasts know where coins and other goodies from shipwrecks are found, but they are generally as closed-mouth as most local divers. When there's a good storm you can be sure they will be out searching their best hunting grounds. It becomes just a matter of covering as much ground as possible to find where these treasure hunters are busily searching. I found the most efficient way to do this is in a light plane. When someone is spotted searching, I photograph the surroundings so I can easily find them on the ground.

Salvage and survivors' camps are usually on the shore as close as possible to a shipwreck site. Finding them will also led you to a shipwreck. Each of the 1715 shipwrecks had a salvors' camp site, and several have been found and worked by metal detector hobbyists. The camp for the flagship of this fleet has been excavated by archaeologists working for the State of Florida. Many bodies were washed ashore from old shipwrecks and sometimes these can also be located and tied to a shipwreck. Brazilian Indians led me to an area they called "haunted ground" because many human bones are scattered there. It turned out to be the burial site from the wreck of the *Santa Clara*, a Portuguese East Indiaman lost in 1571 while returning from the Far East. The ship's remains were less than 100 yards offshore.

I found another Portuguese East Indiaman, the *Rosario e Sant Andres*, by going to church...yes, going to church. Not by praying (which may have helped) but by noticing an old tile painting of a sailing ship on the church wall. An inscription noted that the church had been built in 1737 with funds contributed by the survivors of the *Rosario*. After mass I talked to the priest about the tile mosaic and asked if he knew where the wreck occurred. He answered,

"Stand on the church steps and throw a stone. It will land right on top of the wreck."

I was so excited I didn't bother returning to my boat several miles away. Stripping to my shorts I borrowed a pair of homemade goggles from a little boy and was in the water looking at a stack of cannon and timbers in a matter of seconds. Here was a shipwreck right off a popular swimming beach and yet no one had ever bothered to salvage her in modern times. We found thousands of intact pieces of Chinese porcelain and many other treasures before moving on to an older wreck nearby, which I found even more interesting.

Many times when survivors got ashore they carved on rocks the name of their ship and date of her loss...sometimes even the names of all of the survivors. One Dutch merchantman I worked on off the west coast of Australia was discovered through such an inscription. I myself found the remains of the *HMS Roebuck*, the ship of Captain William Dampier, a pirate turned cartographer, which was lost in 1702 on Ascencion Island in the middle of the South Atlantic. A friend of mine who lives in Providenciales, one of the many islands of the Turks and Caicos chain, has compiled the names and dates of over 45 ships lost in those waters by locating rock inscriptions made by survivors.

Two of the strangest accidental shipwreck discoveries occurred off the French coast. A Brittany fisherman noticed that every time he brought up lobsters from one area they were an unusual green in color. A local diver who heard about the lobsters investigated and found that these crustaceans made their home under a pile of bronze can-

This aerial photograph showing the remains of an 18th-century British ship in the Bahamas illustrates how easy it sometimes is to spot shipwrecks from the air.

non. Their green color came from the copper content of the cannon which had leached into the marine growth growing on them that was being eaten by the lobsters. This proved to be the site of the *Soleil Royal*, the flagship of a French fleet which lost some 20 ships in a battle against the British in 1759.

Another serendipitous discovery was made by a fisherman off Bordeaux who lowers clay jugs tied to a line and leaves them on the bottom long enough for unwary octopus to move into the jars, thinking they've found a new home. One octopus the fisherman pulled out of a jar had a Roman gold coin in his grasp. The tale spread through the local taverns and an enterprising diver made himself over a million dollars from the rest of the gold coins and other antiques he found on the nearby shipwreck.

Sometimes you can find intriguing clues but are never able to trace their source. In a small fishing village in Nova Scotia I found a stack of early 15th-century Portuguese iron cannon. These predated Columbus' arrival by 75 years. Did a Portuguese reach the New World before Columbus, or were these cannon carried as ballast on a later vintage ship? Unfortunately, I couldn't discover where they had come from because the fishermen who had brought them up many years before had drowned just months before my visit.

Because weather causes many expeditions to fail, you should gather as much meteorological data as possible about an area while planning a search or salvage expedition. Of course, nobody can control the weather, but you can at least put the odds in your favor by selecting times

Treasure diver John de Bry surfaces with a double handful of gold coins he recovered from one of the 1715 fleet of ships lost off the east coast of Florida.

that offer the best weather conditions and the calmest seas. Throughout the Western Hemisphere summer months are generally the best, but there are exceptions. Off Texas' Padre Island winter months offer calmer water and better underwater visibility. The rainy season is not a good time to work, especially in rivers or estuaries where rain-washed sediment clouds the water. And, of course, in planning a project in the Southern Hemisphere remember that the seasons are reversed.

Hurricanes and other violent storms can help or hinder the underwater explorer. Some storms uncover sites buried for years. This happened in 1962 when a hurricane lashed coastal North Carolina. High winds whipped up surging waves which uncovered the remains of the *Modern Greece,* a British steamer wrecked in 1862 trying to run the Federal blockade into Wilmington with supplies for the Confederacy. The wreck's general location was common knowledge, but it had been covered by shifting sands and was inaccessible until the hurricane. Navy divers working with state archaeologists have excavated it.

On the other hand, hurricanes have often deposited as much as 15 fifteen feet of sand over known wreck sites or altered the bottom seascape of an area so drastically that a site could not be relocated. Because of the huge seas associated with hurricanes artifacts buried on an offshore site can be thrown up on adjacent beaches. In addition, when beaches are eroded by strong wave action, vestiges of an offshore wreck washed ashore and buried in a previous storm may be revealed. Finding a silver coin on a beach can be the first clue that a wreck lies nearby. If you are interested in an area, ask the local people whether any such items have ever been found. Most of the shipwrecks of the 1715 fleet were discovered by Kip Wagner, who first found coins and artifacts from them washed up on the beaches.

A careful review of hydrographic and oceanographic data should precede any search attempt in a new area.

Charts published by the U.S. Hydrographic Office and the U.S. Coast and Geodetic Survey provide information relevant to water depth, positions of reefs and other shallow or hazardous areas. They give the directions of prevailing winds and currents and other data useful in determining the most promising areas to search and the type of equipment that will prove most suitable. Sailing directions and coastal pilot books furnish further information such as indications of areas where it might be difficult or impossible to work, (areas restricted to military use, fishing grounds or shipping lanes with heavy traffic). The charts are essential in defining the nature of the sea floor in your search area. Chances of locating a site depend a great deal on the topography of the bottom and local sediment conditions. About 95% of all ships that are lost in shallow waters are found on sandy bottoms. The rest lie on or under mud, silt, coral or combinations of them.

The National Ocean Survey Department of the National Oceanic and Atmospheric Administration, U.S. Department of Commerce, has useful tools that can help prepare for a search. You should purchase all relevant charts and a copy of the Sailing Direction Guide for your area for essential oceanographic and meteorological information. Then from the same agency you can purchase aerial photographs in both black and white and color. Infrared photographs are available for some areas as well. Using a magnifying glass you can sometimes spot actual shipwrecks and even smaller objects like cannon in these photographs.

Approximately 98% of all ships lost in the Western Hemisphere prior to 1825 were wrecked in shallow waters at depths of 30 feet or less, which makes them much easier to locate and salvage. In the Mediterranean Sea, however, the reverse is true. At least 95% of Med shipwrecks lie in depths of over 100 feet.

The major causes of shallow-water shipwrecks were storms and faulty navigation. It is easy to understand how foul weather could drive a ship onto reefs, shoals or coastlines. Results of faulty navigation may seem somewhat harder to comprehend until we see the primitive navigational equipment and inaccurate charts early mariners used. Of the 2% lost in deep waters, the major causes were ships breaking up or capsizing in storms, fires at sea, ships sunk in battle, and ships either scuttled to prevent capture or scuttled by their captors after being stripped of all valuables. About 95% of all ships lost in shallow waters are located on sandy bottoms. The remaining 5% are almost equally divided between those covered by mud and silt in harbors such as Havana and Veracruz and at the mouths of rivers and those wrecks covered by coral growth on reefs.

You need to consider what happens to ships that wreck in shallow water. When a ship struck on shallow reefs, sometimes it was so badly broken up that no traces of its wooden hull remain, for the wood either floated away or has since been completely devoured by the teredo. The *Matanceros* site which I worked off the coast of Yucatan, is a good example where we found only a few pieces of ship timbers buried under sand. Other ships wrecked on shallow reefs sometimes had all or part of their hulls carried by wave action or currents to sandy bottoms or small sand pockets, so that their timbers were covered by sand before the worms could totally destroy them.

Coral growth varies a great deal in different areas of tropic and subtropic waters, determining factors being water temperature, current, salinity of the water and wave action. In areas where coral growth is slow most of the items on the ship are carried away varying distances, depending on their weight and shape, and very little--in some cases nothing at all--can be found on the reef where the ship was wrecked. Yet along the Caribbean coastline of Yucatan, where coral growth is rapid, the major portion of a ship's cargo would be buried under coral growth before it could be washed ashore or away from the area of the wreck site. Another good example of rapid coral growth is on Silver Shoals on the eastern edge of the Bahama archipelago. When the divers of Sir William Phips located a richly laden treasure galleon in 1682, only 41 years after it had been wrecked, they reported that the wreck was completely buried in coral and that in some places the coral growth was five feet thick which prevented them from entirely salvaging the wreck.

The Best Preserved Wrecks

Ships lost in mud or silt are generally the best preserved, because the weight of the ship forces the vessel's lower hull down into the sediment relatively quickly, preventing attacks on the wood by the teredo. In the harbor of Cartageña, Colombia, I dived on two large Spanish warships scuttled in 1740 to prevent capture by the English. Several months before my arrival, both wrecks had been uncovered during dredging operations. I found them to have most of their hulls in a remarkable state of preservation. Other examples are the two ships run aground in 1504 by Columbus in St. Anne's Bay on the northern coast of Jamaica. Since bad leaks on both ships had filled them with water, a great part of their lower hulls were pushed down into the soft silt of the bay, preserving them to this day. The main disadvantage of excavating a wreck lying on a mud or silt bottom is that during the actual excavation, underwater visibility is generally reduced to nil because of sediment that is stirred up.

Ships wrecked on sandy bottoms are preserved to varying degrees, depending on how quickly the weight of the wreck pushes the hull into the sand, and the time it takes for ocean or tidal currents to build up sand over the wreck. In areas where only a few inches of sand covers a limestone or coquina bottom, very little of a ship's hull will be preserved. Sometimes wrecks were covered over so quickly that even contemporary salvors were prevented from salvaging them, despite the fact that they knew their precise locations. The *Atocha,* lost in 1622 in the Florida Keys, is a prime example. Since it sank on the edge of the Gulf Stream where the currents run between one and three knots, the sand built up so rapidly over the wreck that within two months Spanish divers reported only the masts remained above the sea floor and there was an average of two fathoms of sand over the main deck of the wreck. Documentary evidence exists to prove that this occurred on many other wrecks.

When ships are wrecked during hurricanes, their hulls and cargoes are usually scattered over wide areas, sometimes covering several square miles. But there are exceptions. During the disaster of the 1715 fleet, 10 of the ships were completely broken up. Very little of their hulls exists today and cargoes are scattered over large areas. Yet, the eleventh ship of this fleet was wrecked close to shore, and its hull remained intact for a long period, thus enabling the Spaniards to salvage her complete cargo.

During the hurricane of 1733 in which 21 Spanish ships were wrecked off the Florida Keys, the majority of them remained almost totally intact until salvaged. Then the Spaniards burned those parts of the wrecks that remained above the waterline.

When I spent several months excavating the 1733 *San Jose,* I discovered that the ship apparently struck an offshore reef with an average depth of ten feet, or it may have been thrown completely clear over the reef by the high seas during the hurricane. About a quarter of a mile shoreward of the reef the ship struck on a sandy bottom approximately 20 feet deep, losing its rudder, five cannons which were possibly carried on the stern, and a substantial amount of cargo that spilled out of the ship in this general area. The main hull of the ship was carried about 250 feet farther, sinking in 30 feet of water, probably after losing her stern section.

Most of the cannon she carried were found either on top of the ballast on the lower deck or relatively close to the main section of the lower hull. Most of the starboard section of the hull was lying between 10 and 20 feet from the lower section of the wreck, which consisted of the lower deck over the ship's keel. Covering the lower deck, we discovered about 200 tons of ballast, with a trail of rock leading to the area where the ship had lost its rudder and part of its stern.

From these discoveries we can assume that the *San Jose* was one of those ships that remained intact after wrecking; otherwise, we wouldn't have discovered most (if not all) of her cannon so close to the main section of the wreck. This would also indicate that most of the cargo she carried would have remained inside the hull of the wreck, or fairly close to it.

In cases such as the ships of the 1715 fleet, we know, both from contemporary documents and actual salvaging of the wrecks, that when they broke up during the hurricane the lower sections of the hulls, containing the ballast and most of the bulky cargoes, sank farther offshore than the upper decks and superstructures. This is verified by the fact that most of the cannon, carried on the upper decks of the ships, was discovered closer to shore than the main ballast piles and by the fact that most of the gold jewelry was discovered close to shore. Unless they were smuggled contraband, the most valuable items, such as gold and silver, were a!ways carried in the cabins of the captain or ranking officers in the superstructure of the old ships, generally in the stern castle. This was done so that chests of valuable treasure could be kept under close surveillance. When a vast amount of silver, either in specie or bullion, was carried, it was always stored in the main hold over the ballast.

There are also instances in which ships were wrecked during good weather with their cargoes lost over large areas. Sometimes when a ship struck a reef, sustaining holes in the hull, the captain kept his sails up trying to run the ship as close to shore as possible to lessen the loss of lives and facilitate salvage operations. When this happened, a great deal of the ballast and cargo spilled out of the ship between the area where she had hit and where she finally sank.

I worked on a 1641 Portuguese shipwreck which illustrates this type of disaster. The ship struck on a shallow reef fairly close to shore trying to elude Spanish warships near Providencia off the coast of Nicaragua. To escape pursuit the captain kept the ship sailing, staying right over the dangerous reef, either hoping that the Spaniards would also wreck on it or that they would abandon the chase to avoid the danger. The ship traveled over two miles before it finally sank. I was searching for the wreck using snorkeling equipment and discovered the area where the ship had first struck the reef. I followed the trail of ballast stones until reaching the main section of the wreck. Mixed in with the trail of ballast rock were a large number of artifacts that had fallen out through the hole in the ship's hull.

After checking out all the locations supplied by your contacts, your next step should be to make an aerial survey of the area...if the water is clear. The preferred tool for this is a balloon. Also useful are either a seaplane, a Bensen Gyrocopter or helicopter and a light single-engine plane. The balloon and the Bensen Gyrocopter can be made compact enough to enable the explorer to ship it to the area he plans to search. Remember that since helium is virtually impossible to obtain outside the United States, a hot-air balloon may be a better bet. The reason I prefer the balloon is that it has to be towed by a surface vessel, and it is always easier to obtain a good position with electronic equipment from a surface vessel than from an aircraft. Furthermore, as soon as something is sighted from a balloon, divers can investigate the suspected area.

If a balloon is not available, I suggest using either a seaplane, a Gyrocopter or a helicopter with floats, which enables the explorer to land right over the suspected area and inspect it immediately, provided sea conditions are good. Prior to obtaining his balloon, Teddy Tucker used a small, light seaplane around Bermuda, locating over 50 wrecks by this method. Dimitri Rebikoff has used a Sea-B seaplane, and aboard it he not only carries sufficient diving equipment but a small portable air-compressor for refilling his scuba tanks.

When an aircraft cannot land on suspicious areas, then I suggest that a surface vessel be used in conjunction with the search. The surface vessel can be directed by radio to suspect areas and divers sent down to investigate, or a vessel can assist in placing buoys over the area for future investigation. Without the aid of a surface vessel it is often difficult to establish the precise position of a shipwreck when you sight it from the air, especially if the location is not close to some noteworthy landmark.

If you are operating alone in the air, there are several different methods that can be used. A loran or lorac set is your best tool. Flying several timed compass headings

Outline of a ship shows clearly in this side-scan sonar record of a Spanish galleon in deep water off Cape Canaveral on the Atlantic coast of Florida.

from the wreck site to known positions is another method. Still another is the use of a radio directional finder, but it is not as accurate as the other methods. From the Gyrocopter or helicopter, buoys can be dropped on top of the wreck, but it is more difficult to do this from a circling plane. Small sonar transmitters are now available. Dropped over a wreck site, some produce a continuous sonar signal for as long as 2,000 hours, and with the use of a boat and sonar-receiving equipment the position can be located.

To obtain the best results from an aerial survey the sea should be flat calm and the altitude between 100 and 500 feet. Polaroid glasses are a must, as is a good chart of the area in order to mark the approximate position of anything you might sight. Not only can items such as ballast piles, cannon, and anchors be sighted, I have also located wrecks that were completely buried under sand. On wreck sites that have a great deal of metal such as large cannon the iron oxide from the metal masses generally darkens sand over a site. Another good indication is a small, solitary coral reef, or several small patches of coral reefs, in areas where there are no others. In most instances these small reefs started building up when some part of a shipwreck was exposed above the sand and they continued to grow after the wreck was buried.

Photography can also be very helpful in locating shipwrecks. Using infrared film in a 35mm still camera, I located three shipwrecks on a reef along the northern coast of Jamaica that I had not seen from a light plane. Regular color film used with a Polaroid filter occasionally produces good results. The main difficulty with aerial photography lies in establishing the precise location of the photographed wreck.

If a wreck is not buried under sand, sediment or coral growth, there are many simple methods that can be used to search for it. I shall begin with the simplest and cheapest methods and progress up to the more elaborate and costly. If the water is reasonably clear and you have good eyes and have had considerable experience, you can use the "Teddy Tucker Method," which is to stand either on the bow or a higher spot on a boat and search for large objects like ballast piles, cannon, etc. The sea must be flat calm, as it is in Bermuda for months at a time. Once, using this method under ideal conditions, I located 14 old wrecks on the Little Bahama Bank in less than three hours. Polaroid glasses are very useful when using this method.

I have always preferred to search for wrecks either by snorkeling on the surface or by being dragged behind a small boat holding on to a line. I have located over 200 old wrecks with this simple method and still use it whenever feasible. Its two disadvantages are that it is more time-consuming than most other methods and that it is dangerous in areas with heavy concentrations of sharks. Whenever sharks have forced me to abandon snorkeling or "riding the shark line" I have usually resorted to a glass-bottom boat.

Other divers like using sea sleds or towing vanes, but I prefer the greater freedom of movement afforded by snorkeling or riding a towline behind a boat. There are now many makes and models of sea scooters. Their big disadvantage is that the maximum length of time they can operate is two hours, after which they usually require from eight to twenty-four hours for recharging. To overcome this major problem, Rebikoff Underwater Products developed another type of Pegasus, which I have found much more adaptable to searching for shipwrecks in shallow water. It is powered by a surface engine that is floated on a small pontoon and connected by an umbilical power line to the underwater vehicle, which drags it behind on the surface. In recent tests we mounted a magnetometer on this new Pegasus and it worked quite well.

Wet submarines offer no advantage over any of the above methods other than giving the diver some protection in the event of a shark or barracuda attack. And while I highly recommend dry submarines for locating deep shipwrecks, I have found them practically useless on shallow-water searches. Not only are they expensive to operate and maintain, but they require constant maintenance. Because of weight they also generally require large surface support vessels and are difficult to launch or retrieve in rough seas.

In 1963 I rented the original Perry Cubmarine for a month, and from the start it was a headache. Before sailing for our wreck location in the Caribbean we decided to test it at Fort Lauderdale. During the test, it ventured too close to the salt-water-intake system of the city's electric power plant and was sucked against the huge pipe's protective screen. The two men inside were trapped for eight hours before we finally located it and had the plant intake pump stopped for a few minutes. On the few occasions we got to use it, we constantly suffered electric shocks from minor water leaks that reached the batteries located under both seats. Navigating it in shallow water, we repeatedly collided with coral reefs.

More sophisticated methods must be used to locate shipwrecks that are completely buried or lying in areas with poor underwater visibility. These same methods are sometimes appropriate for clear water since they reduce considerably the time involved in locating a wreck. Some of them will also locate the shipwreck whether it is visible or buried. In areas of poor visibility, especially bays and harbors, the old method of locating a shipwreck, providing some part of it protruded above the sea floor, was to drag a cable between two vessels or to drag a line with grappling hooks from a single vessel. The big disadvantage of this method was that it could be used only when the sea floor was flat and when reefs and rocks were not prevalent. Otherwise the drag line was constantly snagging on underwater obstructions.

I suggest that every search boat carry a good

fathometer...not only to indicate depth but to prevent the salvage vessel from becoming a shipwreck statistic itself in shallow, reef or rock-strewn waters. A fathometer also helps to locate shoals, rocks and reefs where ships may have wrecked. As a search tool it is mainly useful for locating 19th and 20th-century shipwrecks or older ships which went down in deep water and have remained more or less intact. In recent years two of the richest Chinese porcelain wrecks, both lying between 120 and 140 feet deep, were located using only a fathometer...or echo sounder as they are called in Asia.

Although professional treasure hunting firms have been known to spend as much as $10,000 a day, particularly on the search phase of deep water projects, there are many ways that searches can be conducted for a great deal less money. First, equipment can be rented or even borrowed for a cut of the action. Some equipment companies will even loan expensive equipment for its publicity value to them. Oil exploration firms usually have the latest and most sophisticated electronic equipment available, and they can sometimes be convinced to loan not only equipment but technicians to operate it.

Personnel can be costly, but I have found that there is seldom a shortage of enthusiastic, qualified volunteers available to join a treasure hunt and serve as divers, deck hands, photographers and in other capacities. Many university students working for degrees in archaeology and related subjects also jump at the chance to join a well planned expedition. Local yachtsmen are a good source for finding a suitable boat, and my only cost has usually been the fuel and victuals.

Sophisticated equipment is not as important as thorough research before starting a search or excavation. The idea is to keep overhead down, keep things simple and operate as efficiently as possible with whatever means are available. The two men who discovered the Civil War ironclad *Cairo* in the Yazoo River used a rowboat as a search vessel and a war surplus compass as their only scientific instrument.

Aware that a large mass of metal would affect the earth's magnetic field in the area of the wreck, they passed over the general area holding the compass. When they crossed over the wreck the compass needle swung around 180 degrees and remained in that position until they rowed away. They shoved a long metal rod into the muddy river bottom and knew they had located a wreck when the rod struck metal.

Magnetometers, which detect the presence of ferrous metal, are the main search tool used universally for old shipwrecks, especially those which are buried under sediment or coral and for shipwrecks where visual search is restricted for whatever reason. Magnetometers are also used for confirming targets which may be picked up on side scan sonar when the sonar operator is not sure if a target is a pile of rocks or a shipwreck. Almost every major discovery in the past 30 years was made with a magnetometer. Any magnetometer, however, is only as good as the skill of the operator running it. Many shipwrecks have been missed by incompetent magnetometer users. Before going after a specific target a new mag user should get as many hours of experience under his belt as possible with instruction from an experienced operator.

Magnetometers were developed during World War II to detect submerged submarines. Basically, a magnetometer detects gradients in the earth's magnetic field produced by local concentrations of ferro-magnetic materials such as cannon, anchors or any other ferrous metal objects on a shipwreck. The larger the object is and the longer it has remained in the same position, the better the chances are of locating it. There are four types of magnetometers, each working on a different principle: the rubidium, proton, cesium and differential fluxgate. The usual method of operating a magnetometer is to tow it behind a boat at speeds of from two to ten knots, depending on the sensitivity of the particular instrument and the size of the object being sought. On several occasions shipwrecks have been located by using a magnetometer from a helicopter, from which the sensing probe of the magnetometer was lowered until it was just over the surface of the water.

During the 1950's a few attempts were made to utilize magnetometers to locate shipwrecks, but none of them met with much success until Fay Fields, formerly with Treasure Salvors, developed one with which he located more than 100 shipwrecks off the coast of Florida alone.

Until a few years ago a good magnetometer cost from $15,000 to $30,000. Today some sell for as little as $500, but, of course, they are not as sensitive as the costlier ones. Recently a magnetometer came on the market that is as sensitive, if not more so, than the $30,000 models. Called a Differential Flux Gate magnetometer, it sells for $3,500 and has several important features that many other magnetometers lack. It operates at full efficiency regardless of geographic location, it eliminates problems resulting from orientation in the earth's magnetic field and it is unaffected by ignition interference and atmospheric conditions. The control unit is watertight and tested to a depth of 200 feet. It has negative buoyancy and, with an optional sensing probe, can be operated by a diver in an underwater environment. Indications of magnetic anomalies are provided both visually and aurally.

Power is provided by the power case and consists of rechargeable nickel cadmium cells. Total drain is approximately 4.5 watts. The power case will provide 20-hour operation between charges. A charger operating from 115v A.C., with overcharge protection and undervoltage protection, is part of the power case.

This magnetometer senses gradients in the earth's magnetic field produced by local concentrations of ferro-magnetic material. It employs two sensors, elements that are mounted in a rigid submersible container, and measures the difference between the two sensor outputs. These sensors are balanced, so that orientation in the earth's magnetic field is not critical. The instrument is also insensitive to ignition interference and atmospherics. This device can detect magnetic-field strength at the two sensors less than 0.5 gamma, independent of the external-field strength, as long as this field does not exceed three times the maximum value of the earth's field. This makes the unit's operation independent of geographic location.

This magnetometer consists of three basic components: sensing probe, control unit and power supply. The sensing probe is designed to be towed behind a search vessel from a 100-foot cable connected to the control unit on the vessel. The probe is extremely stable and can be adjusted to run at predetermined depths to 200 feet by controlling the speed of the vessel or by attaching weights to it. The unit will operate at full efficiency regardless of geographic location. It eliminates problems caused by orientation of the earth's magnetic field and unlike other types of magnetometers the proton magnetometer is unaffected by ignition...interference from the boat's engine and atmospheric conditions. Like the sonar instruments, it can be run continuously under most sea conditions.

The usual method in using the magnetometer is to set up a search pattern using buoys, which can be quite time consuming, or by controlling their spacing and navigation

Above
Gregg and Scott Stemm and John Morris, from left, examine bronze ship's bell they recovered with an ROV (see over) in 1500 feet of water off the Dry Tortugas.

Below
These Spanish gold two escudo coins came from the 1656 wreck of the *Maravilla* in the Bahamas.

with various types of computer-oriented systems such as the Motorola Mini-Ranger. Some treasure hunters prefer using an optical transit or theodolite, stationed ashore or on a portable tower placed in the water. The survey vessel runs out predetermined compass courses, and the operator uses a hand-held radio to keep the vessel on course. In areas where loran is effective the magnetometer runs can also be obtained by navigating along a particular loran bearing.

In shallow-water searches for large targets such as cannon or anchors, the sensing probe is pulled on the surface at between 5 to 10 knots. The sensing probe must be pulled close to the sea floor and the width of each search lane narrowed considerably, however, when the amount of detectable ferrous metal is suspected to be small. Examples of such conditions would be a ship that carried bronze cannons, which do not register on the magnetometer, or a ship that might have lost all its anchors in another area before wrecking.

A target like a Civil War blockade runner, which may have had as much as 100 tons of iron used in its construction, can be detected at a distance of 400 to 600 feet. An older shipwreck site with a large number of cannon and anchors may be detected from 250 to 300 feet away if the iron objects are confined in a small area. When the wreck has been scattered and large ferrous articles broadcast over a large area, each piece will probably be detected individually at a maximum range of 100 feet. In cases where a shipwreck has only small ferrous items such as

Above is the *Merlin*, a remote-operated vehicle to be used by wreck hunters on the preceding page to salvage a Spanish galleon in 1500 feet of water. Below is the *Phantom*, which recovered their ship's bell and is typical of an ROV, the best tool for salvaging deepwater shipwrecks.

cannonballs, tools, weapons and bits of rigging, the location will be detected only if the sensing probe passes within 30 to 40 feet of the site. If very small items are widely scattered, the probe must come within 10 to 15 feet to detect them.

During the past 30 years magnetometers have been used to locate hundreds of shipwrecks and other types of submerged objects such as airplanes or pieces of military equipment. On the east coast of Florida and in the Florida Keys treasure hunters have found more than 500 shipwreck sites in the past 10 years alone. The magnetometer is not practical for use in an area like the Mediterranean, since ancient ships carried little ferrous material.

I used a proton magnetometer to find the *Maravilla* on the Little Bahama Bank. We spent four months conducting a thorough magnetometer survey in the summer of 1972. We covered 35 square miles, averaging a quarter of a square mile per day. Usually when looking for a Spanish wreck, searchers space each run about 200 feet apart in hopes of locating a cannon or anchor, since the sensing probe is detecting off to both sides while being towed.

Although various treasure hunters had covered this same area previously without finding the site, my research had convinced me that the wreck was in this area. Consequently, I decided to space each of our runs at only 100 feet, which meant the probe would pass within 50 feet of every object in the search area and could detect ferrous articles much smaller than cannon or anchors. I knew that the *Maravilla* had carried only bronze cannon which would make her difficult to find. Even though she was buried under 25 feet of sand, we were able to find her and 24 other wrecks as well as 76 anchors, some with chains, and even such odd items such as a fisherman's tackle box.

Many sites buried under the sea floor, such as ancient shipwrecks and sunken buildings, have little or no ferrous material on them. None of the search methods described above will reveal them. The only sure way to search for such a site is with a special sonar instrument, the sub-bottom profiler. Two of the best available are the "Pinger" and the "Boomer," both designed by Harold Edgerton. They have been used as the principal search tools on dozens of underwater archaeological sites all over the world. The sub-bottom profiler works on the same principle as other types of sonar, except that by using a lower frequency signal it can penetrate through the sediment interfaces and produce a profile of objects buried in the sediment or beneath it on bedrock. Like the echo sounder, this instrument must pass directly over a buried object to detect it. The unit shows not only a profile of buried objects but reveals their size and shape, how deep they are buried, the depth of the water and the thickness of different types of sediment lying on bedrock.

Sonar Surveys Valuable

During January and February of 1968, I was fortunate to have Dr. Edgerton run sub-bottom sonar surveys in Jamaica at both St. Anne's Bay and the sunken city of Port Royal where I was working. Most of his efforts were devoted to surveying and mapping Port Royal. A series of shore points, all about 10 feet apart, were located, numbered and plotted on a map. Buoys were spaced about 10 feet apart in lines running offshore. Then the survey boat with sub-bottom profiler made runs at a constant speed. Since the site was almost a mile long, this sonar survey took about three weeks. Results were excellent. With the aid of several draftsmen we used the hundreds of feet of sonar-recording paper to produce four large charts covering the entire site and showing the precise positions of hundreds of walls of the old buildings as well as of several shipwrecks. An important feature of this survey was that it defined the extent of the whole site.

The sub-bottom profiler can also pinpoint a wreck when its approximate position has been determined, but when it is buried and can be found no other way. One of the most famous ships in British naval history was the *Mary Rose,* which sank in Portsmouth harbor in England in 1545. Research established she was in an area of about 1,200 square feet, but attempts to locate her through visual and magnetometer search failed. A sub-bottom profiler produced a three-dimensional seismic sonar profile which proved to be the *Mary Rose* under 10 feet of harbor mud.

More recently, Barry Clifford reported discovering the *HMS Hussar,* a Revolutionary War British payship lost in New York's East River. The 619-ton, 114-foot-long warship was located on the first pass using a sub-bottom profiling sonar with six other old shipwrecks then located in the same area. A wreck was distinctly outlined on a sonograph, even showing the superstructure and a beam lying across the bow and two forward holds that Clifford and Garry Kozak, an engineer with Klein Associates, said were most likely the hold openings typical of a ship of the *Hussar's* design. The masts appeared to be missing. Unfortunately, Clifford has failed to obtain salvage permits from the State of New York and the Army Corps of Engineers and thus the treasure still lies under the mud in 80 feet of river water. Dozens of previous attempts had been made to find this wreck since the early part of the 19th century, but except for a few gold coins and an anchor inscribed with the ship's name, all failed to find the elusive remains.

Recently Klein Associates developed an extremely efficient high-resolution profiler, the Klein Microprofiler, which is superior to similar instruments available to the wreck hunter. By using a much higher frequency, a narrower beam and shorter pulses, plus having the sensor head towed right close to the bottom, it produces a more sharply detailed outline of the sea floor topography and objects hidden in the sediment. Subtle features, such as bronze cannon, which on more profilers are hardly distinguishable from other bottom features, are more clearly defined and identifiable.

In areas where ships sank, were buried under sediment in mud or silt and don't have any ferrous materials to be picked up by a magnetometer, the profiler is the answer. It has limitations, however, for most shipwrecks are buried in sand. No profiler can penetrate deeper than 10 feet in coarse, compact sand. For wrecks covered in coral the instrument is useless. Prior to his recent death Dr. Edgerton was developing a profiler designed for use in deep sand. It is hoped that someone else will continue this important work.

Sidescan sonar, developed in World War II to detect submerged submarines, is the best way to locate sunken objects projecting above the bottom. It has the advantage of not missing anything as the cable sweep sometimes does. A cable could slide right over a smooth object without snagging. Sidescan covers large areas in a much shorter period than the echo sounder. It operates on the same principle, but the sonic signal is directed obliquely toward the bottom, and a sensitive instrument can cover an area 1,200 feet wide on each pass over deep water if the bottom is flat or has only a gentle slope. In depths of 50 feet, up to 500 feet can be swept at a time. Thus, if a boat is moving at 10 knots, one square mile of sea floor can be covered in a little over an hour. Unlike visual search systems, which are affected by bad weather, dirty water and darkness, the sidescan unit can be operated around the clock. The silhouette of any protruding object is recorded on graph paper and shipwrecks or walls of sunken buildings are easily distinguishable from other objects.

Side-scan sonar is mainly used for ships lost in waters deeper than 100 feet since most remains of such a ship will be laying on the sea floor and not buried under bottom sediment. Exceptions occur, however, that make this type of sonar useful for shallow water shipwrecks. When Mel Fisher's team finally found the main site of the *Atocha,* they described it as a "reef of silver bars" sticking above the sea floor. If Fisher had used a side-scan sonar, he might have found the *Atocha* years earlier. All of the major deep-water discoveries in recent years such as the *HMS Edinburgh,* the *Central America,* and six other deep-water wrecks discovered by the Seahawk group of Tampa were found with side-scan sonar.

Underwater beacon transponders have recently found great acceptance in treasure hunting, and I highly recommend their use...especially since buoys left on a shipwreck have a nasty habit of disappearing. Some are accidentally cut by passing boats, others break loose in heavy seas and still others are lost for a number of different reasons, including sabotage. Even with the most elaborate electronics equipment, a considerable amount of time is required to relocate the position of any shipwreck...provided that it was plotted accurately in the first place.

The beacon transponder eliminates this problem as well as the possibility of pirate divers sighting your buoys on a wreck site and diving when you are not there. This problem is especially troublesome in the Florida Keys, where there are a number of divers who make a living poaching on wrecks belonging to others. The beacon with an operational life of up to several years depending on the size of its battery power source can be attached to any part of the wreck and hidden from surface view. A salvage vessel returning to the general area by regular navigational means can then activate the beacon transponder from the and home in on it easily to the wreck site.

Cannon and Anchors

The three main signposts in locating an old shipwreck are the cannon, anchors and ballast. Merely finding any of these three, however, does not always indicate that you have located a ship wreck. Often when a ship was in danger of capsizing during a storm, some or all of its cannon were thrown overboard. When a ship ran aground on a reef or shallow area, cannon were thrown overboard to lighten the ship, and sometimes the ships could be refloated. At times even large amounts of a ship's ballast and cargoes of the least value were thrown overboard to lighten and refloat a stranded ship. I have dived off several areas close to old forts on Caribbean islands and discovered large numbers of cannon that were not from shipwrecks but from the forts. They could have gotten into the sea for a number of reasons...fallen during hurricanes and earthquakes, discarded as too old and dangerous or to prevent their capture by an enemy, or thrown in by an enemy after capture of the fort.

Old cannon were sometimes used as ballast on ships and occasionally jettisoned when not needed. An instance of this is found off the eastern end of the Bonaire Island. Diving there some years ago I located over 200 cannon in a relatively small area. What amazed me was the fact that their age ranged over a period of 250 years! A local historian cleared up the mystery by explaining that this had been the area where ships from Holland anchored to load cargoes of salt from the island. The submerged cannon had been used as ballast on various ships and jettisoned when the ships took on heavy cargoes of salt.

Generally, finding anchors that are not near cannon or

a ballast pile simply signifies that a ship lost an anchor. As usual, however, there are exceptions to this rule. When a storm drove a ship toward a dangerous reef or coastline, anchors were naturally thrown out to prevent the ship from wrecking. In these situations one or more anchors could have been lost seaward from the shipwreck and can provide a clue that leads to the location of a wreck.

Anchors can also be found shoreward from a wreck, providing a clue in locating the main site. We know that most, and in some cases all, of a ship's anchors were carried high on the bow and stern, and in many cases these sections of a shipwreck were carried closer toward shore than the main section of a shipwreck. In either event, whether the anchor is seaward or shoreward from a wreck, knowing the wind and sea direction as well as the direction of prevailing currents in the area is extremely useful in determining the approximate position of the wreck site.

Finding a ballast pile does not always indicate a shipwreck, especially when it is discovered near or in ports or harbors. Ships occasionally sailed without cargoes in which case they needed to load large amounts of ballast to stabilize. Before or after entering a port where a heavy cargo was to be loaded aboard a ship, most and sometimes all of the ballast was thrown overboard. If the ship remained in the same position when this operation was underway, the ballast pile would resemble one similar to that of a shipwreck site. If the ship was swinging on its anchor, then the ballast would be scattered as it is on a wreck site where the wreck was badly broken up and the ballast strewn over a large area.

In an age when mariners were not overly concerned about sanitation, the Spaniards had the reputation for the dirtiest ships afloat. Since many seamen and the poorer passengers lived below deck on these long voyages, a great amount of fish, animal, and fowl bones, broken pieces of ceramic, glassware, etc. were thrown into the hold with the ballast. This resulted in items that a modern-day salvor might associate with artifacts from a shipwreck being mixed in with ballast rock. Thus, these items would also be thrown overboard with the ballast rock and can mislead a salvor into believing that the ballast pile is indeed associated with a shipwreck.

Old ships carried round ballast rocks ranging in size from several ounces to 200 pounds. The larger rocks were usually placed over the lowest deck, then smaller rocks filled in the spaces between the larger ones. On some of the early French and English ships, a substantial amount of ballast rock was cemented together with mortar for use as permanent ballast. I have not discovered whether ships of other nationalities followed this practice.

Since most ships took on their ballast in ports or harbors, most of which had rivers or streams emptying into them, the round "pebble" or "river rock" ballast was the

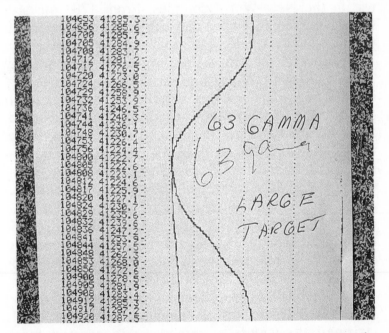

Chart showing the reading of an iron-seeking magnetometer that proved to be a one-ton anchor illustrates how this electronic instrument can help locate shipwrecks.

type most commonly used. There were many instances where this type of rock was not available, and they were forced to use other types of rock. Their preference was naturally round rocks, which did not have sharp edges that could pierce wooden hulls in rough weather.

A late 16th-century wreck, either of Spanish or French origin, salvaged by Teddy Tucker in Bermuda contained flint rock for ballast. Documents dated 1570 tell of a Spanish merchantman sailing from Cuba to Spain with copper ore for ballast...of another Spanish ship sailing in 1638 from Venezuela to Spain with saltpeter for ballast...and still another sailing in 1760 from Cadiz to Venezuela with gypsum rock for ballast.

As early as 1614 there are mentions of Spanish ships carrying bars of iron from Spain to America as ballast, but this was done only when iron was being carried for sale or use in the New World colonies. From 1700 onward, English warships used bar-shaped pigs of iron as ballast, a practice that took hold with French warships from 1707.

For several reasons, a wreck site may not have any ballast on it at all. When ships carried heavy cargoes they avoided being dangerously overweighted by not taking on ballast. When ballast rocks were scarce, sand was used. Also, on small vessels the limited space below decks necessitated an alternate means of carrying ballast. Therefore, as casks and barrels containing water, beer, wine, vinegar, etc., were consumed, they were filled with sea water. This method permitted quick and easy lightening of a ship during a storm. The casks and barrels could either be emptied into the bilges and the salt water pumped overboard, or they could be jettisoned easily, unlike ships carrying ballast in the form of rocks or pig iron.

Responding to a great demand for scrap metal during World War II, dozens of commercial salvage vessels stripped thousands of anchors and cannon from shipwrecks all along the shores of the United States and throughout the Bahamas and Caribbean. This created the

216

same kind of problem that the Bahamian government did when they removed similar objects from the wrecks on the Little Bahama Bank. Cannon and anchors are the main signposts that indicate the presence of an old shipwreck...whether sought visually or electronically. People all over the world today still recover cannon and anchors for scrap metal which aggravates the problem for future generations of wreck hunters. One character I ran into in the Bahamas has been recovering old anchors and cannon for years and selling them to marinas to use as mooring anchors.

Even though contemporary salvors rarely were able to recover all of a ship's treasures for many different reasons, salvors generally grabbed all the anchors and cannon off these wrecks, which again makes it extremely difficult until better search equipment is developed, to find such shipwrecks.

Twice in the last 20 years I have discovered treasure-laden shipwrecks only to lose them because poachers removed from the wreck the exposed anchors on which I depended to relocate the sites. In 1970 I found new documentation on one of the major shipwrecks of the 1715 fleet and discovered that the main section of the wreck lay three miles offshore. I convinced Mel Fisher to join me in getting a team together to go after this wreck. Fisher had been working for the previous two seasons close to shore where a section of the wreck had been thrown during the hurricane. Since the main section of the ship contained a fortune, we set off to locate it.

Although it was winter and the seas were rough, we got a strong magnetometer reading in one spot. Tom Gore, the State of Florida's representative on the project, and I went down to investigate. Sticking up from the bottom was a giant galleon anchor and scattered all over the sea floor around it were Spanish-type ballast stones. We were thrilled because we had just located the remains of one of the flagships of the 1715 fleet! It was too late in the season to contemplate any salvage and the prospect of having to wait for the spring killed us! From the bouncing boat we took numerous compass bearings on land objects and then placed a submerged buoy with a steel cable on the anchor.

Spring finally arrived. Excitement normally associated with beginning of the season greatly enhanced by the knowledge that we had already found our target, we rushed to the site. We first discovered that during the winter months a huge condominium development had resulted in demolition of five of the six objects we had used for our compass bearings. Running out on the one remaining bearing, we expected no trouble in finding the buoy. No such luck. I went ashore and rented a small plane, hoping to find it from the air. No luck again. Well, since we had originally found the wreck by "magging," we tried that again. What followed were six of the most frustrating weeks of my life. We couldn't find either the anchor or the site. We later learned that on the day following our discovery the previous winter a rival diving group had gone out and stolen our anchor. Fisher and many others have tried in vain to relocate this spot but for now, it is just as lost as it was before we found it.

The second time this happened caused an even greater heartbreak for me. I had been obsessed for years with finding a very rich galleon named *San Anton do Brasil*, also known as the *El Dorado*. This ship had been a Portuguese slaver which was nabbed by the Spaniards to transport an enormous Inca treasure discovered in Ecuador in 1551. I had known for years that she sank in the vicinity of Bimini, but I also knew that such a vague location was not sufficient to warrant going after her. Then quite by accident I located a 17th-century chart in London which denoted a place north of Bimini as El Dorado Shoals. This had to be my dream wreck site! I was prepared to spend the entire summer of 1981 searching for her.

I first gridded an area of five miles square because I knew that old charts are not too accurate. This entire area was white sand for miles around without any reefs or rocks. As we were dropping buoys prior to making our first magnetometer run, I noticed a dark spot in the water. Although I believed it to be modern debris, I went down to check it out anyway. To my great surprise and joy it turned out to be a sponge attached to the fluke of an old anchor, which subsequently proved to be one of three anchors of the *El Dorado*. Although the remainder of the shipwreck was under 30 feet of fine sand, these three anchors lay buried just beneath the surface of the sea's floor because their wooden stocks of Brazilian hardwood had proved impervious to the shipworm. By remaining intact they gave the anchors almost neutral buoyancy and kept them near the surface.

After uncovering all three anchors we dug one test hole and found several pieces of gold and a handful of red coral rosary beads, which convinced me this was indeed the *El Dorado*. Because we were out of sight of land, I relied on loran bearings...unaware that loran was quite unstable in this area and not very accurate. Since my vessel was not suitable for a salvage project of this magnitude, I planned a quick return to Florida for a larger one that could help me to bring up the treasure of my dreams.

A different fate lay in store for both me and the *El Dorado*.

While sailing for the larger boat, we stopped to check out another location a fisherman had revealed to us. After having written all my life that sharks don't bite divers, I was made a liar when I ran into a mako shark that apparently hadn't read my books. I ended up with 262 stitches in my upper right arm and a healthy respect for sharks.

While recuperating, I learned that one of my divers had robbed some gold coins from me on an earlier expedition. Naturally, I dismissed him immediately. This proved to be disastrous. While I lay in bed dreaming of the great wealth we would soon be pulling off the *El Dorado,* he went back to the site...which was a piece of cake to find with those anchors exposed on the surface. He removed all three of them. The next time I was to see these particular anchors was in a photograph on the cover of the *Smithsonian* magazine illustrating an article on underwater archaeology. I have since used every type of search tool available, but I've never been able to relocate this site, nor have any of the others who have been searching for it as well.

Although *El Dorado* carried 48 bronze cannon, they are laying under 30 feet of sand, and there is no way to find them. A magnetometer will not detect bronze, and neither metal detectors nor sub-bottom profiling sonar can find objects this deep. The only objects that a magnetometer could locate were the three iron anchors which were removed. This is the kind of problem wreck hunters face with many other shipwrecks, especially rich ones that generally carried bronze cannon.

Anchors always make great magnetometer targets but unfortunately a ship's anchors are usually a long way from the main site. When a ship found itself in danger too close to shore or a dangerous reef, it generally dropped an anchor or in many cases all of its anchors to lighten ship and sail away. When anchors were lost after cables were severed by sharp coral, the ship was carried at the mercy of wind and current and lost a considerable distance from the anchors. Two of the most sought-after treasure ships in the Bahamas suffered such a fate. The *Santiago el Grande* was lost in 1765 south of Bimini and her location is shown on numerous charts as "Galleon lost 1765," yet lots of us, including Mel Fisher, have searched in vain for this very rich galleon.

During a hurricane she dropped anchor right on the edge of the dropoff, lost her anchors and was carried for miles up on the Great Bahama Bank before finally sinking. We have found her anchors but it's another case of bronze cannon and heaps of silver and gold that are all buried too deep for any other type of search equipment to find.

Another such site was the *Genovese,* lost in 1669 on the Little Bahama Bank north of Grand Bahama Island. I found her three anchors and the reef which took out her bottom where she dropped some ballast and coinage. Then the trail was lost because she was carried far onto the sandy banks. Fortunately, the *Maravillas,* lost in 1656 just several miles to the north, went down with all five anchors aboard; otherwise, I might never have been able to locate her. Holed in a collision with another galleon, the ship took on water so rapidly that she sank intact.

Diver inspects the encrusted remains of a large iron cannon whose presence helped to locate the wreck of a Spanish galleon off Bermuda.

Documenting A Site

With fantasies of deep sea divers fighting for their lives as they grapple with the giant octopus guarding a chest spilling over with gems and gold, television and the movies have portrayed wreck hunting as one of the moşt dangerous occupations on the face of the earth. Actually the greatest dangers are those caused by man's carelessness and lack of respect for an alien environment. There is always the remote possibility of a shark or barracuda attack, or of a moray eel trying to eat one of your fingers, and I've experienced all of these. Over the years, however, I have found it safer to work under water than to drive on any Los Angeles freeway. Since noise of excavation tools generally scares away large marine creatures, spiny sea urchins and stinging fire coral cause more problems than the larger fish. Caution and common sense will prevent underwater accidents. There is no reason why underwater work should be particularly hazardous to a qualified diver.

Scuba equipment is the best underwater breathing gear to use for most survey and search activities...particularly for the shallow water where most shipwrecks in which readers of this book are interested can be found. Wearing

Compact and easily portable Third Lung, a modern method for providing air to divers, is particularly satisfactory in areas where no facilities exist for refilling scuba tanks.

a heavy, bulky scuba tank on your back, however, can be less than ideal for salvage work. Scuba can hamper an operation on most sites which are shallower than 30 feet deep and where bottom time is not limited. Coming up every hour for a fresh tank and having to fill tanks at the end of a long day's work is tedious and time consuming. Surface-supplied air is the only answer.

Back in the 1930's when treasure hunters like Art McKee were combing the Florida Keys and Caribbean for shipwrecks, standard diving gear was the bulky shallow-water helmet, which required the diver to keep his head erect lest the air escape and water enter. After WWII this rig was superseded by the Desco diving mask, a full face mask connected to an air compressor on the surface by a rubber hose. Teddy Tucker still swears by the Desco rig. Around 1955 the Hookah equipment came into use and is still used on deeper shipwrecks in many areas of the world. Similar to scuba gear, the regulator is, however, connected to an air hose going to the surface rather than a tank on your back. The advantage of using either the Desco or Hookah rigs is that the same compressor used for providing breathing air can also supply air for running such excavation equipment as airlifts or pneumatic hammers. High pressure air compressors used for refilling scuba tanks cannot be used this way.

In 1965 the Outboard Marine Corporation introduced a new SAS (Surface Air Supply) diving system called the Aquanaut which I found far superior to any other for work in water up to 50 feet deep. It consisted of an engine-air compressor assembly encircled and floated on the surface by an inflatable tube, with hoses connecting to a full face mask worn by the diver. During the three-year excavation of the sunken city of Port Royal my divers and I logged over 13,000 hours using the Aquanaut.

Today the Aquanaut is no longer on the market, but similar and more advanced SAS systems are available to the wreck hunter. I have found the Third Lung, manufactured and sold by Brownie's of Fort Lauderdale, to be the best. Its compact form and light weight enable me to take it on planes when I must travel to faraway places. Too, in many of the remote corners of the world where I work there are no facilities for refilling scuba tanks. These Third Lung units are similar to the Aquanaut except that they use a scuba regulator instead of the full face mask. The floating models are good for depths up to 75 feet. A larger model, which is still relatively light weight and compact, can be placed aboard a vessel. This type has two oil-less air compressors providing air for two divers to 90 feet, four divers to 60 feet or six divers to 30 feet. Recently I used one on a shipwreck in the Philippines in 80 feet of water with one other diver and a four-inch diameter airlift and had plenty of good breathing air.

After a wreck site has been located by either visual or electronic methods, there is still a great deal of work to be done before a salvor gets into actual excavation. For example, the target has to be pinpointed, then the overall extent of the site established and its parameters recorded. There are many other preparations as well. Nothing is more frustrating than to find a shipwreck or some part of it on the bottom, only to lose it because of failure to mark the site properly. I can't remember the number of times that one of my divers has surfaced to report an important find and then been either unable to relocate it or took a great deal of time to do so. If only he had left a buoy, this would not have happened! I have become so paranoid over this problem that I now fine my divers $100 when I find them entering the water without a diver's personal buoy...even if they are just going after a lobster for dinner.

One of the most important things to remember during a search is that nothing should be removed from the bottom where it has been found until the spot is marked in some way so that it can be found again.

More than one wreck has been found by location of an artifact or cannon on the bottom only to be lost again

227

because the artifact was removed or the cannon covered when sand shifted to bury it during a windy night. If the broken neck of an amphora, for example, were lying on a sandy bottom in clear water, a diver might feel safe in rushing it to the surface to display to excited comrades. Yet, within minutes the surging sea could cause sand to fill the depression made by the amphora fragment and the diver wouldn't be able to find the same spot again. Because the open sea is so vast that landmarks on it don't really exist, it isn't safe to leave even a large object on the bottom. To make sure of finding a particular area again, a buoy or other marker should always be placed on it before the diver surfaces.

During a search operation three different kinds of buoys should be used. All should be well built and self-unwinding. A diver can carry several small buoys which can be quickly dropped during a visual search when he sights something that seems interesting. They must be small enough to be attached to a weight belt without causing discomfort, yet large enough to be spotted on the surface from at least 100 yards. In my work I use a float cut from balsa wood. It is about six inches long, the thickness of a broom handle and painted an easily-visible fluorescent orange. A length of strong fishing line is attached and wrapped around it and a four-ounce fishing weight is tied to the other end of the line. An elastic band holds it all together. When the buoy is dropped, the elastic band is first pulled off and the weight drops to the bottom as the line unwinds and the float races to the surface.

The largest buoys needed on a search operation are those for defining the outer limits of the area to be searched. Usually placed at the four corners of the area, they should be visible for at least one mile. Empty 55-gallon fuel drums attached to three-quarter-inch line and a heavy anchor are a good choice. They should be painted fluorescent orange or red and white like peppermint candy canes. When rough seas make it more difficult to sight them, six to ten-foot poles flying brightly colored pennants can be attached to the drums.

During any kind of electronic or surface search when divers are not actually in the water, large numbers of smaller buoys will be required for laying out search patterns (the lines that the boat must follow on each run to cover a specific area) and to mark a spot when something is discovered. The best buoys are the eight to twelve- inch styrofoam floats used by fishermen on fishnets and lobster pots. They should be attached to quarter-inch line and standard building blocks weighing from 10 to 15 pounds. The line on all of these buoys should be considerably longer than the water is deep so that when the seas get rough the buoys will not be lifted and carried away.

One of the major mistakes made by modern-day salvors is their failure to make a proper survey of a wreck site after it has been located and *before* beginning excavation. This has repeatedly resulted in expeditions failing, causing the loss of great expenditures of capital and effort. A prime example took place quite recently. A group from Miami, armed with historical documents giving the location of a rich galleon wreck in the Bahamas, first used a magnetometer dragged from a helicopter. In less than a week they located a wreck in the general area given in the documents as the location of the sunken galleon. Instead of first making a survey of the site to determine if the wreck was the one they sought, this group rushed to outfit a large vessel for salvaging the galleon, then quickly realized their mistake. The wreck turned out to be a late 19th-century vessel with nothing of value on it, and these salvors lost over $20,000.

This group should have learned from this venture, but they repeated the fiasco. After returning their salvage vessel to Miami, they resumed a magnetometer search from the helicopter and *again* located what they believed to be their galleon wreck. For a second time they failed to make a survey of the suspected area and brought their large salvage vessel back to the Bahamas. Their discovery proved to be a modern missile cone rather than a Spanish galleon. In both cases they could have invested a small amount of capital and time in a survey of the suspected areas by renting a small vessel and taking a minimum of diving and excavating equipment.

And, there are other reasons why a wreck site should be surveyed before bringing in a salvage vessel. Establishing the overall extent of the site is important because it will be a partial indication of how long the excavation will take and determine the economic feasibility of salvage. A wreck contained in a small area...say, about the size of a football field...is certainly more economical to excavate than one spread over an area of several square miles. Another reason for surveying is to determine the type of excavation equipment required.

An expedition in the Bahamas paid the price for failing to prepare adequately. Salvors located a wreck site visually from the air, sighting a large number of cannon on a sandy bottom. Believing that the wreck was buried in sand they outfitted their salvage vessel with airlifts and a prop-wash. Arriving at the wreck site, they were shocked to find that the sand was only several inches deep and that the wreck was buried in thick coral growth. They lacked the proper pneumatic hammers or powerful water-jets to salvage the wreck effectively.

In areas like Florida, where salvors must obtain a pinpoint lease on a wreck site, it is imperative that the total extent of a site be known, since the salvor may not get a lease covering the total area. When this occurs--as it has on several occasions--others are able to obtain leases adjacent to those of the original discoverers of the shipwrecks.

The initial step of any survey should be to locate all visual traces of the wreck by diving and placing buoys over the objects located. In doing this, I make it a practice to have someone follow me in a small skiff. After I place a buoy over each object, I surface and identify the object. The person in the skiff records my discovery and carefully plots it on a chart. Mapping and identifying the objects as they are located eliminates the danger of not relocating them if the buoys are lost.

To pinpoint your discovery and also to identify it you should always start with a visual survey, whenever possible. Since buoys dropped during a side-scan sonar or magnetometer search are rarely directly on top of the target, further searching is generally required. When you enter the water to make a visual inspection, make sure you are wearing a depth gauge, an underwater compass and carry at least one personal buoy. I like to grab a line with a buoy floating on the surface so that the men in the search vessel can monitor and plot the areas I have covered in my search. This same buoy can also be used to tie to whatever object you locate.

If the target you seek is a magnetometer anomaly, keep in mind that there is a good chance it is buried. Magnetometer anomalies buried in sandy areas can sometimes be spotted by discoloration of the sand. Since iron oxide bleeds from large iron objects close to the surface, the sand will be darker than the surrounding sand. This also occurs with large metallic objects buried in coral growth. Iron will turn coral brown or black; brass, bronze and copper will turn coral greenish; and lead tends to turn coral white or gray. Although a single silver coin will be difficult to spot in the coral, silver sulphite leaching from large numbers of them will discolor the coral black, or sometimes a greenish color if the coins contain a large amount of copper.

There are no chemical changes in gold, pottery or ballast rock. These and other objects can be spotted only by a trained eye noticing strange shapes in the coral. Remember that Mother Nature does not make straight lines in reefs or sand. Coral grows at different rates depending upon factors including depth, currents, and

231

salinity of the water. I have found that the fastest coral growth is in the breaker zone and that coral grows faster in rougher seas. It may have something to do with the movement of the oxygen in an area of fast moving water.

In pinpointing a target I usually set up a search pattern using a compass and space each search line to overlap the previous one to prevent missing anything...depending on underwater visibility. Another method, good in both clear and turbid water, is the circle sweep. After the search boat reaches the vicinity of a likely target, a heavy anchor is dropped on a line. Another line is also attached to some part of the anchor. If the search is to be visual, this line is marked at intervals to let a diver know how far to space each circle he will make. If the underwater visibility is only five feet in each direction, each mark on the line should be spaced about eight feet apart. The marks can be made by knotting or tying a piece of cloth to the line. The diver starts by swimming a complete circle around the anchor holding the first mark, then moves out further in progressively larger circles until the target has been located.

When the target is large, a faster method is for the diver to swim out to the far end of the search line, holding it taut and swimming a large circle...circumference depending on the length of the line. Once the target is snagged by the line, the diver, still holding the line taut, swims back toward the anchor until he runs into the target. He quickly drops a small marker buoy which serves until a larger buoy can be dropped from the search vessel.

In rivers or streams where there is a strong current, the best way to locate a target is with the traverse sweep search. The anchor and line are dropped upcurrent of the likely area and the diver operates in the same manner he would in executing the circle sweep search...except, to avoid fighting the current he swims a pattern in a relatively flat arc on each sweep, which increases in size the farther he moves from the starting point near the anchor. After each sweep, he drops back a bit farther to the next marker before starting on another sweep in the opposite direction.

The most efficient way to zero in on a side-scan sonar target is with a hand-held sonar unit, no larger than an underwater camera, which can locate objects 200 feet away. After descending along the buoy line the diver sweeps the surrounding area in a 360-degree arc, until the sonar unit emits a beep which indicates the direction of an object protruding above the sea floor. The beep will grow stronger as the diver gets closer to the object. The latest model from Scubapro has an illuminated scope to show the distance from the target to the diver. This unit named Sonar Vision can be used to depths of 300 feet. Recently I mounted one on a scooter and found it to be very effective for finding sonar targets.

In the past we had to rely on submersibles and submarines--expensive and sometimes dangerous--to locate wrecks in deep water. Thanks to great advances in oceanographic technology we now have the ROVs (remote-operated vehicles). Since even the cheapest models are in the $35-$50,000 range, these ROVs are not for the average wreck hunter, unless he is able to rent or borrow a unit. The ROVs are powered by a series of thrusters and carry low-light-level color television and still cameras. The units are connected to the surface by an umbilical cable which provides power and transmits commands from the surface, as well as relaying video images to surface screens and recorders.

Operating an ROV is similar to playing a television video game and you don't even have to get wet. You simply sit facing a video screen and control the movements of the ROV and the cameras by manipulating several joysticks. Many models come equipped with manipulator arms for picking up samples. The most widely used ROV are the Phantoms manufactured by Deep Ocean Engineering of San Leandro, CA.

Using one of the Phantoms, the Seahawk group from Tampa last year recovered a ship's bronze bell from a late

16th-century Spanish galleon in 1,500 feet of water off the Dry Tortugas. They used a manipulator arm attached to the Phantom.

A recently developed unmanned deep water search and survey system is now marketed by Sea Inc. of San Diego. Their Sea Search MKII unit is equipped with an integrated side scan sonar and low-light-level video camera that permits the operator to confirm sonar targets visually. This vehicle which can also carry still cameras, a sub-bottom profiler sensor and a magnetometer operates at depths up to 1,000 feet. A transponder beacon can also be attached and dropped from it right onto a target.

Returning to shallow water again, another important factor must be considered when pinpointing and establishing parameters of a shipwreck site. Many shipwrecks are contaminated by modern debris which can confuse a wreck hunter...even to discounting an interesting shipwreck. This has happened to me a number of times. Once while searching for a galleon off Panama, I obtained a promising magnetometer reading. When I dove to inspect the anomaly, I found a large fishing net with steel cable attached. Deciding that this had caused the anomaly, I continued my search and failed to locate the galleon. It was only when I returned to inspect this same area more closely a month late that I found that the cable had snagged on the fluke of an old anchor. My galleon was right under the modern debris. Another time in the Bahamas I had a modern barge loaded with steel irrigation pipe right on top of another galleon wreck.

One of my most frustrating experiences with contamination occurred 10 years ago in Brazil. My main target was the *Hollandia,* flagship of the Dutch privateer Piet Heyn, which was lost in 1627 during a sea battle. From historical documents I knew her location to within several hundred square yards, but I realized that she would be tough to pinpoint. Magnetometers and sub-bottom profiling sonar were useless because the remains of dozens of other ships were buried in the mud in this area. I was faced with a tidal current of up to four knots, very poor underwater visibility and--to top it all off--the area lay in the center of a busy shipping channel.

We spent over 900 hours underwater and found 19 shipwrecks of various other periods, but there was no sign of the Admiral's flagship. Could it have devoured by the hungry jaws of a dredge boat? The following year I returned and resumed the search, again to no avail. Finally, the director of the Naval Museum requested that we recover some artifacts from the many wrecks we had found during our futile search. While digging a ceramic jar from mud on the site of a 19th-century British merchantman, I felt a mass of metal below. Thinking that it was part of the 19th-century wreck, I dug deeper and, to my great surprise, discovered it was a large iron cannon...not a 19th-century gun but a Dutch cannon of the early 17th century. By a fluke the merchantman had sunk some 250 years later than the *Hollandia*...right on top of her.

Occasionally there have been times when wrecks were

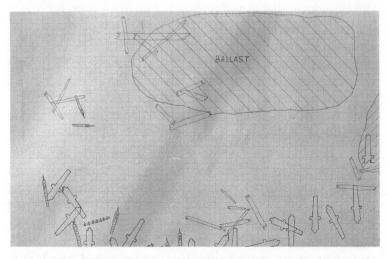

Plot charts such as this one that indicates the precise layout of a Portuguese ship that was lost in a wreck off the coast of Brazil in 1690 facilitate proper recovery from a shipwreck.

contaminated by *older* shipwrecks. I've encountered this numerous times not only in harbors, but also in the open sea where hurricanes stir up the bottom a great deal. The area where the wreck of the flagship of the 1715 fleet lies, commonly called the Cabin Site, is contaminated by both older and more recent vintage shipwrecks. A late 16th-century Spanish merchantman was lost on the same spot, as well as two 19th-century ships and three modern fishing vessels.

Sometimes treasure hunters are responsible for contaminating shipwrecks...occasionally, deliberately. To disguise the real identity of a shipwreck they've thrown rivals off by placing wreckage from more modern shipwrecks over a site. I know of one instance where one group had a permit for an area off the east coast of Florida which was coveted by another group. They went to a great deal of effort to dig up a much later wreck from another area and litter the old shipwreck site with the debris.

Another type of contamination, usually unintentional, occurs when treasure hunters drop objects from one shipwreck on the site of another. During a search objects are picked up and placed on board a boat for later examination. Then while diving on another site, they fling overboard some of the previously found objects that wouldn't pass inspection after coral growth was removed.

Some ships were contaminated even as they were being lost. When I discovered the 1656 *Maravillas* galleon, one of my first finds was a cannonball. Upon removing coral growth I found that it bore the British "board arrow" mark, signifying it was property of the British Admiralty. I was almost convinced that this was the wrong ship and was ready to move on to another area. But I changed my mind when almost immediately afterward we found some Spanish silver coins.

During the excavation of the sunken city of Port Royal I discovered a Latin-inscribed pedestal which no doubt was carried as ballast on a ship that had visited this port.

The pedestal was most likely picked up along with ballast rock from some river bed. On one Portuguese shipwreck off the Cape Verde Islands I found a number of iron cannon which were more than 150 years older than the ship which had been carrying them...probably as ballast.

After you have completed a thorough visual survey of a site, the next step is to locate all concentrations of metal, which is necessary when no trace of a wreck is visible above the sea floor. A magnetometer will locate the metallic objects and from the size of the anomalies recorded, a good operator can determine the size or mass of the metallic concentrations. This information should also be plotted on a chart. Sub-bottom profiling sonar can also be used to locate large non-ferrous objects such as wooden remains and ballast piles, as well as a large pile of silver bars if you are on a Spanish galleon.

An underwater metal detector should be used to comb every inch of a site after its perimeters have been established, not only to find large objects like bronze cannon if a profiler is not employed, but to find the smaller concentrations of coins and other metallic objects. The penetration depth of any metal detector depends on the performance of the detector and the size of objects and their depth in sediment or coral.

The nature of the sea floor itself determines the next step in surveying a wreck site. Objects that are buried in coral growth are the most difficult to survey, since many test holes must be made over the area until the overall extent of the site is determined. This can be a lengthy undertaking. If the coral growth is soft, you can use either a strong water-jet or coring device. It goes without saying that you should make every effort not to harm coral reefs or any part of the underwater environment. The small holes you make will not cause undue damage to the reef.

In hard coral growth, such as we experienced on the *Matanceros* wreck off the coast of Yucatan, small pneumatic hammers should be used. If they are not available, small sledge hammers and chisels can be used. On most reefs where wrecks are located there are generally many small pockets of sand not more than a few inches deep. I have found that a scuba tank with several feet of hose attached proves quite effective as an air-jet for blowing away the sand. You can also fan sand away by hand...more time consuming, but the best way to work small pockets, especially if you suspect there are delicate artifacts beneath the sand.

Various other methods can be used to survey a site in mud or silt after magnetometer and sub-bottom sonar surveys have been completed (or when these sophisticated instruments are not available). The fastest, but not always most effective, method would be to make test holes on the site using an airlift, hydrolift or small prop-wash. In some areas these can be used when there is only a few feet of sediment over the site. Small test holes can be made quickly. If the sediment is hard and compact, small test holes that reach quite deep can be made with these tools.

When the sediment is soft and silty, however, much larger test holes have to be made because the holes continually cave in. At Port Royal I found areas where the sediment was so soft that in order to make a test hole with an airlift to a depth of 20 feet, the diameter of the hole had to be over 60 feet. To overcome the problem I used five sections of concrete water pipe which were four feet in diameter and five feet long. After driving the first section as far down into the sediment as possible, I began excavating with a small airlift. As I went deeper the pipe also sank. When it sank below the level of the sea floor, I attached the next length of pipe and continued this method until I reached the desired depth. This method had one big disadvantage...it was almost impossible to retrieve the concrete water pipes without excavating a large hole around them, which didn't really matter, since I had unlimited access to the pipes.

I learned a simpler way to obtain the same results from

Art McKee, who developed his method by making test holes on wreck sites located in deep sand. Instead of water pipes, he used a long metal tube and an airlift. The diameter of the tube should be a few inches wider than the airlift-tube diameter. His method is quicker and safer than mine, for the diameter of his test hole is smaller...requiring less time but obtaining the same results. The metal tube is easier to handle than the larger water pipes, and instead of the diver operating the airlift in the water pipe as I did at Port Royal, he remains on the sea floor operating the airlift as it and the metal tube sink deeper into the sediment. He doesn't run the risk of the water pipe collapsing and trapping him under tons of sediment.

Depth Beneath Sea Floor

To determine the depth beneath the sea floor in which items are located by the airlift, the diver simply measures the length of the metal tube remaining above the sea floor and subtracts it from the total length of the tube. The metal tube can be recovered from the sediment with the aid of lifting bags or lifting equipment from a boat, such as an anchor winch.

At Port Royal I used a 12-foot iron rod, one-quarter inch thick with a wooden handle, to locate large objects buried beneath up to 10 feet of mud and found it to be quite effective. This method located hundreds of brick walls of old buildings as well as large artifacts and even two shipwrecks. With a little experience I was able to tell whether the object I had struck was brick, ballast stone, wood or iron just by the sound of the rod striking and the hardness of the object.

After we had located the Columbus ships with Dr. Edgerton's sonar equipment, I first attempted to determine the overall extent of both wrecks by using the metal probe method. The sonar indicated that both wrecks were under 10 to 12 feet of sediment. In some areas on both wrecks I was able to reach these stratigraphic levels and discovered the presence of wood and ballast rock. In others my probe would not penetrate more than several feet through concentrations of very hard mud.

In compact sand, a probe is more difficult to use unless the target is fairly close to the surface. In looking for something under more than four feet of sand, an air probe should be used. It is also useful where mud is hard and difficult to penetrate with a metal probe. I usually use a 20-foot length of one-inch diameter galvanized iron water pipe, the kind plumbers use. On one end I attach a hose connected to a surface air compressor which sends down a continuous stream of air to blow away the sand or mud around the mouth of the tube and facilitate its penetration. After something solid is encountered, the same method as used with a metal probe to indicate the type of material.

Dr. George Bass assisted me in obtaining a coring device from Columbia University for bringing up test samples of the Columbus' wreck. While Bob Judd from Columbia was helping operate it, he saw the problems I was having with my metal probe and invented an air probe right on the spot. It consisted of a 20-foot section of galvanized iron water pipe of one-inch diameter. The air hose of an Aquanaut diving unit was attached to the top of the pipe, sending down a continuous stream of compressed air that cut through the concentrations of hard mud. It not only penetrated the sediment quickly but was also easy to pull back out because of the compressed air blowing from the bottom of the pipe.

Coring tubes, useful in mud or silt, can also be effective on sandy bottoms and even in soft coral growth. Those

Wrecks of the 1715 fleet off the east coast of Florida continue to yield treasure, such as these gold disks, gold doubloons and silver plate.

generally used by marine geologists are driven into the sea floor by explosives or other equipment operated from a surface vessel. Those used by divers can be much simpler, like the one I used on the two Columbus shipwrecks. It consisted of four-foot sections of four-inch diameter iron tubing. One diver held the tube vertically while another drove it into the sediment by hitting the top of the tube with a heavy sledge hammer. As each section sank into the sediment, another was attached and the operation continued until we reached a depth of 20 feet beneath the sea floor.

Before the coring tube was pulled up with a lifting bag, a rubber plug was inserted into the top of the coring tube to maintain suction in the tube. This kept the sediment and artifacts in the tube from falling out when the tube was pulled up through the sediment. Either aboard a vessel or ashore, the sample in the tube was recovered by simply removing the plug and holding the tube almost horizontally and shaking it lightly. We were able to recover artifacts such as wood, glass, flint, iron nails and tacks, small ballast rock, animal bones, ceramic shards and beans and to determine their exact stratigraphic depth as well. This method also eliminated the danger of disturbing the archaeological nature of the site.

If a coring tube is used in coral growth, the bottom of the tube will require a sharp edge for cutting through the coral and will often have to be sharpened during the operation. The length of each section of the coring tube should not exceed four feet, a length that enables the diver

Younger and leaner author, far right, with part of team that helped recover these trade goods in 1956 from a Spanish merchant ship that sank in 1739 off the coast of Yucatan.

who is pounding the tube into the sediment to stand on the sea floor. This gives him more power in swinging the sledge hammer than if he had to swing it while swimming underwater.

It is easier to survey a wreck site on a sandy bottom than those in coral growth or on mud or silt bottoms. Test holes can be made with small airlifts, hydrolifts or small prop-washes on small boats. I have operated both small airlifts and hydrolifts without the use of even a small boat when the sites were located relatively close to shore. The air compressor for an airlift and the water pump for the hydrolifts were mounted on a platform floated on an inner tube of a truck. A small prop-wash, which would be effective only on a shallow-water site no deeper than 10 or 12 feet, can even be mounted over the propeller of an outboard engine. The advantage of the airlift and hydrolift in making test holes is that they can be used in any reasonable depth of water; however, an airlift will not work in less than 10 feet of water.

Test holes can also be made in areas of shallow sand over a wreck by using an air-jet or water-jet, both of which can be operated from a small float or boat. In shallow water the air hose from an Aquanaut diving unit can be used effectively. Since the unit has two hoses, one can provide the diver with air to breathe and the other to make test holes. I do not recommend the use of air or water-jets in muddy areas because they quickly reduce your underwater visibility to nothing.

A common mistake made by modern-day salvors is failure to *map* a wreck site. They consider it time-consuming and believe that the information obtained is useful only to archaeologists. They are wrong! By mapping and recording all information gathered during survey of a wreck site, the salvor not only determines the overall extent of his site but gains a great deal of other information. The pattern in which the wreck lies can enable the salvor to determine the cause of the sinking, which is useful in trying to establish whether it was salvaged by contemporary salvors.

For example, a wreck that has remained intact for a long period is more likely to have been salvaged than one that is scattered over a large area. A wreck lying on the surface of the sea floor or not buried very deeply was most likely salvaged soon after being lost and again over the centuries by other salvors, while a deeply buried wreck was most probably covered over before anyone could have salvaged it. Another reason for mapping a wreck is to establish its size, which is useful in identifying a wreck if its size, tonnage or the number of cannon it carried is known. This can be done by measuring the length of the keel of a wreck (when it exists), estimating the amount of ballast the ship carried or discovering the number and size of cannon.

Several salvage groups are now using a good system of surveying a wreck site. With a prop-wash mounted on a large vessel, they dig long test trenches by continually excavating with the prop-wash and "walking" the vessel on a straight course over a large area. This is done by first determining the length of time needed to excavate to the desired depth in the sand and by playing out the stern anchor lines and taking in on the two bow anchors respectively. While the vessel is "walking" and excavating the trench, divers follow behind the vessel at a safe distance and search in the trench. The advantage of this system lies in covering a larger area much faster than by using any of the other equipment mentioned in making test holes. Its disadvantage is that it requires a large vessel, which increases the cost of the survey.

Mapping or plotting the location of major artifacts discovered during the actual excavation aids the salvor in a variety of ways. From the nature of the different items recovered, the salvor can determine which end of the wreck is the bow and stern. Since the largest anchors were generally carried on the bow of the ship, anchors found at one end of a ballast pile or section of a wreck normally indicate that this was the bow...provided the ship was wrecked more or less intact. But this is not always a safe assumption, since anchors were also carried on the stern, and sometimes several were stored in the hold as spares. If a ship threw several over off her bow before wrecking, she might wreck with some on her stern, further confusing the issue. Most salvors make an attempt to distinguish the bow and stern of a wreck as quickly as possible. Knowing that most of the important treasure carried on old ships was carried in the stern castle, they naturally want to excavate that section of a wreck first.

In many cases the most likely areas for finding treasure on a wreck, provided it was not badly scattered, can also be determined through mapping the position of the artifacts recovered. Because officers and rich passengers lived in the stern castle, where the most valuable treasure was kept, this is the most likely area in which silver or pewter, fine china or similar items are discovered. The salvor should take many facts into consideration, however, before making assumptions. If the items show no sign of use, such as knife marks on a pewter or silver plate, they may have been carried as cargo elsewhere on the ship.

There are various ways to map a wreck. The method the salvor selects will depend on a variety of factors, including underwater visibility, current, depth and distance from shore. The grid system commonly used by land archaeologists has also been used on underwater excavations. When underwater visibility is good, the sea floor more or less level, the wreck contained in a relatively small area and a prop-wash not used (the prop-wash will blow the lines away), the grid system usually works well. Grid lines can be laid out in a predetermined pattern, generally running on a north-south and east-west axis and spaced from 10 to 20 feet apart, making squares of equal size. Each square is marked with a number and plotted on a chart. As each square is excavated, locations of artifacts, ballast rock, ship's timber and other items that cannot be raised (like a heavy cannon) are plotted on the chart.

Unfortunately, this simple grid system is neither practical nor economically feasible in most cases. On wrecks that are scattered over large areas, with parts lying even in the shore breakers, the system obviously cannot be used. Mendel Peterson, formerly with the Smithsonian Institution, developed a fairly simple method of mapping wrecks contained in a relatively small area that is less time-consuming and less expensive than the grid system. It consists of an azimuth circle marked with the degrees of the compass and mounted on a brass rod driven into the bottom near the center of the wreck site. This becomes the *datum point*. Using an underwater compass, the azimuth circle is lined up with magnetic north. A chain is connected to the center of the circle and distances are marked on the whole length of the chain. After the chain is stretched to a cannon, or whatever object is to be mapped, the diver notes the compass bearing on the azimuth circle to the object, plus the distance from the datum point, and the information is then plotted. This system has an advantage over the grid when the bottom is not uniformly level. The device is compact and can be built for only a few dollars.

If the wreck site is close to shore, the best method is to erect shore markers and plot their positions on a chart. Compass bearings taken on these shore markers will indicate the position of the items that must be plotted on the chart. Taking compass bearings from a rocking boat is neither easy nor accurate. After first surveying the wreck site, buoys should be placed on all important items. Their locations can be determined by taking compass bearings from the shore. During the salvage operation someone could also take compass bearings whenever required. This requires some method of communicating between the person ashore and the salvage vessel.

At Port Royal I used the method of shore markers which were erected by the Jamaican Survey Department and plotted on special grid charts for my use. When major finds were made, one of my team on shore established the precise position of the find by taking compass bearings from three or more shore markers to the top of the airlift tube, which protruded vertically above the water right over the position of the recovery. Since stratigraphic information was useful on this particular site, the depth of the recovered item was simultaneously established by determining the length of the airlift tube remaining above the surface of the water. Taking the water depth and state of the tide into consideration, the exact stratigraphic depth could be determined.

Mapping a wreck site that is scattered over a large area and not close to shore is the most difficult. First, using good electronic equipment and a sextant, a datum point must be established. A buoy placed on the datum point would provide one compass-bearing source, but at least two others would be required, preferably forming a triangle. Other buoys would then have to be placed in precisely known locations, possibly by measuring the distance and bearing from the datum point. I used this method on the excavation of the *San Jose* (wrecked in 1733 in the Florida Keys).

Since we were, fortunately, in sight of land, we were able to figure the precise position of the actual hull of the shipwreck and its ballast pile. A datum point was established on the seaward end of the wreck and buoys positioned over other areas of the overall wreck site. The State of Florida official aboard the salvage boat used these buoys to take compass bearings and map our excavation. On several occasions when one or more of these buoys disappeared during bad weather, it was easy to locate their original position and put new buoys out by simply establishing their compass bearing and distance from the datum point.

Sextants are used by navigators on the high seas to establish positions through latitude and longitude, but they can also be used for finding positions and distances from shore. At least three landmarks should be selected and the sextant then used to find the degree of angle between two of these points at a time. These angles are plotted on a chart indicating the position of the boat. Even though it is then simple to measure the distance on the chart between the position of the boat or site and the shore, you should verify accuracy of the angles by using the sextant again for determining distance. If the height above sea level of a particular landmark, such as a lighthouse or tower, is known by using the sextant in a vertical plane, it is possible to obtain the angle between the highest point of the object and the water level. This can be equated to a distance by referring to tables in all navigational books.

There are simple, inexpensive instruments called range finders which are not as accurate as sextants in fixing distance between objects ashore and a boat but which can be used when you don't know the elevation of the landmark you are sighting. The most accurate way to map a site is with a Brunton transit or other sophisticated land surveying equipment, but this method is too complicated and expensive for the average salvor. It was utilized on the two Columbus shipwrecks in St. Ann's Bay because of their great historical importance.

Underwater photography can be used in mapping a wreck site, but only when visibility is good and the wreck site is contained in a small area. Generally, the wreck is first marked with the grid system. A grid frame is then used to hold the camera, and photographs are taken of each square grid. The photographs are made into a large mosaic showing the entire area of the wreck. Marine archaeologists have photographs taken of each square at a number of stratigraphic levels. Provided the wreck sank relatively intact in deep water and has not been disturbed by man or nature over the years, this furnishes valuable information concerning the ship's construction, how and where the cargo was carried, and other pertinent data.

On shallow-water wreck sites, however, the same information cannot be obtained. I recommend that salvors make a photographic mosaic of wreck sites when large sections of the actual ship may exist, which helps to establish the type, size and (sometimes) nationality and identity. This is done after the wreck has been uncovered and all of the ballast stones removed from it. The best method for making a good mosaic of a wreck site, and one that is not too expensive, is to use the Pegasus or a similar underwater vehicle with a pulse camera mounted on it.

The focal width of the camera lens and the clarity of the water will determine the elevation above the wreck from which the photographs will be taken and the total number of photographs required to make a complete mosaic. In making a complete mosaic of the *San Jose* site, which encompassed a 200-by-100-foot area, only 14 individual photographs were required. With good underwater visibility and the depth of the wreck averaging only 30 feet, we could use the wide-angle corrected Rebikoff lens on a camera from a height of 25 feet over the wreck.

Hand-held cameras can also be used to make a photographic mosaic of a wreck site, but the diver must remain at a constant elevation over the site and swim on a straight course. Otherwise, the photographs will not be accurate and it will be difficult to match them when putting the mosaic together. The Pegasus eliminates this problem because it has a complete navigational system and can be flown at a constant depth while keeping a straight course.

Underwater Excavation

Many divers think the most difficult part of finding a sunken treasure is locating the wreck on which it was carried. This isn't always the case. Some wrecks are found relatively easily but require months or even years to excavate properly, depending on a variety of factors. The depth of a wreck, tides, weather conditions and a number of other problems can restrict the amount of time a salvor can spend working on a site. For example, off the east coast of Florida salvage divers are only able to work between early May and the middle of September...some years they even have to quit earlier because of hurricanes. The summer months seem to be the main season for shipwreck work worldwide. To work year around some professionals like myself work in the Northern Hemisphere during half the year and spend the other six months in the Southern Hemisphere where the seasons are reversed.

Sometimes when a wreck hunter thinks he has found a good wreck, it turns out that he has only found a section and it may take months, or even years, before he finds the remainder. Mel Fisher experienced this problem with the *Atocha*. After locating the galleon's anchor and a considerable amount of silver coinage, his divers had to follow a trail for 12 frustrating miles before finding the mother lode. Fifteen long years and almost $20 million went into this venture before Fisher and his investors were to get rich.

Many other shipwrecks in the Florida Keys and Bahamas ended up similarly...after striking a reef the ships were carried for miles, dropping ballast and artifacts along the way, before coming to their final resting place. The wider spread the scatter pattern of a shipwreck, the more time-consuming and costly it will be to salvage. One galleon lost in 1669 in the Bahamas hit a reef and was carried almost 20 miles eastward on the shallow bank, dribbling ballast and goodies along the way, before finally sinking and being covered by a blanket of sand 30 feet deep. Picking up the trail and staying on it is challenging. Sometimes there may be a gap of half a mile where nothing fell out of the ship, and it is quite a feat to trace the trail to doom.

Even ships wrecked close to shore can be widely scattered for many miles. Take the 1715 *Cabin Site* for example. The ship struck on a reef 350 yards offshore, and her main ballast pile is 150 yards out, but the main deck and superstructure was carried by the storm waves to and along the shore. A few of her cannon are around the ballast pile, but most are spread along a two-and-one-half-mile length of the coast in only a few feet of water in the breaker line. Treasure and artifacts are found all along this two-mile stretch. During northeasters some of this treasure usually ends up on the beach to the great joy of beach hunters. Another of the 1715 galleons off Vero Beach is scattered from shore to a half-mile offshore, and its remains stretch six miles along the coast line. This is the reason that the 1715 fleet shipwrecks--which have been continually worked for the past 30 years with sometimes as many as six salvage vessels on each site--are still producing significant amounts of treasure.

Depth of the water in which a shipwreck lies is a major factor in determining the duration and cost of a successful salvage effort. On most sites in this hemisphere wrecks lie in depths of 30 feet or less, and divers can work all day with no decompression problems. In such other areas where I have worked as the Mediterranean, Philippines and Guam, most of my wrecks were deeper than 100 feet, reducing bottom time to only an hour or an hour and a half per diver each day. This increases costs a great deal because you must either get more divers or set up a saturation diving system.

The amount of sediment or coral covering a wreck is another important factor. I have found some wrecks on coral reefs covered with only a few inches of coral growth and many of the goodies in small sand pockets. Excavation and salvage here can be accomplished with only a metal detector, prying tool and hand-fanning to pick up the goodies. Teddy Tucker excavated many of the Bermuda wrecks he located in sand pockets, using only a ping pong paddle. On occasions when a wreck was covered by only a thin blanket of sand I've been able to use an underwater scooter as my main excavation tool. By wearing extra lead weights I was able to stand on the bottom and hold the scooter in my hands with the propellers pointing downwards, blowing away the sand and exposing the goodies. Unfortunately, these "dream wrecks" are few and far between. Most are deeply buried in either sediment or coral, and more elaborate equipment is required to make them reveal their secrets.

Off the coast of Yucatan I located wrecks buried under more than eight feet of hard coral growth, and I have heard of other shipwrecks in the South Pacific with as much as 12 feet of coral growing over them. Unlike wrecks buried in the sand, which sometimes is removed during hurricanes and storms, those embedded in coral just become deeper each year.

Generally we think of wrecks buried in mud as being in harbors or near river mouths. Recently, however, I found an early 16th-century Portuguese shipwreck in the Far East which defies excavation--at least for the present--because of the mud that encases it. The ship hit a shallow reef, opened up and lost some of her contents before being carried 250 yards and sinking in 80 feet of water. The magnetometer and sub-bottom profiling sonar easily located her remains under the mud, but she lies on a hard pan rock bottom beneath 45 feet of mud. Mud is normally easy to remove, but in this case the mud was hard as concrete. Even after we had spent 300 hours with an airlift and done our best with powerful water jets to soften the mud, we had made a hole 40 feet in diameter and only 20 feet deep. We found ourselves still 25 tantalizing feet from the remains of the wreck, a depth which ruled out the use of a prop-wash. In some harbors mud is even deeper, but generally not as hard and compact.

Lighter objects such as ceramics and wood are sometimes found closer to the surface, but generally everything else on a wreck site precipitates down through the mud, silt or sand and eventually rests on the hard pan rock bottom. Off the east coast of Florida we find what we call a "false bottom" because there are layers of coquina rock from one to three inches thick that formed after a ship was lost, and parts of a wreck may lay under this layer.

When Kip Wagner and his team first dove on the *Cabin Site,* after spending several non-productive years on another of the 1715 wrecks that proved to have been already salvaged by the Spaniards, a winter storm had just removed almost all sand from the site and treasure was laying exposed all over the bottom. Divers alternated between grabbing large clumps of coins and filling buckets with handfuls of loose coins. They even used garden rakes to pull the loose coins into piles. Easy come, easy go! Several weeks later another storm deposited six to eight feet of sand on the same site, leaving only the tip of the ballast pile uncovered.

On average, most of Florida's east coast wrecks have from six to eight feet of sand on top of them. In the Keys the sand is generally deeper, from 12 to 20 feet and in the Bahamas things get progressively more difficult with most of the wrecks under 20 to 30 feet of sand and some even more deeply buried. During our search for the *Maravillas* in 1972 we encountered a wreck site that was impossible to reach after we found it with a magnetometer. Using the most powerful prop-wash then available, we dug and we dug but could never reach the depth of the anomaly. We could make a hole 40 feet deep and over 100 feet in diameter but couldn't get any deeper with the prop-wash. After reaching that depth we employed an airlift, but no matter how much we dug, the sides of the hole kept collapsing. Needless to say, that wreck is still there.

This wreck was in coarse sand, but I experienced the same problem with the *El Dorado* site under 30 feet of very fine sand. We could reach the hard pan bottom but only by digging a hole which, although 100 feet in diameter at the top, was only a foot or two across at the bottom. It was impossible to enlarge this hole at the bottom without digging again and expanding one of the sides of the entire hole.

In some cases unorthodox tools have been useful. In 1865 the Confederate ram *CSS Neuse* was scuttled and burned in the shallow Neuse River near Kingston, NC.

This photograph of a prop-wash in action shows how power from a ship's propellors generates a wash that literally digs into the sand and displaces it in large quantities.

255

After it was accidentally discovered by a fisherman in 1961, a group of citizens in Kingston began salvage operations. Because of swift currents and a lack of visibility, divers couldn't be used to excavate the ship. Airlifts were tried, but holes filled immediately with mud. Finally, a cofferdam was constructed around the site, and the water and mud overburden was removed with a combination of pumps, dragline buckets and shovels. The hull was reassembled and placed on permanent exhibit with artifacts salvaged from the *Neuse.*

Frederic Dumas, the noted French underwater explorer, came up with a unique solution to a similar situation. His wreck was in clear water, but a four-knot current made digging out of the sand nearly impossible. During a brief period when the current wasn't as strong, he erected a corrugated steel wall at right angles to the swift current, 30 feet long and six feet high. Deflecting the current at great velocity, the wall created a prop-wash effect which removed several feet of sand that covered the wreck, exposing amphoras and other artifacts.

As the saying goes…"necessity is the mother of invention." Underwater photographer Luis Marden resorted to an unusual but effective system to obtain clear photographs in the murky waters of Port Royal. He took what looked like a giant aquarium tank made of clear glass, filled it with clear water and sank it right next to where I was working on the bottom, By shooting through the clear waters in the glass tank, he was able to obtain excellent photographs.

After a site has been completely surveyed to determine its overall extent as well as those conditions that will affect its excavation, it must be decided how the wreck can best be excavated…even if excavation is economical or realistic. The survey also indicates where to begin on the site and the techniques to be employed.

Failure to make a survey, which they considered too

time-consuming, proved costly for an expedition in the Bahamas. The salvors located a wreck site from a small plane, sighting a number of cannon on a sandy bottom. Assuming the wreck was buried in sand, they outfitted their salvage vessel with airlifts and a prop-wash. To their dismay, they discovered that under a mantle of sand a few inches deep the wreck was cemented in a thick coral matrix they couldn't excavate with the equipment they had brought.

The Sea Causes Changes

Divers engaged in excavating a wreck need to know how different items will appear after centuries under the sea. A silver coin, for example, is easily mistaken for a dark, corroded sea shell. Kip Wagner made this mistake for years. He used to find coins on the beaches where the 1715 and other ships were lost. Thinking they were sea shells or stones, he delighted in skipping them across the water to see how many times they would hit before sinking. Even after he realized they were silver coins, he was unaware of their value and melted them down to make toy soldiers for children. *Many objects are not what they appear to be.* Once I found what looked like an iron cannon ball and gave it to a friend. Years later it was dropped and spilt opened to reveal over 50 silver coins.

A standing rule on my salvage vessels is for divers to bring to the surface everything found. *Don't play expert underwater.* At the end of each day's salvage the team discusses the day's work while carefully examining all the coral-encrusted objects that were retrieved. Some are shorn of their coral encrustation at this time, while others are set aside for x-raying ashore. Some wreck hunters think that just passing a metal detector over a coral encrusted object will reveal anything of value inside. Priceless porcelain cups and gem stones are missed this way. On the *Maravillas* we picked up thousands of iron objects with silver coins and even emeralds attached, most of which weren't always visible to the naked eye.

The leader of a treasure hunt has the responsibility for making sure his divers clearly understand not only what to look for on the bottom but how to handle what they find. You obviously don't put a fragile porcelain plate in a lift basket and then fill it with cannon balls. Fragile objects should be placed in jars, plastic bags or a bucket and hand-carried to the surface. Larger items can be wrapped in blankets or towels and placed in a lifting basket with the diver surfacing with the object to direct the surface crew in taking it aboard the salvage vessel properly. Divers should carry a ziplock bag for small items such as coins. Many divers have surfaced announcing discovery of a gold coin only to find that it fell out of their gloves or suits. Larger goodie bags are carried for silver coins and other small artifacts.

The most important hand tool is a diver's knife which has myriad uses and is particularly useful in digging around an object to speed its exposure by another excavation tool. It can pry loose objects which are attached to bedrock, ballast stones or the ship's hull. Crowbars, chisels and hammers are handy tools, but must be used with care and only if they will not damage the site. A variety of scrapers help remove coral growth from heavy objects before they are lifted to the surface. In areas where marine vegetation flourishes, a sickle may be helpful in clearing an area. Small tweezers or hypodermic needles are useful for recovering very small things such as flecks of gold dust and tiny gem stones.

Diving suits are needed even in the warm waters of the Caribbean because a diver will get chilled after several hours in the water. They also offer protection from coral cuts and scratches, burns from fire coral, stings from jel-

Wreck hunters using an airlift to clean out an area of seabottom and bring objects to the surface illustrate various aspects of this excavation tool and technique.

lyfish, and bites from small fish. During the actual excavation of a wreck, large amounts of sea worms and other marine life are uncovered. This provides a feast for small fish who hover around and during their feeding frenzies it is not uncommon for them to take bites out of a diver. Triggerfish are especially aggressive, and I have several scars to prove it. Since a diver's fingers look like worms to these fish, gloves are essential when they are in the vicinity...and a good idea in any case on most sites. Sea urchins and moray eels need to be cleared from any area you are working on. The deeper you excavate into a wreck, the more areas you uncover that have made attractive homes for the eels.

Non-fragile items are usually lifted in metal buckets or baskets made of wire mesh. Heavy objects can be raised by pulling them aboard the salvage vessel by lines or lifting bags. Some salvage vessels are rigged with heavy-lifting equipment to raise cannon, anchors and other items. There are also lifting bags on the market with a lifting capacity as heavy as a ton. The use of 55-gallon fuel drums is the most common method of raising large items to the surface. The drums are sunk and attached by steel cables or lines to the object to be lifted, then filled with compressed air, to raise them to the surface. Using this method, I have seen salvors recover large cannon and anchors while operating from a small boat. After the drums and objects attached to them are lifted to the surface they are towed to shore, where they can be raised out of the water by one of several methods.

Above are divers hand-fanning a ballast pile in search of coins and other artifacts. Below is a rare Spanish piece of eight, dated 1733, valued at approximately $10,000.

Surveying the wreck site helps the salvors decide the best way to tackle the project and determine which excavation tools and methods are required. Surface and tidal currents are a factor to consider when excavating in areas with an overburden of sand, silt or mud. The currents should be used to carry sediments *away* from the wreck site, or at least into areas that have already been excavated. A common mistake of salvors is to begin excavating in the middle of the site. This usually leads to the excavated sediment being deposited on areas not yet examined, with the same sediment then having to be moved more than once.

Moving ballast is the hardest, most time-consuming task on any wreck excavation. Caution is also important here since more divers are hurt when ballast is being moved than at any other time during an excavation. Yet, every ballast pile *must* be thoroughly investigated because valuable artifacts are almost always mixed in with the ballast rock. The best method is to excavate all the areas adjacent to a ballast pile and then move the ballast rock into these areas. Sending the ballast rock to the surface vessel in baskets can eat up months of time, and it isn't really necessary...provided the same ballast rock can be moved on the bottom to an area already excavated. A friend of mine is currently developing a system of moving ballast rock on a wreck site to other areas by means of a conveyer belt.

The most difficult wreck site to excavate is one embedded in coral growth, like the *Matanceros* off Yucatan. On this wreck our main excavation tools were sledge hammers and chisels to chop into the coral. We usually attempted to chop or cut out pieces of coral about the size of a basketball or larger. These pieces were raised aboard the salvage vessel and later broken apart to extract the artifacts they contained.

In many instances we had no idea of the contents of a chunk until it was broken apart. We extracted over 200 individual artifacts from one clump of coral alone which weighed about 20 pounds. Since parts of artifacts could be seen embedded in the surface growth in most areas, we would dug sometimes as deep as five feet into the coral, until there were no more artifacts to be recovered. In areas where no artifacts were seen in the coral's surface, we dug as deep as three feet before finding any. Large artifacts (pewter plates, wine bottles, etc.) were carefully excavated from the coral on the bottom because it was too difficult to dig out a large enough section of the coral growth that contained the artifact.

During my third year on the *Matanceros,* I used three pneumatic hammers, which proved quite effective in chopping through the coral growth and freeing artifacts. The largest hammer was used for recovering cannons and anchors. The medium one, which was only 12 inches long and had a cutting chisel six inches long and two inches wide, was used to excavate the basketball-size chunks of coral which contained the smallest artifacts. For excavating fragile items like glass wine bottles or small items like a brass medallion or crucifix, the smallest pneumatic hammer with a chisel only 4 inches long and three-fourths of an inch wide was used.

The overall area of the *Matanceros* wreck site is smaller in extent than a football field, and although over the years thousands of hours have been spent by hundreds of divers chopping into the coral growth on this wreck, it is far from being completely excavated. This wreck was the most difficult to excavate that I have ever seen or heard about. Most wrecks located in coral growth have been easier to excavate because a large portion of the wreck was actually buried in sand pockets on a reef and most of the parts buried under coral growth were in much softer coral than that at the *Matanceros* site, permitting use of high-pressure water-jets.

When excavating on muddy or silty bottoms, the only recommended tool is an airlift. It consists of a metal tube into which a continuous stream of compressed air is injected through one or more holes, depending on the size (diameter) of the tube, which also determines pressure and volume of the air required. A three-inch diameter airlift requires between 20 and 50 cubic feet of air per minute at a pressure of about 50psi. One of six-inch diameter requires 50 to 200 cubic feet of air per minute at about 100psi. The effective working depth of an airlift depends on the air pressure being provided, which must be greater than the surrounding water pressure. For example, maximum effective depth for an airlift using only 50psi of air pressure is 40 feet, whereas one using 100psi of air pressure is effective in depths to 100 feet.

The principle of the airlift is that when air is forced into its bottom, it rises rapidly to create suction and suck up bottom sediment and small artifacts. There should be a control valve on all airlift tubes so the diver can control the amount of air entering the tube. When removing overburden, the airlift is run at full power to remove as much sediment as possible. When areas containing artifacts are reached, however, the speed of the suction is reduced to permit the diver to grab artifacts before they are sucked up by the tube or damaged by striking against its bottom. When small objects such as coins, buttons, musket balls, etc. are sucked up by the tube, spill from its top should be directed onto a floating screen or onto a boat or barge containing a screen.

Under no circumstances do I recommend that anyone use an airlift with a diameter larger than six inches. Because they are difficult to control, artifacts will be destroyed or lost. This happened during a six-week excavation of the sunken city of Port Royal in 1959 led by Edwin Link when a 12-inch diameter airlift was used.

The chart at the top of the following page indicates the diameters of tubes and hoses required at various depths and the amount of air pressure and volume of air needed to work efficiently:

264

Airlift Diameters/Volumes/PSIs

Airlift diameter	Hose diameter	Max. Depth to be used (in feet)	Air Volume (in cubic feet per minute)	Air Pressure (in pounds per sq inch)
3 inch	1/2 inch	40	20-40	50
3 inch	1/2 inch	65	30-50	75
3 inch	1/2 inch	90	10-60	100
4 inch	3/4 inch	40	30-50	50
4 inch	3/4 inch	65	40-60	75
4 inch	3/4 inch	90	50-70	100
6 inch	1 1/4 inch	40	75-100	50
6 inch	1 1/4 inch	65	100-125	75
6 inch	1 1/4 inch	90	125-150	100

I used a four-inch diameter airlift with good results during my excavation of Port Royal. On the bottom of the tube I had two wires attached across the metal tube in opposite directions, which permitted only the smallest artifacts to go up it. These then landed on a screen on the barge where two men stood guard to recover them the moment they emerged from the tube. Using only 50psi of air pressure meant it took longer to remove the sediment than if I had used a higher pressure, but it prevented artifacts from being damaged by being sucked against the bottom of the tube.

The advantage of using the airlift on muddy or silty bottoms is that spill can be directed and carried away by the current. Thus, underwater visibility isn't affected. Since there was rarely *any* underwater visibility at Port Royal...and then for only a few inches, the only advantage in using currents to carry away pumped-up sediment was to prevent it from sinking back on unexcavated areas. Until the development of the prop-wash, the airlift was the main excavation tool used on wrecks in sandy areas, and it is still used on many wrecks today, especially on those lying in waters below the effective working depths of the prop-wash.

The airlift cannot be used effectively in water less than 15 feet deep because the differential between atmospheric pressure on the surface and water pressure on the bottom is not sufficient to create much suction in the tube. Nor is the airlift useful on sites widely scattered or buried under deep, sedimentary deposits. In these situations work that might take years with an airlift could be accomplished in a fraction of the time with a prop-wash. Depending on size and the depth of a site, the prop-wash can be as much as 100 times more effective than an airlift. There are a number of restrictions to its use, however, and it is not suited to all types of sites.

The prop-wash, also called the "blaster" or "mailbox" by some divers, was invented early in the century to blow away sediment covering oyster beds in Chesapeake Bay. In 1962 salvors working on the 1715 wrecks off the coast of Florida accidentally discovered its use as an effective excavation tool. Confronted with having to dive in murky waters with very little visibility, they devised a type of prop-wash to push clear water from the surface down to the bottom, where it is always dirtier and darker. To their great surprise, they discovered that it was a much better excavation tool than the airlifts and hydrolifts they had been using.

None of the surface-air-supply diving rigs should be used when excavating with a prop-wash. There is the danger of the air hose being caught in the vessel's turning propeller which could cut the hose cut or, even worse, cause it to wrap around the propeller and pull the diver into it. Instead, scuba-diving equipment should be used.

A prop-wash is simple and inexpensive to construct and easy to operate. It consists of an elbow-shaped metal tube several inches larger in diameter than the vessel's propeller diameter and is attached to the transom of the salvage vessel so that the wash of the propeller is forced into the tube and deflected downward to the sea bottom. Generally, the upper end of the tube is attached from one to three feet behind the propeller, and a wire-mesh cage covers the propeller area to prevent divers from being cut.

On twin-screw vessels, two prop-washes can be used side-by-side. The length of the prop-wash will depend on the diameter of the tube. On a small prop-wash such as those used on outboard engines, they are generally about three feet in length. On larger vessels, such as those having propellers as large as four feet in diameter, the length of the tube is usually six to eight feet, and half of this length runs out horizontally from the propeller to the elbow part of the tube.

Four anchors must be put out to hold the salvage vessel in place when the prop-wash is being used. The vessel's propeller turns at varying speeds, depending on the depth of water and amount of sediment that must be blasted away. The wash of the prop as it is deflected downward creates a whirlpool action that forces water to the bottom at a terrific velocity and blasts away the sediment at a rapid rate. It is so powerful that it also cuts through coquina, a type of limestone coral growth, almost as fast as through sand.

Its effective depth depends on two factors...the size of the prop-wash tube and the highest velocity at which the vessel's propeller can be run. A small prop-wash on an outboard engine is effective only up to 15 feet. Those on a vessel with a propeller two to three feet in diameter can be used up to 35 feet, and on one with a four-foot diameter propeller it can be used up to 50 feet. In 20 feet of water a prop-wash two to three feet in diameter can excavate a hole 20 feet across and 15 feet deep in only a few minutes. A larger prop-wash can excavate a hole in 50 feet of water to a diameter of 50 feet and a depth of 20 feet in the same period of time.

The secret in using a prop-wash is being able to control its speed, fine-tuning it...running it at high speeds to remove overburden on a wreck...and knowing to slow it down when the level of the wreck is reached, which prevents the artifacts from being blown away. I have learned that removing 12 feet of sand over a wreck requires running the engine so that the propeller makes 1,200 revolutions per minute for a period of exactly three minutes. Then I reduce the speed to 400rpm and send divers down to operate under this slow speed, picking up artifacts as they are uncovered.

At this speed the prop-wash will remove approximately an inch of sand per minute, which is slow enough to enable divers to catch all the artifacts before they are blown away. If the prop-wash is not properly controlled, artifacts will be destroyed or blasted into other areas. With a prop-wash running at full speed I have seen a six-pound cannonball blasted over 50 feet from its original position. Some prop-washes are so powerful that they could be used to remove ballast stones from a wreck, but I do not recommend this. Mixed with ballast piles are generally many valuable artifacts which would be lost.

When a good area...for example, one where many pieces of jewelry or gold coins, or priceless porcelain...is uncovered by the propeller, it is advisable to stop the prop-wash and use a method of excavation that gives the diver on the bottom more control. I have had several experiences where a prop-wash uncovered a layer containing a large number of coins and other items and, even while it was running at its slow speed, I was unable to grab all the items before they were swept away by the prop-wash. Stopping the prop-wash and continuing an excavation, either fanning by hand or using a small airlift or hydrolift, is advisable.

The major disadvantage in using the prop-wash is that as it excavates a hole, sediment is thrown or blasted over unexcavated areas. This overburden must always be removed from the virgin areas, but, given the speed in which the prop-wash can excavate, this is usually a minor problem.

To work in depths greater than 50 feet or to dig in shallow water where there is deep sand and an airlift is not effective and where a salvage vessel can't approach, hand-held blasters are the answer. They work at any depth a diver can reach. I constructed one using a two-foot diameter piece of thick PVC pipe, four-feet long, with one propeller pointing downward which is used to blow away the sediment. Another propeller faces upward which prevents counter-torque and counter-thrust, enabling me finger-tip control of the unit without having to fight the power of the blaster. It runs on hydraulic fluid circulated through two hoses connected to the middle of the blaster and to an oil reservoir and the engine on the boat. The blaster is given neutral buoyancy on the bottom by filling two small ballast cylinders with just the right amount of air from whatever breathing source I am using at the time. Lying on the bottom I use one hand to control the blaster and the other to pick up the goodies uncovered.

An air jet is an excavation tool used chiefly when nothing better is available or during a survey of a site. A hose from a Third Lung or any other SAS breathing unit can be used as an air jet. It is nothing more than a hose connected to a surface compressor which forces high pressure air out into the water to permit the diver holding it to direct its business end to blow away small amounts of sediment. The strength of the air pressure dissipates so rapidly on the bottom that the jet can move the sediment only a few feet. It is useful, however, in very shallow water to remove small amounts of sediment from potholes in coral reefs.

Using a Water-Jet

A water-jet is similar, except that water instead of air is pumped down at high pressure and used to blow away sand or sediment. It can also be a great deal more powerful than the air jet. A small high-pressure pump, costing a few hundred dollars, makes an inexpensive excavation tool since it can be run from a small float on the surface and doesn't necessarily require a boat. The working end of the hose is fitted with a special nozzle with small jets feeding part of the water-flow backward to counteract the tendency of the hose to recoil which would fling the diver about.

The nozzle should have a valve with which the operator can control water pressure.

The water-jet is a specialized tool for use only in limited circumstances. In areas where sediment is but a few feet deep it can excavate faster than an airlift (but not a prop-wash) yet there is always the danger that it will blow objects away. On wreck sites where there is a thick covering of eel grass, the jet is useful in breaking up the matrix holding the grass which enables an airlift or prop-wash to dig more effectively. It is also capable of digging tunnels under a ship that is going to be raised as were the *Vasa* and *Cairo*. A jet can be useful in removing overburden that might pile up around the lip of a hole being dug by an airlift or prop-wash, but it decreases underwater visibility so drastically that it can't be effective unless a current is flowing to carry the turbid water away.

A hydrolift, also known as a transfer tube, underwater dredge or gold dredge, was first developed to aid prospectors recover placer deposits of gold which collected in crevices on river bottoms. It has a limited application in very shallow areas where it might be the only effective excavation tool. It is also useful for making test holes in sediment more than six feet deep. The hydrolift consists of a six-foot length of metal or plastic tube, like that on an airlift, and four to six inches in diameter. At the working end about a foot of the tube is bent like an elbow in a 90-degree angle.

A water jet from a surface pump is attached at the apex of the outside bend. This jet is pointed straight up the centerline of the tube and forces the flow along the length of the tube, creating what is known as a venturi effect, causing sediment and small objects to be sucked through the length of the tube and discharged several feet away. The spill should either be directed to fall into a screen basket, so that small artifacts can be found, or a diver should be stationed at the exhaust end of the tube to cull artifacts as they spew forth. The hydrolift can remove only one quarter as much sediment as an airlift with the same diameter tube.

Nothing is more frustrating than to excavate a hole only to discover a beer can that one of your crew has flung overboard. This can be avoided by keeping proper records. Systematically excavating and mapping a wreck is the best method, but unfortunately many modern-day salvors fail to do this. Using intuition and ESP to decide where to excavate, they jump from one spot to another...in many cases, of course, missing the best finds. When a wreck is worked systematically, salvors can easily keep track of the areas excavated each day. Mapping or plotting locations of major artifacts can aid salvors in other ways too. From the disposition of the various items recovered, they can determine which end of the site is a ship's stern where most of the most valuable treasure was carried aboard ships.

Mapping and recording the site as it is being excavated

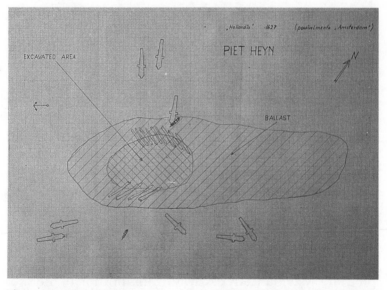

This plot chart illustrates an important aspect of underwater recovery by showing how a Dutch warship lost in 1627 was mapped during an excavation.

can also enable the salvor to determine the size of a ship, number of cannon she carried and other pertinent data, all of which helps determine if he has found the target he is seeking. Remember that the stern section of a ship was not only where important treasure was carried; it was also the area where the ship's officers and wealthier passengers lived. This is where most of the contraband was carried, treasure and other items not listed on the cargo manifest. Here you are most likely to find fine silver and pewterware and other valuable personal objects. It is never safe to assume, however, that these kinds of items were carried only in the stern castles. Items showing no signs of use, such as scratch marks on plates, could have been carried in the ship's hold as cargo.

When I was mapping the *Maravillas* site on the Little Bahama Bank, I was compelled by the large area of the site to employ a system of mapping which might not meet with approval of professional archaeologists. The ship had broken in three pieces, and the stern and main sections lay more than two miles from the bow section which we were then excavating. Even the bow section had been badly broken up and scattered over an area 600 by 900 feet with only a few traces of the wooden hull still left. Normally I would have used the grid system, but neither that nor any other orthodox mapping system was possible since the wreck lay under 25 feet of sand. I considered removing all the overburden first and then erecting a grid, but this would have taken years and, even then, been impossible because there is a never-ending movement of sand on the bank caused by strong currents running on it.

Following a thorough survey, I decided on the following method. Buoys were placed at 20-foot intervals around the perimeter. They served as reference points both for mapping and systematically excavating this portion of the site. Excavation began in the northeast corner and progressed on a north-south heading until we reached the southern extremity. We then moved 20 feet to the west and started moving due north until the northern extremity was reached. This system ensured that we would cover every inch of the bottom. We assigned a code number to each hole dug, and the chart was marked accordingly. Overburden was removed and artifacts and bits of the wreck were exposed on the bottom.

With a wide-angle lens on a still camera I was able to photograph everything *in situ* before anything was removed from the hole. When a large object such as a cannon or anchor was uncovered, buoys were attached directly to them and their positions reckoned by taking bearings between the buoys and several buoys on the outer perimeter of the site. Since each hole had a diameter at the bottom of about 25 feet, everything raised had to come from within a 12 1/2-foot radius from the hole's center, the position of which we had already fixed. We recorded all major artifacts recovered from each hole, and at the end of the day were able to plot their relative positions on a chart. From photographs that showed what we had uncovered in each hole, I was able to produce a more accurate chart of the site and a good photographic mosaic of the whole bottom as if it had all been exposed at the same time.

Since the State of Florida first began controlling shipwreck salvage in the early 1960's they have required all salvors to follow certain procedures in mapping sites and recording where all finds were made. At the start of each salvage season the State of Florida erects markers ashore for establishing horizontal control on wreck sites. A sextant is utilized for obtaining the angle of two or more markers to enable plotting major discoveries of a wreck, such as cannon, anchors and ballast piles. This is far more effective than trying to use a hand-held compass on a rocking boat. These angle- bearings are also required to record each hole dug. As an artifact is recovered, the salvor attaches a numbered tag and then records these tag numbers in relation to each hole dug. This enables the state archaeologists to prepare a site plan of each wreck and the disposition of the objects recovered assists the salvor as well by preventing him from digging in places where he or other salvors may already have excavated.

Historical Research and Development Inc., one of the many salvage firms working off the east coast of Florida, has developed a new system that is more accurate and efficient and does the job the state archaeologists have been doing in far less time. Using a new prototype high-accuracy loran unit connected to a lap-top computer, it calculates latitude, longitude and plot points, then generates maps and dispersion patterns without the cumbersome effort required to do this by hand. The computer accomplishes in minutes calculations that would require days to figure manually. Regular loran units are only accurate to within 20 or 30 feet but this new type of loran has an accuracy rate of two or three feet.

By entering everything into the computer as it is discovered, the salvor can have instant data in print-out maps showing the exact locations where he has found objects, where he has worked and what areas have been missed. This system has taken the guesswork out of treasure hunting. Using this system that he helped develop for the first time, John de Bry proved that it worth its weight in gold. By plotting where he and other salvors had made recoveries over the years, the computer-generated map revealed an area that had never been worked. John and his divers rushed to this spot last summer and picked up 821 gold coins from one of the 1715 wrecks.

In the records that salvors keep for the State of Florida only a brief description is required to cover each tagged object. For their own records many salvors also photograph each of the finds, but this can become very costly. A better system has been developed using video cameras to take individual still photographs of each artifact. These images are then stored on a laser disk in a computer along with data such as size, age, shape and location. This system allows a salvor with computer access to recall data or call up the image of any object recovered and display it on a monitor, where it can be enhanced, magnified, superimposed over other objects or otherwise compared. Treasure hunting is really coming into the Space Age!

Archaeological Data Required

Along with these changes states are demanding that more and more archaeological data be gathered by shipwreck permit holders. Until recently a would-be salvor was only required to fill out a few forms to get a salvage permit to work in California waters. Recently this state passed a new law which requires that each salvage operation be supervised by a qualified archaeologist, paid for by the salvor, and the project must be undertaken under the strictest of archaeological standards.

Before I was even able to start my search for the Manila Galleon *San Agustin,* I had to submit a 200-page archaeological design plan which was analyzed by a bevy of bureaucratic archaeologists, both state and federal. Since I located this shipwreck I have been required to submit a 600-to 800-page archaeological design plan...just to make test holes and confirm my discovery. They will probably want a three-volume book written before I ever get the salvage permit.

Basically what this all amounts to is that since the new Abandoned Shipwreck Act was passed, requiring states to work with commercial salvors, the bureaucratic archaeologists have convinced those authorities running the state shipwreck programs to change their rules and make it extremely difficult for anyone to work on shipwrecks. Some states like Texas have decided against giving any permits to salvors for search or salvage activities.

Since a potential salvor today must know proper archaeological excavation and recording techniques, one solution would be to hire an archaeologist...just as Mel

275

Fisher did on his *Margarita* and *Atocha* projects. This is easier said than done. First of all there are very few qualified underwater archaeologists, and the bureaucrats have made it almost impossible for these people to work with commercial salvors. Not only have they prevented all archaeologists who have ever worked on commercial projects from presenting reports at archaeological conferences, but they make life very difficult for any archaeologist who works with a salvor.

Archaeologists rely a great deal on federal and state grants, and proposals for these funds pass through the hands of the bureaucratic archaeologists. Making money from archaeology is considered a serious breech of ethics, yet they don't look at their own salaries in the same light. Another solution would be for the states to assign archaeologists to work with commercial salvors, but then we are faced with the same problem...not enough archaeologists available. Even if they were, the states most likely wouldn't be able to pay them. This would be a major problem in Florida if the state ever changes its law and demands that every salvor have an archaeologist aboard his vessel. To meet this demand each diving season would require nearly every underwater archaeologist in the world to work with the 50 or more salvage operations in Florida waters.

Archaeologists are demanding a great deal more accuracy in data collecting than that furnished by the present system being used in Florida. Not content with just learning that an artifact came out of a specific hole, they want a record of both where an artifact was found and its stratigraphic depth. After all, a hole may be 20 or more

Diver at top uses an underwater scooter to search the seabottom, while diver below inspects coral-encrusted iron fittings of a wreck located visually on a Caribbean reef.

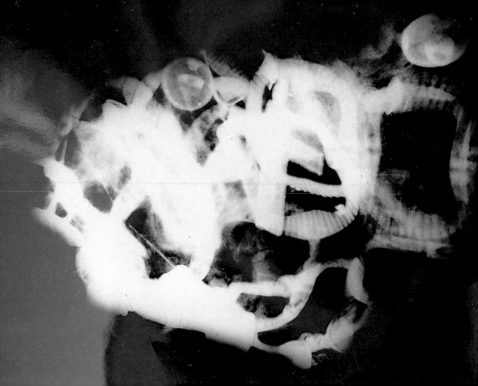

feet in diameter. Unfortunately the majority of these archaeologists seem to have little idea of what happens after a ship is lost. They insist that discovery location data can reveal valuable bits of information such as where individual objects were stored on a ship. The fact is, however, that since the sea floor is constantly changed by storms, currents and other factors, artifacts constantly move from one place to another.

During hurricanes and other severe storms many of the smaller items such as coins are even cast up on the beach and then reclaimed by the sea again to be deposited in a new area. Artifacts are moved around on the bottom by other means as well. At Port Royal I found artifacts from the time of the 1692 earthquake and even earlier right on the surface and I found modern Coke bottles and a kitchen sink of recent vintage at a depth of 20 feet. Ships anchoring over the site caused this stratigraphical confusion. When their anchors act as "plows" and dig trenches, some of the older materials are dragged to the surface, while more recent objects fall into the trenches made by anchors.

On important underwater archaeology sites strict adherence to standard archaeological procedure is certainly merited. But this is neither fruitful nor practical for the majority of shipwrecks which are found in shallow, warm water where artifacts may be scattered over a large area and the remains of the ship itself completely disappeared. Since it is impossible to convince the bureaucrats of the folly of plotting and measuring each artifact *in situ* on every site, the salvor must comply and hope that more archaeologists will actually work on shipwreck sites themselves so that they can better understand the situation.

Two views of a coral-encrusted clump: how it looks when brought up from the seabottom and how it looks under x-ray, showing buttons, buckles, pins and coins.

279

The earliest mapping methods used on underwater archaeological sites relied on tape measurements and underwater compasses to establish horizontal relationships between objects. Later, grid frames were introduced which are used to make vertical measurements in addition to horizontal calculations. A grid system can be used efficiently, however, only on a site covering a relatively small area and should be used only when vertical measurements are relevant...rarely the case on Western Hemisphere shipwreck sites. In addition, precisely recording every single item and fragment found on a widely scattered site is not essential.

The first step in excavating a shallow water shipwreck is establishing a datum point, or reference center, from which all subsequent measurements will be taken. It should be located in the center of the site as determined from a preliminary survey. Buoys alone cannot be relied upon to make sure this point remains constant because they are subject to shifting or loss. The best method is to use an air probe to drive a long metal pipe as far down into the sediment as possible. After the pipe has reached bottom, the air hose is detached. The pipe should be painted yellow, which is highly visible, and have one or more brilliantly colored pennants attached. As each artifact is recovered, its location in relation to the datum point can be established by using an underwater compass and distance from the datum point can be measured. A small plastic tag with an identification number is attached to each object before it is raised. All this data is marked on a clipboard and later, after the object has been properly identified, transferred to a chart of the entire site.

The azimuth circle system described in Chapter 8 can also be used.

If the site covers a very large area, such as several square miles, it is gridded off on the site chart into many sections and a datum point is established in the center of each section as it is excavated. The size of each section depends in great part on the underwater visibility. If there is unlimited visibility of some 200 feet, each section can be 300x300 feet. The datum point would be in the center with all mapping in a 150-foot radius from the datum point.

Trying to map a site in murky water is at best very difficult and sometimes impossible. If the site is relatively close to shore, divers can place buoys on the major objects, and bearings can be taken from shore points. If this is not possible, a surface buoy placed in the middle of the site can be established as a datum point. Bearings and distance from this point to the surface buoys which mark the objects can then be taken by compass and measuring tape.

Since taking compass bearings from a rocking boat is neither easy nor accurate whenever possible, bearings should be taken from shore to the buoys placed on objects to be plotted. The bearings should be taken with a surveyor's transit or theodolite, which are more precise than a compass. Radio communication is necessary between the man on shore and the vessel.

In clear waters of the Mediterranean archaeologists often use a system of triangulation for plotting positions of objects excavated. Although this is a more accurate means of measurement, it requires a larger number of workers and much more time. A simple device called a plane table, similar to a surveyor's transit, can be used. It has two units: a form of underwater drawing table and a sighting device. The sighting tube is of plastic or metal pipe, about 10 inches long and two inches in diameter. Two wires are stretched at both ends of the tube, crossing each other and resembling a telescopic gunsight without magnification.

The sighting device is mounted on a base plate and a mark is made on the front end of the plate corresponding to the line of sight of the device. A pipe or something connected to the bottom of the base plate is fitted into a hole in the middle of the drawing table in such a way that it can rotate 360 degrees. An azimuth circle or protractor

281

is then marked off in degrees and attached or painted on the top of the table so that the sighting device and base plate are enclosed inside.

In normal operation three plane tables are used at once. They are placed in a pattern forming a triangle, and their precise positions are established and plotted on the site chart. North on the azimuth circle is lined up with magnetic north on an underwater compass before the table is weighted down to keep it from moving during the operation. A diver with a range pole, usually a plastic or metal pipe two meters long and graduated in sections of 10 centimeters using alternate red and white paint, positions himself directly over the object to be mapped, holding a numbered identification tag. The operators of the three plane tables then sight onto the range pole and the bearing from each position is obtained by noting where the mark on the base plate either points to or touches the azimuth circle. The number tag is then attached to the object and the diver moves to another object and the process is repeated. When the information is plotted on the site chart, it gives the accurate position of everything mapped.

If both the table and sighting device are perfectly level, this method can also furnish the datum height or elevation level of objects in relation to one another or to a fixed horizontal level for the whole site. At the same time that each operator is sighting to establish the horizontal position of the object by recording where the cross hairs line up on the range pole, the elevation level can be ascertained. To calibrate this information one must know the depth of the water, the precise depth at which the sighting device was used and the measurement on the range pole to establish the difference between the top of the object and the line of sight of the sighting device.

For those who can afford it, there is a relatively new system for collecting data *in situ* which is faster and better. Marine Telepresence Inc. of Pocasset, MA, developed the

SHARPS (Sonic High Accuracy Ranging and Positioning System), which provides fast and accurate three-dimensional acoustical mapping of a shipwreck site. Four transceivers are used; three are positioned in a triangular arrangement, while the fourth is held by a diver. The three stationary transceivers, which track the one in the diver's hand, are connected to the surface by a coaxial cable, feeding the data into the SHARPS control unit and then passed into a computer. Each time the diver wants to plot the position of another object, he activates a transmitting button which relays the information to the surface through the other three transceivers and the precise position of the object is recorded with X, Y and Z coordinates. During this operation a map is traced on a computer screen and stored for later use or printed out on recorder paper.

A photographic mosaic of a shipwreck site, especially when it is in a compact area or is one on which some parts of the wooden hull remain, can be useful in trying to determine the type, size and some times the nationality and identity of the ship. Experts on old ship construction can deduce a great deal from an accurate photographic record of this type. Mosaics can be made during different phases of the excavation, but the most important will be those taken when the site has been completely uncovered and the anchors, cannon, ballast, wood and other remaining features and objects can be seen in relation to one another.

Considerably more information on mosaics and other aspects of mapping by photography can be found in Chapter 12.

Identifying Shipwrecks

Identification and dating of shipwrecks and the equipment and cargoes they carried is a fascinating process but often difficult and time consuming. When assistance from experts is available, the salvor should make use of their expertise. I realized a long time ago that I could not become an expert on identifying and dating the thousands of different items that might be found on a shipwreck, even though I have spent decades studying and have a comprehensive library of books and reports dealing with shipwrecks. Books and reports can result in positively identifying and dating an item, particularly when a great deal of material has been published on it. Still, to avoid any possibility of error, I often consult specialists for confirmation. On items about which little has been published, I rely on the assistance of experts. I've come to know many interesting people this way and made friends around the world. These men and women share my passion for bringing the past to light and filling in historical shadows with rich details of fact gleaned from research.

There are many problems associated with identifying and dating a shipwreck and its associated artifacts. Some items can't be positively identified because not enough is known about them, nothing has been published or because there are no experts on such subjects as ship's pumps or sewing thimbles. The more sources the salvor has to refer to, the better his chances are of establishing a positive identification and date. Of course, contamination of artifacts in the years following a shipwreck is always possible. Items from other wrecks lost in the same area might be mixed in with an earlier shipwreck. Articles thrown off a passing ship or from a ship salvaging the shipwreck may also contaminate a site. During a recent salvage operation in the Florida Keys, the first item recovered was an anchor dating from the second half of the 19th century. If the salvors had dated their shipwreck from just this one item, they would have made a grave mistake. The anchor had apparently been lost after snagging on a 17th-century wreck, thus contaminating the shipwreck site.

On the other hand, many shipwrecks will have items predating the period of the shipwreck. From reading old documents I have found many instances in which items carried on ships were much older than the ships and men sailing them. A Spanish sea captain wrote to the king in 1728 that he would defend his ship against any enemy attacks with the same sword that one of his ancestors had used during the famous Battle of Lepanto in 1571. Another captain reported in 1682 that since he was unable to procure the required number of cannon for his ship making a voyage to Mexico, he had hired divers to recover several from a shipwreck in Cadiz Bay dating from the mid-16th century. He knew they could not be fired and admitted that he carried them only to make his ship appear heavily armed to enemy ships he might encounter. An English ship was lost without a trace in 1794 somewhere in the Caribbean during a hurricane. Its principal cargo consisted of treasure recovered from a Spanish galleon that had sunk on the coast of Panama around 1560.

This book attempts to assist the salvor in establishing the possible identification and date of some of the items found on shipwrecks. The average salvor may not have a reference library or access to library books he needs to identify and date a shipwreck, and weeks or even months might be required to obtain an answer from an expert, In some instances, however, I can only recommend obtaining assistance from such experts.

I have had firsthand experience with the problem.

While I was living in Seville, the director of the local archaeological museum asked me to make a survey on a shipwreck found by fishermen near Malaga. The fishermen reported seeing a large marble statue on the shipwreck. When I explored the site, we learned that although he statue was of Roman origin, the rest of the ship's cargo as well as the ship itself dated from the latter part of the 19th century. Through research we discovered that the ship had been sailing from Sicily to Spain with a general cargo. Either the statue was being brought to Spain to be sold or was being used as ballast.

Establishing the nationality of a shipwreck from the items discovered on it is often impossible. The majority of cargoes brought from Spain to the New World were manufactured in many different countries. This also applies to ships of other nationalities. Even during times of war, when the rulers prohibited trade between their subjects and the enemy, commerce continued as usual, sometimes by using merchants of neutral nationals as middlemen. A good example of this was discovered on the *Matanceros* shipwreck. Although Spain and England were at war at this time, over 50% of the cargo carried on the ship was of British origin. To further complicate the identification of this wreck, the major portion of the remainder of the ship's cargo came from countries other than Spain, such as France, Germany, England, Holland and Brazil.

At the close of our first season of excavation on the *Matanceros* we sought assistance from the Smithsonian in identifying and dating the wreck. Their expert assured us the wreck was definitely an English merchantman. My partners and I disagreed, mainly because the ship carried a vast number of Catholic religious articles, which we felt certain no English ship would have carried. Consequently, through our own research efforts we were able to identify the shipwreck as a Spanish merchantman. After obtaining copies of the original ship's cargo manifest from the Archives of the Indies in Seville, we were able to compare

287

the majority of the items we recovered from this wreck with those listed on the cargo manifest.

There are many cases in which ships of other European nations also carried cargoes manufactured in various other countries. In 1620 a Dutch merchantman was captured after entering a small port in Cuba to carry on illegal trade with the local residents. The bulk of its cargo consisted of merchandise from England, France and Italy. Many ships of different nations sailing from Europe to the New World made it a practice to stop at one of the Canary Islands to take on fresh water and victuals before making the long ocean crossing. Since they often also purchased Spanish wine and other spirits, it would not be unusual to find large numbers of Spanish jars in which such liquids were carried on non-Spanish ships. The highly prized swords made in Toledo and other items manufactured in Spain were also available in the Canaries.

Ships of all nations returning from the Western Hemisphere to Europe also carried manufactured goods from various countries. Items such as navigational equipment might be carried throughout the life of the ship, whereas other items had been obtained by trade in the ports they visited. Items were also obtained when one ship captured another.

Discovering Spanish specie or bullion on a shipwreck cannot identify it definitely as a Spanish ship. Spanish coinage was the chief currency circulated by European nations with settlements in the New World. In fact, it circulated around the globe and was legal tender in the United States into the 19th century. When we talk about "two bits" or "four bits," referring to a quarter or half-dollar, we are recalling Spanish pieces of two and pieces of four, subdivisions of the famous pieces of eight. Spanish currency was universally circulated because of the vast amount of silver and gold mined and minted by the Spaniards and the scarcity of these precious metals in all the other European nations.

Through trade, legal and illegal, as well as plunder most of the precious metals mined in Spanish America eventually reached other European countries who benefited far more than the Spaniards. In many of these nations, rather than melt the precious metals down to make new coins, Spanish coinage was used on a large scale. On various occasions the English Crown melted and minted tremendous amounts of Spanish coinage into English coins, but very few of these coins ever reached the New World.

Spanish Silver in Asia

Spanish money made its way to Asia as well. Each year huge sums were shipped from Mexico to the Philippines to purchase goods to be shipped to Acapulco from the Orient. Large amounts of this specie filtered down to other nations. A Dutch ship, the *Golden Dragon,* wrecked in 1656 on the west side of Australia, was recently salvaged. Among the items recovered were 7,500 silver coins dated 1654-55 from the Mexico City and Potosi mints.

The nationality and date of some shipwrecks can be established by the size of the vessel and the objects found on them, but caution must be exercised...there are many exceptions to confuse a salvor. Small caravels and pinnaces used by early explorers should be fairly easy to identify by the artillery they carried, as they differed a great deal in size and construction from all types of later-period ships. Because of the risk involved in sailing in uncharted waters, the officers and crew usually avoided bringing such valuable items as silverware or glassware. Instead they ate and drank from wooden or ceramic objects. An exception occurred when one of these ships carried colonists or government officials to a newly settled area, in which case they brought all their possessions with them. Such a ship also carried agricultural, mining, masonry and carpentry tools. These items should enable the salvor to differentiate between an exploratory vessel and one transporting colonists. If any treasure is found on one of the early shipwrecks which was homeward bound, it will most likely be gold or silver of an unrefined and unminted nature or items manufactured by the Indians.

Advice and mail boats--and even reconnaissance boats, for that matter--appear very similar in appearance under water. Unlike the early exploratory or colonizing vessels, these carried more armament which aids in identification. They were not armed to fight large vessels but rather to repel ships their own size and smaller ones that might overtake them. Their lightness and construction enabled them to outrun larger vessels. Since these vessels had to be light to maintain fast speeds, they rarely carried any cargo at all. On occasion, advice boats returning to Spain carried small amounts of treasure to drop off at places along the way to pay officials or garrisons. Sometimes, too, they carried it to hard-pressed Spanish kings to tide them over until the treasure fleets arrived later.

Small pirate and privateering vessels also fit this description and are difficult to distinguish. Salvage vessels, too, carried a substantial amount of armament to protect treasure they might have recovered. Finding diving bells or any of the many instruments used in early salvage operations might aid the modern-day salvor to identifying the type of ship he has located as well as provide a thrilling discovery. If the early salvors were successful, a diversified cargo of treasure and artifacts might also be found on this wreck.

Because of the constant shortage of artillery throughout the Western Hemisphere during the entire period covered in this book, very few small trading vessels carried it. If they did, the pieces were rarely ever larger than swivel guns used for repelling boarders. Since this lack of armament and slow speeds from the weight of their cargoes made trading vessels vulnerable to attack by all other shipping, they sailed only when it was safe. And, even when they did sail, they usually carried cargoes of relatively little value because of the risk of capture involved. Small Spanish vessels were forbidden by the Crown from carrying any treasure; however, documents telling of many lost with treasure aboard reveal that this rule was not always strictly enforced.

Occasionally these small trading vessels were used to carry large amounts of treasure, but only when they were guarded by armed galleys or other warships. The gold and emeralds that were sent annually from Bogota to Cartageña for transshipment to Spain were brought down the Magdalena River in small vessels which then sailed along the coast to Cartageña. When the Chagres River was used to transport the treasure by raft from the Pacific to the Caribbean side of the isthmus, small trading ships carried the treasure from the mouth of the river to Nombre de Dios or Porto Bello. Virtually all non-precious cargoes such as lumber and agricultural products these small traders carried would have disappeared long ago from a shipwreck with few traces remaining...especially if the ship carried no armament or ballast.

Many of the larger merchant ships suffered the same fate over the years, since cargoes they carried back to Europe consisted of perishable products such as tobacco, cocoa, sugar, rum, cotton, drugs, indigo, cochineal and lumber. Finding a shipwreck that fits this description could lead a salvor to mistakenly think he has found a ship that sailed without cargo, since only shipboard items, cannon, anchors, weapons, and cooking and eating utensils would be found.

When no trace of cargo, colonists or treasure are found on a wreck, the ship most likely was a warship. Generally, warships of all nations were forbidden to carry cargo of any description, and the scarcity of artifacts normally found on merchantmen will aid in identifying a wreck as a warship. In most cases it is impossible to distinguish between a Spanish treasure galleon sailing from Europe to a New World port and a warship. Neither would be carrying cargo and both would carry large numbers of cannon and hand weapons. Since mercury was occasionally shipped from Spain to the New World on the treasure galleons, discovery of this on a wreck site would normally identify it as a treasure galleon arriving from Spain.

British warships are easily identifiable because of the broad-arrow mark on many objects found on shipwrecks of this type. I have seen the broad arrow on cannon, weapons, copper sheathing, cutlery, bottles and many other articles. The origin of the mark is obscure, but it was in regular use by the second half of the 16th century to denote all Crown property and continued until the end of the 19th century. Finding a few items with the broad arrow on a shipwreck will certainly indicate that the items once belonged to the British admiralty, but not necessarily that the shipwreck is British. Items marked with the broad arrow were found not only on several of the 1715 Spanish shipwrecks but also on wrecks that proved to be non-British.

Slave ships sailing to or from the New World are usually identifiable by the equipment found on them. One located recently near Panama contained hundreds of leg and arm bracelets attached to chains, used on the hapless human cargoes these ships carried. Because almost every inch of a slave ship was used to carry the slaves and water and victuals to maintain them, most ships of this type carried only a few cannon. Other than the slaves, the only cargo these ships carried was ivory and gold dust, also obtained on the African coast. After selling its cargo on this side of the Atlantic, the ship returned to Europe with gold or silver specie or bullion received as payment.

Before discussing the identification and dating of items discovered on shipwrecks by their physical appearance, I shall mention the various scientific methods that can be utilized on various materials discovered on a wreck to establish place of origin or date or both. Carbon-dating using radiocarbon 14 (C-14) is the best known method of dating an old object, but it is limited to organic material such as wood, bone, charcoal, peat, shell and plant. This method was conceived by the noted nuclear physicist W. F. Libby, who discovered that all organic material absorbs C-14 from the earth's atmosphere until it dies, and that this absorption ceases and disintegrates at a known rate over periods of time. By measuring the amount of C-14 remaining in organic material, scientists can determine the length of time that has elapsed since the object died. Only small samples of the materials are required for this method, but the object should be kept wet (if discovered in the sea) until the tests are performed. Many universities have facilities for C-14 dating and there are also a number of commercial laboratories that do it. Testing requires from two to six weeks.

Date Lacks Certainty

The main disadvantage in using this method to date shipwrecks located in the Western Hemisphere lies in the uncertainty of the date obtained. Recently I submitted a wood sample from a shipwreck and received a date of 420 years, plus or minus 150 years. This meant that the wood sample could date from 1400 to 1700, which was no help at all. When C-14 dating is used on items that are many thousands of years old, the plus or minus factor is of little significance; but on items only several hundreds of years old, it is critical. Furthermore, in many cases the date obtained by this method will have no relationship to the date of the shipwreck The ship may have been many decades old...some were used for as long as fifty years...when it sank, and the ambiguous date obtained would relate to the date when the tree which supplied timbers for the ships was cut. There are many instances when a ship was constructed from timbers from older ships, which in turn could have been constructed from the timbers of an even older ship.

Dendrologists, scientists who study trees, can establish wood's origin, In many cases they not only can identify the type of wood and the country from which it came but even narrow its source to a small section of the country. This information is extremely useful in establishing the country in which the ship was constructed and was one of the factors that contributed to the positive identification of the two Columbus shipwrecks discovered in St. Ann's Bay, Jamaica.

Botanists are another resource. During our preliminary survey of the St. Anne's Bay site we found several black beans that botanists identified as a species grown only in Spain. On another occasion a botanist identified tobacco leaves I had found on a shipwreck as coming from Venezuela, thus aiding me in identifying it. Most plants or seeds discovered on shipwrecks can also be identified as to their species and place of origin.

Zoologists can be helpful in identifying bones of animals, birds and fish. Finding large numbers of human bones on a shipwreck might indicate either that there was a sea battle or that the ship sank in a storm. Investigating a shipwreck site near Jamaica, I noticed that there were a many fish bones mixed in with the ballast. At the time I assumed that they were either from fish that had died over the years on the wreck or were the remains of meals eaten by the ship's crew. The latter assumption was correct. I took a selection of the fish bones to a marine zoologist, who identified them as belonging to a species of herring caught in the North Sea. This information, combined with the discovery of many Dutch items on the wreck, identified it as being a Dutch merchantman.

Information obtained from geologists, who can establish the source of most ballast rock found on a shipwreck, can be helpful in identifying a ship's origin. There are certainly exceptions to the rule, but generally a ship car-

Earthenware jars such as these being pulled from a Spanish wreck off the coast of Panama are one means by which salvors can try to identify a ship.

ried ballast rock from its home port or other ports belonging to the same country either in the Old or New World. Scientists specializing in metallurgy can determine through microscopic study and other means, the exact origin of minerals and alloys used in metallic items. This will not necessarily identify the particular nationality of a wreck but will give the precise origin of the metallic objects carried on it. Where metal fastenings were used in the construction of a ship's hull, this information is especially useful, since these fittings were probably manufactured near the source of the minerals of which they are composed.

The Corning Glass Museum of Corning, NY, has conducted extensive research in methods of identifying and dating glassware. Throughout history different methods and minerals have been used to make glassware, and scientific analysis can identify the place of manufacture of most glassware. Several years ago, Corning's Dr. Robert Brill developed a method of precisely dating glass recovered from the sea. By counting the number of layers of the weathering crust on the glass fragment, he established the length of time it had been under the sea. I have submitted many samples of glassware from dated shipwrecks, and his findings have been accurate to within a year or two of the known date of the wreck.

Thermoluminescence, which was developed at the Oxford Research Laboratory in England only a few years ago, can be helpful in determining the dates of ceramic materials such as dinnerware or building bricks. This process uses the fact that radioactivity from certain isotopes in clay is trapped in the material until a ceramic object is fired in a kiln. The firing releases the electrons in

Diver surfaces, above, holding aloft his find of a coral-encrusted Spanish sword. Below are Spanish eight real Pillar dollar coins, dating from 1742.

a thermoluminescent glow. When the object cools, the electrons are again trapped but continue to increase with the process of decay, and the number of electrons released increases with the length of time. By measuring the number remaining in the test object, an approximate date of origin can be established.

Size of Ships

As a result of studying hundreds of documents concerning size and tonnage of ships of different types and nationalities, I have devised the following table to aid in establishing size and draft of old ships. The salvor may know from documentary sources that his ship was of 500 tons and, provided he locates the correct shipwreck, the length of the keel should be about 92 feet. This information can be used in reverse. Locating a shipwreck, the salvor might discover that the keel length was 120 feet. This would indicate that his ship was 1,400-1,500 tons, which would aid him greatly in identifying the ship. All figures in the table are given in feet.

Tonnage	Length of Keel	Width of Beam	Draft
100	52	19	7 1/2
200	66	24	9 1/2
300	76	27 1/3	10 1/2
400	84	30	12
500	92	33	13
600	98	35	14
700	102	36 3/4	14 5/8
800	104	37 1/2	15
900	107 1/2	38 1/2	15 1/4
1,000	109	39 1/5	15
1,100	110	40	15 1/2
1,400-1,500	120	44	16
1,600	132	48	16
2,000	152	60	18

Establishing the nationality of a ship from a visual inspection of the remains is difficult for many reasons.

Ships were subject to a change of flag throughout the Colonial era when European nations in varying patterns of alliances were almost constantly at war with one another. Warfare, privateering and piracy meant that a ship built in Spain might be captured by French corsairs and they in turn might lose it to English privateers. Captured ships were used in navies and merchant fleets; others were bought or hired from different nations. A scarcity of Spanish shipping in 1593 caused the King to seize all foreign ships in Spanish ports so that a full fleet could sail on schedule to the New World. Of the 62 ships in this fleet, only 14 were Spanish-built. The others came from 12 nations, including Greece and Sweden.

On almost all shallow-water sites too little remains of a shipwreck to aid in establishing the place where the ship was constructed. Even if it were established, it would not indicate the nationality of the ship at the time it was lost. One of the 1715 ships, originally built in England, served as a warship for many years until it was captured by the French and converted into a merchantman. She was eventually sold to the Spaniards, who converted her to a treasure galleon.

The spikes, nails, tacks and other metal fastenings found in association with a shipwreck are no help in identifying its date or nationality because their shapes and sizes changed very little over the centuries. Brass tacks discovered on a Roman shipwreck dating from the 3d century A.D. were identical to those found on an 18th-century French warship. Treenails (wooden pegs) used to fasten the planking to the frame of the ship, are no help either in dating a ship, since they remained the same over centuries. If they were turned on a lathe rather than shaped by hand, it indicates only that the wreck is dated after 1825. Nor will the types of wood used in a ship's construction provide the salvor with any valuable clues. The wood used depended on what was most readily available. Earliest mention of a ship built in Europe using teakwood was in 1821. A ship built with mahogany planking might indicate that it was built near Honduras, which was the major source of mahogany in the old days.

Preventing boring of the teredo and the accumulation of barnacles on the hulls was a constant problem. One method used by most of the European nations was to careen their ships and burn the ships' bottoms, then apply any of a number of protective compounds, basically consisting of a tar and pitch base. The Spaniards generally used a mixture of tar and lime. Some Spanish ships in the 18th century used a layer of wooden sheathing and placed a compound of tar and animal hair between the sheathing and hull. The English used too many different mixtures to enumerate here. In 1745 the mix consisted of 100 parts of pitch, 30 parts of brimstone, and 35 parts of brick or marble dust.

Earliest mention of Spanish ships sheathed in lead dates to 1508. This practice was continued until 1567 when the King ordered it to cease, claiming that added weight caused his ships to sail too slowly. In 1605 lead sheathing was again applied to Spanish ships sailing to the New World, but only to those going to Mexico. The reason for this was to protect their hulls from the teredo during long months when these ships wintered in the warm waters of Veracruz. Those going to other Spanish settlements were still forbidden to use lead sheathing. The only other nation that used lead sheathing was England, and only on a small scale, mainly as an experiment on their warships in the Caribbean during different periods.

There was a brief mention in 1735 of 20 sheathed English warships, but the material used was not mentioned. In 1766 several English warships were sheathed with copper, and by 1780 so were all English ships, both naval and merchantmen. The first French ships to use copper sheathing sailed in 1775, but this practice did not catch on with the Spaniards or Portuguese until the first decade of the 19th century.

300

The majority of the masts, yards, spars and rigging used on all ships came from the Baltic region. Their shapes differed so little over the years that they are not useful in identifying nationality or age. However, their dimensions can aid in figuring the size of the ship.

Anchors That Were Used

Anchors are very difficult to date because their shapes changed so little over the centuries and their place of origin can't be determined by shape. From the time of the Vikings until about 1825, all anchors were hand-forged from several pieces of iron. After this period many were cast in one piece. The stocks were made of wood until the middle of the 19th century, when they were replaced by iron bars. The first mention of chains being used on an anchor occurred in 1817 and referred to those on an English warship.

The number and size of anchors a ship carried depended on her size and type. Since anchors were routinely lost, many extras were carried. Until 1579 there was no regulation as to the number of anchors a ship must carry, but that year the king issued an order stating that ships over 100 tons going to *Tierra Firme* must carry five anchors and those going to Mexico must carry seven. The first mention of their sizes occurred in 1620, when a galleon of 500 tons carried seven anchors on a voyage to Veracruz: one of a ton weight, two of 1,800 pounds, two of 1,600 pounds, one of 450 pounds and one of 350 pounds. In 1709 an order was issued that the total weight of anchors on all Spanish warships must be equal to 5% of the total weight of the ship.

After 1634 French merchantmen were required to carry a minimum of four large anchors and warships, at least six. One large French warship lost in the Caribbean near the end of the 17th century was carrying 10 anchors at the time, while another, lost during the same hurricane, had only two available, resulting in her loss when both of their cables parted and she wrecked on a reef.

In 1688 English warships were required to carry the following number of anchors: a ship of 2,000 tons, known as a first-rater, carried nine anchors weighing a total of 17 tons; a second-rater of 1,500 tons carried nine weighing a total of 12 1/2 tons; a third-rater of 1,000 tons carried six weighing a total of 8 1/2 tons; a fourth rater of 700 tons carried six weighing a total of 5 1/2 tons; and a fifth-rater of 500 tons carried five weighing a total of 4 1/2 tons.

The grapple (multi-armed iron anchor) is believed to have been developed by the Greeks and was used until modern times. Various sizes and shapes can be seen in religious illuminated works of the Medieval period and in paintings of the 15th and 16th centuries. In the New World they were widely used during the first half of the 16th century on smaller vessels with some erroneously identified as grappling hooks used when boarding an enemy vessel.

With the introduction of the iron anchor with a wooden stock, there were very few changes or improvements on them until the 19th century. Records in 1514 list anchors by name and show that the *Henri Grace Adieu* had four bower anchors, four destrelles, one shot anchor and a cadger or kedge anchor. By the time of Elizabeth I, anchors had taken on their present names of bower, sheet, stream and kedge. Bower anchors were for ordinary use such as mooring and were stored in the bow for ready use, hence their name. Sheet anchors were heavier and used in emergencies such as to prevent a ship from going up on a lee shore. Stream anchors were small anchors used mainly as stern anchors or to supplement the bowers.

Kedge anchors were the smallest and used for light work such as maneuvering a vessel, bringing around the head, and sometimes for navigation...by rowing it out ahead of the ship and having the ship haul up to it if the ship was becalmed or steering through hazardous waterways. Another type of anchor used throughout this period was the mooring anchor, which is easily identified since it head, and sometimes for navigation...by rowing it out ahead of the ship and having the ship haul up to it if the ship was becalmed or steering through hazardous waterways. Another type of anchor used throughout this period was the mooring anchor which is easily identified since it has one of its arms bent back to the vertical shank or stem. It was generally used in anchorages to attach permanent mooring buoys, the good arm digging into the bottom and the other bent back to prevent damage to a vessel tying up to the mooring.

With a few exceptions, most anchors of the 16th and 17th centuries had curved arms, but as larger anchors came into use the straight-arm anchor was introduced, first by the English and soon after by other nations. The flukes were generally the shape of equilateral triangles and about half the length of the arms. The anchor ring was usually smaller in diameter than the fluke. Rope wrapping on the rings was in general use and probably dates back in antiquity. In Mainwaring's *Seamen's Directory,* first published in 1622, he states that the shank was twice as long as one of the flukes plus half the distance between the tips of the flukes.

The anchor stock was more or less the length of the shank, except in Portuguese and Spanish anchors where it

Markings and numerals on this anchor stock reveal the 1773 date of manufacture of the anchor, and indicate that it was the property of the Dutch East India Company of Amsterdam.

was from 25% to 40% longer. The stock was made from timbers bound with iron hoops which were driven on when heated. Sutherland in *Britain's Glory or Shipbuilding Unveiled,* writing in 1717, states that Royal Navy regulations specified that the length of the shank of the largest anchor on a naval vessel was two-fifths of the vessel's extreme breadth. Eighteenth century anchors were made from a number of iron bars tied together, heated and then forged under a trip hammer into one bar to form the shank or arms. These parts were then welded together. Since there were no methods then for checking welds, hidden defects resulted in many anchor arms breaking under severe strain.

By 1800 most European anchors were of a standard shape with the shank slightly larger than earlier anchors and about a 60° angle to the arms. The Scandinavians and Dutch used anchors whose arms were about 5% longer than those used by the French and slightly curved, whereas the English were using straight armed anchors. These differences were minor and all anchors looked more or less alike at this time. The bulky wooden stocks were still in use, but many were laminated with thin sheets of copper or lead. The arms were still scarfed and hand-forged to the crown of the shank, which was the weakest joint in the anchor.

To eliminate the great numbers of anchors which were being broken, an Englishman named Richard Pering in 1813 devised and patented a new method of laminating the arms to the shank of an anchor. To permit a smoother flow of the laminated joints he rounded the arms slightly. His anchors were crafted by means of a drop hammer operated by up to 40 men. In 1839 the steam hammer, requiring only one or two men to operate, revolutionized the manufacture of anchors and chains. Following this invention, any new types of anchors were patented, such as the Admiralty Pattern anchor developed in 1841 by

Admiral Sir William Parker. Cotsell's 1850 *Treatise on Anchors* showed 19 different types in use, and by the turn of the 20th century Lloyd's List of approved anchor types showed 80 different varieties. Most of the 19th-century anchors had the wooden stock replaced by an iron one. Stockless anchors also came into use which were stowed by pulling the shank into the hawse pipe, where they were ready for immediate use.

Iron stocks were by no means new. They were used by the Romans. An anchor recovered from one of the Lake Nemi Roman wrecks had a removable iron stock. The anchors shown in the Bayeux tapestry dating from the end of the 11th century also appear to have iron stocks. The first mention in more recent times of iron- stock anchors appears in 1780 when they were being tested on British warships. The British navy was using iron stocks on most anchors weighing less than fifteen hundredweight in 1805, but heavier anchors did not use iron stocks until a few decades later. Iron stocks were not used on British merchant ships until around 1875, and it should be noted at this time that some ships on both sides of the Atlantic were still using wooden stocks at the turn of the present century.

The earliest anchor cables were made of hide, animal membranes, and later flax, jute, hemp and cotton. The advantage in the holding power of a chain cable over a buoyant cable was recognized in earliest times and quite often a few fathoms of chain were bent on next to the anchor. Use of chain meant that the anchor shank could be shortened, both because of the holding power of the chain and because the strengthened crown joint permitted use of a shorter shank for breakout. A carved Greek gemstone of circa 500 B.C. depicts an anchor surrounded by chain cable, and there is some evidence that the Chinese were using chain cable even earlier. Julius Caesar wrote that the Veneti tribe in southern Brittany used iron cable instead of rope fiber cables. A Danish ship dating from 950 A.D. was discovered with an anchor which had

30 feet of chain cable attached. Then for some unknown reason chain cable fell out of use until early in the 19th century, by the end of which it had almost totally replaced fiber cable on the majority of vessels over 100 tons in size.

Caution must be exercised when relying on anchors to date a shipwreck. There have been many instances when anchors have been recovered from the sea, either by divers or when they snagged on other anchors or cables and were brought to the surface and used again, centuries after they were last in use. Even a date on an anchor, which is quite rare, does not necessarily have to be accurate. An example of this is to be seen outside of Ships' Museum in Amsterdam. The anchor dated in the late 18th century is actually an early 17th century anchor which was recovered from the sea and inscribed after it was introduced for use by the Dutch East India Company.

Trying to establish the nationality or place of manufacture of anchors during the Colonial era isn't really possible. Too little data is currently available to enable proper identification as to the place of manufacture. Furthermore, there was such a great trade in anchors throughout this period that all nations were using anchors of foreign manufacture. During the 16th century the manufacture of anchors in northern Spain was a big business, yet a document dated 1557 states that most of the anchors on that year's outward-bound New Spain *flota* were of foreign manufacture. Another document from a few years later stated that over 50 anchors had been seized from Northern European merchantmen then in port for that years outward-bound *flota*. In 1606 most of the anchors used on Portuguese East Indies ships had been purchased in Scandinavia, and in 1678 an English ship with a large cargo of anchors destined for sale in Genoa was seized by the French off Ushant.

Navigation Instruments

Establishing the place and date of manufacture of most navigation instruments is best left to an expert, since very few reference books on the subject are available to the average underwater explorer. The navigation instruments used at the time of Columbus consisted of astrolabes and quadrants to establish latitude, nocturnals to establish the approximate time of night and compass and dividers to mark off distances on charts. About the middle of the 16th century, the cross-staff, or Jacob-staff, came into general use. The sextant was invented simultaneously in 1732 by John Hadley in England and Thomas Godfrey in Philadelphia, but it did not come into general use until about 1750.

Several brass astrolabes and a quite a number of dividers have been recovered from shipwrecks, but none of the other navigation instruments mentioned above have been found with the exception of several sextants dating to the 19th century. Quadrants and the cross-staves were made of wood and probably have not been found because they either floated away or have been devoured by worms. Since nocturnals were made of brass, it is strange that none has been discovered. The same applies to compasses, whose housings were usually made of lead or other non-magnetic metals.

Glass Bottles

Glass bottles are very good for establishing the date of a shipwreck. Their shape changed quite often, and they can be dated to within 10 years of their manufacture. Glass was first made by the Phoenicians and the Egyptians, who crafted many exquisite glass objects. At the time of Columbus' discovery of America, Venice was the center of European glass manufacturing, specializing in drinking glasses and decanters. Glass factories were founded in Antwerp in 1550 and in London in 1557. Another was founded in Jamestown, VA, in 1608, but it went out of business in 1624. One was started in Salem, MA, in 1632, making bottles to transport rum and cider to the West Indies and England. The next glassworks to open was in Brussels in 1662, and soon after others were founded in Spain, France, Holland and Germany.

Glass bottles that contained any type of liquor are generally called "wine bottles." The first ones manufactured we know of were those in Salem in 1632. The exact date they were being manufactured elsewhere is not known, but it is believed that they were being made in England around 1650. Other European nations were not manufacturing wine bottles until well after 1700. At least 95% of all wine bottles discovered on 17th and 18th-century shipwrecks will be of English manufacture, since the English produced them on a large scale and exported them all over Europe. Wine bottles manufactured in Holland are very similar in appearance to those of the English, but those made in other European countries have their own distinct characteristics, permitting nationality to be established.

Some bottles bear the dates of manufacture and others bear identification seals of the persons for whom they were made...the owner of a tavern. Bottles were sealed with wax-covered cork until near the end of the 17th century, when brass wire was used to hold the corks in place. Late in the 18th century, copper wire came into general use to hold corks in place.

All bottles were blown by hand until the second decade of the 19th century, when they began to be manufactured in molds. Thus, any bottle discovered with mold marks or with the maker's or owner's name molded on it must date later than 1810.

There are various books available to identify and date drinking glasses, but I suggest sending photographs and measurements of any glasses discovered on a shipwreck to the Coming Glass Museum. Glass plate for windows and mirrors was first made in England in 1673.

Clay Pipes and Tobacco

White clay smoking pipes are also very valuable for establishing the date, but not for establishing the possible nationality, of a shipwreck. Almost all of them were manufactured either in England or Holland and were exported all over Europe. Most clay pipes can be dated to within 10 years of their date of manufacture, with the exception of a few that were manufactured in Virginia and Jamaica. Unlike many other items discovered on shipwrecks, the lifespan of a fragile clay pipe was short, so those located on a wreck will date very close to the time when the ship was lost. They were very inexpensive to purchase and almost as expendable as cigarettes are today.

The use of tobacco was unknown in Europe until after the discovery of the New World. Columbus and his men saw Indians on various Caribbean islands smoking cigars, and later explorers in North America saw Indians smoking tobacco from clay pipes. Although the Spaniards started cultivating and exporting tobacco to Spain from the colonies about the end of the 16th century, the use of tobacco in Spain was prohibited by the Church until the beginning of the 19th century. Most of the tobacco imported into Spain was sold to England and Holland.

On his voyage to the West Indies in 1565 John Hawkins gathered a large amount of tobacco and introduced it to England upon his return. The first mention of the manufacture of clay pipes in England occurred in 1573, and by the end of the 16th century the use of tobacco and clay pipes was widespread both in England and Holland. By 1619 there were so many manufacturers of clay pipes in England that they incorporated into a guild, with Dutch pipemakers doing the same in 1660. Pipes were first made in Denmark in 1655 and in Switzerland in 1697, but very little is known concerning the dates when they were first manufactured in the other European nations. It is believed, but not known for certain, that small numbers were being manufactured in Virginia and Jamaica in the late 17th century, but it wasn't until about the beginning of the 19th century that the United States first manufactured clay pipes on a massive scale.

There are many distinctive features about clay pipes that aid in dating them. When smoking first came into vogue in England and Holland, the cost of tobacco was prohibitive since all of that used was purchased from the Spaniards. Consequently, pipe bowls were small.

After the English began cultivating tobacco in the New World and exporting it to England, its cost became progressively less and the size of the pipe bowls increased in proportion. As their size increased the shapes of the bowls also changed. Thus, pipe bowls can be dated to within 10 or 20 years by their shapes. Prior to my excavation of the sunken city of Port Royal, it was believed that clay pipes could be dated by the diameters of the bore of their stem. The theory was based on the assumption that as the pipe bowls grew larger the diameter of the bore became smaller. At Port Royal I discovered a total of 7,133 pipes with intact bowls and over 5,000 with semi-intact bowls. From a very thorough examination of these clay pipes, ranging in dates from 1650 to 1850, I found that this theory didn't hold up and stem bore diameters are not a reliable way to date a clay pipe.

A majority of the pipes manufactured in England were marked with either the initials or full name of the manufacturer. Records exist in England listing 3,400 pipe-makers from 1600 onward. Several good reference books on the subject are available to enable a salvor to identify the maker, place of manufacture and dates of any particular pipe. These marks can be found on the bowls, heels, spurs or stems of the pipes. Decorated pipes were made as early as 1600. Some of the earliest had patterns of the fleur-de-lis or rosettes etched on them. Later types bore oak leaves, grapes, flowers, anchors and myriad other designs.

From the end of the 18th century to the middle of the 19th century, decorations on pipes became much more elaborate, with some adorned with busts of the British monarchs, mermaids or coats-of-arms. Practically nothing is known about the markings on the pipes made in other European nations until well into the 19th century. The

310

same applies to the red clay pipes believed to have been made in Virginia or Jamaica.

Discovery of large numbers of pipes on a shipwreck usually identifies it as being English or Dutch, but small numbers have been discovered on a few Spanish shipwrecks. Since snuff came into general use around 1700, the discovery of snuffboxes on a wreck would date it after that. Tobacco stoppers, generally made of brass or pewter, are first mentioned as being used in 1640, and many contain distinctive markings that can be used to establish a date or place of manufacture.

Gold, Silver and Pewter

Items made of gold, silver or pewter are usually easy to identify and date. At Port Royal, for example, I found tankards, spoons, knives, etc., and with only a few exceptions I was able not only to discover the place and date of manufacture but in many cases I identified the names of the actual owners of the items. Some of the objects bore the full name of the owner, but the majority were stamped with the owner's initials. From historical records in the Jamaican archives I was able to match these initials with the names of their owners, thus determining the identity of the owners of buildings I was excavating. I have also been able to do this with items recovered from various shipwrecks by matching the names or initials on items recovered with passenger or crew lists of the ship.

There has been a great deal published on these kinds of artifacts. A salvor can often establish a precise date and place of manufacture of a silver or pewter piece. The majority have hallmarks and touchmarks that can be traced. Those that do not can be identified by their shape or form.

More than 95% of these kinds of things found on shipwrecks are of English manufacture, with the exception of jewelry. A small quantity of silver items, mainly spoons, forks, plates, and cups of Spanish and French manufacture, have been found on various shipwrecks. All

311

contained sufficient markings to identify and date them. Even on most Spanish wrecks the vast majority of items of this type were made by the English. On the *Matanceros* shipwreck, over a hundred pewterware and silverware articles were found, all of English manufacture ...with the exception of one Spanish fork.

All items made of gold, silver or pewter discovered on shipwrecks of all dates were used throughout the period covered in this book, with the exception of snuffboxes and forks. Large serving forks were in use as early as 1300, but the use of small forks to transfer food from the plate to the mouth is not mentioned until the latter part of the 16th century, when they came into general use for the upper class. Their use did not catch on with the lower classes until the end of the 17th century. Cutlery used by the lower classes was usually made of iron or brass until late in the 18th century.

Because only the very rich could afford articles of gold or silver, small quantities of such items will be found on shipwrecks. Items made of pewter were used by the majority of the upper and middle classes. Pewterware, first used by the Romans, has remained in continuous use up to the present.

Pewterware Markings

There are different types of markings on pewterware which help identify it. The touchmark on all pieces identifies the manufacturer. After being admitted to the Pewterers Guild each pewtermaker was given permission to strike a mark of his own choice--generally from one to two inches in height--on all pieces he made. The touch-

A bronze 16th-century astrolabe, the instrument that was used for finding latitude at sea, is quite rare, and some are valued in excess of $500,000.

marks of more than 6,000 English pewter-makers are recorded in a number of excellent books. The majority consist of some type of design...flower, animal, crown, with the maker's name or initials around it. Even the place of manufacture is mentioned on many. The crowned Tudor rose mark signifies that the item was manufactured in London; the letter X with a crown above it denotes items made of extraordinary quality. In addition, many items were stamped with their date of manufacture.

Many articles of pewterware bear hallmarks similar to those used on gold or silverware. These marks were not authorized for use by the Pewterers Guild, however, and were illegally struck by pewtermakers. They were struck in the shapes of shields or cartouches, averaging about three-eighths of an inch in height, and were aligned in a straight row unlike the marks mentioned above. The first hallmark denoted the place of manufacture. The crowned leopard's head was the mark of the London manufacturers, the anchor for those in Birmingham and a plain crown for those in Sheffield. The second mark consisted of a letter of the alphabet and denoted the year of manufacture. Every 27 years they would start the alphabet all over again. The third hallmark denotes that the piece was of good quality. In England the lion was used...elsewhere in the British Isles other devices, such as the thistle in Edinburgh. The fourth hallmark denoted the identity of the maker and usually consisted of his initials.

Gold and silverware used the same kinds of hallmarks described above in addition to other distinctive marks that can easily be identified. American-made silverware of the

Both maker's and owner's marks on the silver plate, above, will identify place of manufacture and the owner. Clay pipe, typical of those found on non-Spanish shipwrecks between 1650 and 1800, can be dated by shape and maker's mark.

17th and 18th centuries contained only the maker's mark; thus these pieces can only be dated as being made sometime during the lifespan of the known craftsman. There are many reference books to consult on the subject. Silver plating on copper items was first done in 1743, but not on a large scale until 1833, when electroplating was invented.

Porcelain and Pottery

Large amounts of porcelain have been found on many different shipwrecks, and most pieces can be identified and dated fairly accurately. The distinguishing feature of porcelain is that it is translucent, as opposed to pottery, which is opaque. All porcelain found on a 16th-century shipwreck and the majority found on shipwrecks of the 17th century is of Chinese or Japanese manufacture. Some of these pieces bear marks of the province in which they were made in addition to the name of the reigning ruler of the country at that time. However a salvor is more likely to find small fragments or shards of porcelain than intact pieces because of porcelain's fragile nature and the nature of shallow water wreck sites which are buffeted by wind, waves and currents.

The first exact date or place of manufacture of porcelain in Europe is not known, but it is believed to have been in Florence around the close of the 16th century where it was produced on a small scale and not for export. The English first began producing small amounts of porcelain about 1745, the Dutch a few years later. Most of these pieces bear manufacturers' marks, making it possible to establish the date and place of manufacture. Most of the other European nations and the United States did not begin manufacturing porcelain until the 19th century. Identification of unmarked porcelain should only be attempted by experts, but approximate dates and places of manufacture can be obtained by amateurs using various references.

The most common type of pottery discovered on

shipwrecks is utilityware, which consists of a coarse hard paste, usually red but sometimes gray or brown. Only small amounts of utilityware were glazed, generally green. This pottery used by the lower classes was rarely decorated or had any other distinctive feature that would facilitate identifying its origin or date of manufacture. Approximate dates can be fixed by the shapes of various vessels of this type, provided the vessel is found intact or enough pieces are found to establish its original shape.

On all Spanish ships and on many of other nations a type of vessel resembling the amphoras used by the Greeks and Romans was used to carry liquids and other things. These vessels, known as Spanish "olive jars," were manufactured in Seville and the surrounding countryside and exported all over Europe and the New World. An approximate date can be obtained from the shape of a vessel and by the maker's mark found on some of them. They were made of utilityware, usually of a gray exterior, and ranged in size from two to six gallons in capacity.

Another type of large vessel that can be dated fairly accurately was the bellarmine jug. These were manufactured in Germany of a type of ceramic known as stoneware. The clay used had flint in its body and was fired at a much higher temperature than utilityware. Bellarmines were coated with a salt-glaze that give it a distinctive whitish-gray interior and brownish exterior. Most of the necks of the jugs were decorated with a human face, which had its origin in a caricature of the Spanish Cardinal Bellarmine, and some have armorial medallions on the bodies.These jugs range in capacity from one pint to five gallons.

Another commonly used type of pottery is known as delftware. It was called that by the English, Dutch and most other northern European countries, but in France and Italy it was called *faience* and in Spain and its New World possessions *majolica*. Widely manufactured in every country and used mainly by the upper and middle classes, it was generally made of the same clay as utilityware but was coated with a glaze of tin oxide, which appeared white in color after firing. The surface of the glaze was then decorated in a wide range of colors and designs.

Most of the pieces manufactured in Europe and some of the later pieces made in the New World have distinctive makers' marks on them which can be used to establish the date and place of origin Experts should be consulted to aid in identification of all unmarked pieces.

Dating by Coinage

Coins can generally be used to date a shipwreck within a few years of its loss, especially when large numbers of coins bearing the same dates or dates that span a short period of time are discovered. Coins have been found, however, that were more than a century older than the shipwreck itself. Remember that a shipwreck must date from the same year, or later, than the latest dated coin found on it. Since almost all coinage carried on ships wrecked prior to 1825 in the waters of the Western Hemisphere was of Spanish-American colonial mintage, I shall describe here only such coins and the means by which they can be dated.

Very little is known about the earliest coins minted in the New World. Several documents mention that private persons minted their own issues of gold and silver coins in Mexico City as early as 1528, but nothing is known concerning their descriptions or how long this practice continued. In 1535 a mint was established in Santo Domingo, where copper maravedi coins were first minted. Practically nothing is known about this coin, except that it was also minted at Mexico City and Panama City, among other places, and was used until the beginning of the 19th century. Very few were stamped with distinctive markings such as dates, mint marks or assayers' initials. Some, dating from the second half of the 16th century and minted in Santo Domingo, had an anchor on one side and a fort

318

on the other. Others, minted there in 1636, had a fort on one side and two ships on the other.

Occasionally, maravedi coins minted in Spain bearing dates and other marks have been discovered on shipwrecks. The known denominations of these coins were 8, 4, and 2 maravedis, but they may have been minted in other denominations as well. Their actual buying value was small and they were basically used as small change in the New World. A silver one-real coin was worth 34 maravedis and an eight-real coin, or piece of eight, was worth 272 maravedis.

Silver coins were first officially minted at Mexico City in 1536, at Lima, 1568; Potosi, 1572; Bogota, 1622; Guatemala City, 1733, and Santiago (Chile), 1751. It is believed that they were also minted at Cartageña and Panama City for short periods at various times during the 17th century. The basic silver coin was the eight-real piece, which weighed an ounce. Other real denominations were the 4, 2, 1, 1/2 and 1/4 coins, smaller in size and weight.

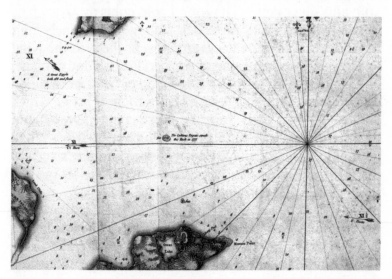

This chart shows the exact location of the French Revolutionary War ship *Cerberus,* which was lost in 1777 in Long Island Sound, just off the coast of New York.

Gold coins were first officially minted at Cartageña in 1615, at Bogota in 1635, at Mexico City in 1679, and at Lima and Potosi about 1697. They were also minted for a six-month period during the year 1698 and again after 1750 at Cuzco, Peru. The gold coins are of the same size and weight as the silver and are in denominations of 8, 4, 2,1, and 1/2 escudos.

Although the screw press was used to mint round milled coins in England as early as 1610, it was not used in Spanish America until 1732, when the first round milled coins were made at the Mexico City mint. The Lima mint did not produce round milled coins until 1752, and the other mints at even later dates.

Prior to 1732 almost all gold and silver coins minted in the New World were not round in shape but of many irregular patterns. There were some exceptions. The silver coins minted in Mexico City during the first 20 or 30 years of operation were almost perfectly round, and over the years all the mints made small numbers of perfectly round gold and silver coins. The round gold coins are known as royals and are quite rare. It is believed that each mint made several royals each year and sent them to the King to show that they were capable of producing good coinage.

The irregularly shaped gold and silver coins were called cobs, a name probably derived from *cabo de barra,* which means "end of a bar." To make these coins molten metal was poured out on a flat surface in long, thin strips. When the metal cooled, pieces of the approximate size and weight of the desired coin were cut from the strip, then trimmed to their proper weight. The planchet was then placed between two dies and struck with a heavy hammer. Since one or both sides of the coin was not perfectly flat, the dies only marked the highest surfaces of these sides. This resulted in the majority of the cob coinage not having full die marks.

Because such large quantities of coins were minted each year, care was not always exercised in marking them.

Thus, many bear only die marks on various sections of their surfaces.

The coins made at the Mexico City mint during the 17th and 18th centuries are poor in quality, show faulty die marks and are the most difficult to date. Of the coins recovered from the 1715 shipwrecks, of which at least 95% are from the Mexico City mint, only 15% of the gold coins and less than 1% of the silver coins show dates. Other mints appeared to have exercised better workmanship, as larger amounts of both their gold and silver coins are found with fuller die marks in addition to bearing dates. At Port Royal I recovered about 2,500 silver coins from the Potosi and Lima mints dated from 1658 to 1690, and 98% of these coins had dates on them.

There are numerous books that can be used to date Spanish-American colonial coins; also, in most large cities there are numismatists who can be consulted. When dates are not visible on the coins, there are other means by which they can be dated fairly accurately. The majority of the coins have the shield or coat-of-arms of the monarch on the obverse side, so the coin can be dated to the period in which the king reigned. From 1772 to 1825, the end of Spanish rule in America, both the gold and silver coins carried the portrait of the Spanish king. All coins were also marked with the initials of the assayer and cover the period in which a particular assayer was in charge of a mint. On small numbers of coins the reigning monarch's name or initials were also marked.

The place in which a coin was minted can be determined from the mint marks on each coin. The letter L for Lima, P for Potosi, M for Mexico City, C for Cartageña, G for Guatemala, S for Santiago, and NR for Bogota. When the mint marks are not visible on the coin, the place where it was minted can be identified by its die markings. Almost all of the Mexico City coins had a Jerusalem cross--a square cross with balls on all four ends--on the reverse side, as did some of the Bogota and Cartageña-minted coins. The Lima and Potosi-minted coins had a plain cross with the arms of Castile and Leon on their reverse sides. Even if only a small amount of the die is visible, the place in which it was minted can generally still be identified, making coins one of the best markers in unraveling the mystery of a shipwreck site.

Cannon and Weapons

Cannon are very useful in identifying the size, type and approximate date of the ship, but not always the nationality...cannon manufactured in many different countries might be found on a single vessel. During the second half of the 16th century the majority of cannon carried on Spanish ships was made in England and Holland, and during the 17th and 18th centuries a large percentage was also of foreign manufacture. A Spanish merchant ship sailing to Veracruz in 1616 had three English, one Italian, three Dutch, two Portuguese, five French and three Spanish cannon aboard. In 1623 the *flotas* and treasure galleons were unable to sail for the New World because of a grave shortage of cannon...not all the ships that had gone to the New World the previous year had returned to Spain. To arm the ships 30 cannon were bought from Portugal, 200 from Denmark and 300 from England. Many of the ships of other European countries also carried cannon of foreign manufacture, most of which were obtained by capturing ships of other nations.

Most bronze and iron cannon were struck with dates at the time they were founded, and many also carried the coat of arms of the monarch of the country of manufacture. English cannon were struck with a crowned rose during the Tudor period and the initials *GR* (George Rex) during King George's reign. On bronze cannon these marks always survive, but by the time many iron cannon are discovered, markings have disappeared. When no date of founding is visible, cannon can still be dated by shapes and other distinctive characteristics. All European nations have artillery museums, and their experts can generally date the pieces to within 50 years. In the United States the Smithsonian and the Metropolitan in New York have experts who can aid a salvor in identifying and dating cannon. Various books have been published on cannon, but the majority are written in foreign languages and are difficult to obtain in the United States.

During his voyages Columbus armed his ships with two types of cannon, Lombards and Versos, also called swivel guns. The Lombards were made of forged-iron strakes running the length of the barrel and held together by iron bands spaced every 4 to 6 inches. The piece was opened at both ends and a breech block loaded with powder was wedged against the back end of the piece after a ball was inserted. The cannon was mounted on a wooden cradle and carried on the main deck of the ship. These pieces varied from six to twelve feet in length, weighed from 500 to 2,000 pounds and fired a ball of stone between four and ten inches in diameter. The weight of the stone depended on the type of rock used in making the ball. A distinctive feature of this type of cannon was the absence of trunnions on the cannon, unlike any other cannon used at later dates.

The Versos were either cast in bronze or made of iron in the same manner as the Lombards, but by the end of the 16th century they were also cast in iron. They were mounted on a pivoting frame and attached to the bulwarks of the ships. They varied in length from four to ten feet, weighed between 150 and 1,800 pounds and fired a stone or iron ball between 1 1/2 and 3 inches in diameter. These small-caliber guns were mainly used to attack the personnel on the decks and castles of an enemy ship rather than a ship's hull could resist the shock of small projectiles. This type of cannon was carried on ships of all types and nations as late as the end of the 18th century. It was also used as a signal gun and by officers at times of mutinies.

As early as 1504 some of the larger Spanish ships sailing to the New World were carrying bigger cannon mounted on two-wheeled wooden gun carriages. A merchant *nao* sailing to Santo Domingo this same year carried one bronze Demiculverin, 11 feet in length, weighing two tons and firing a 12-pound ball; four iron cannon Serpentines, eight feet in length, weighing 2 1/2 tons, and firing a 40-pound ball; one bronze Saker, seven feet in length, weighing 1,200 pounds, and firing a 6-pound ball; and three Versos of unknown size and weight but firing a 4-pound ball.

In 1552 a royal order was issued that all Spanish ships sailing to the New World had to carry a specific amount of armament. Merchant ships between 100 and 170 tons were required to carry one bronze Saker, one bronze Falconet, six iron Lombards and twelve iron Versos. A ship of 170 to 220 tons must carry one bronze Demiculverin, one bronze Saker, one bronze Falconet, eight iron Lombards and 18 iron Versos. Ships of 220 to 320 tons must carry one iron Demiculverin, two bronze Sakers, one bronze Falconet, 10 iron Lombards, and 24 iron Versos. Treasure galleons of between 400 and 600 tons were required to carry all bronze cannon, which consisted of 30 to 50 Culverin cannon, four to six Demiculverins, two to four Sakers, four Falconets and an unknown number of Versos.

The Demiculverins fired balls weighing from seven to 12 pounds, were 25 to 40 times their bore diameter in length, and weighed between 3,000 and 4,000 pounds. The Sakers fired balls weighing from five to 10 pounds, were from five to eight feet in length, and weighed between 1,700 and 2,400 pounds. The Falconets fired a three or four-pound ball, were 30 to 36 times their bore diameter in length and weighed between 1,500 and 2,500 pounds. At this time the Lombards were made with trunnions and were about the same size and weight as the earlier types. The same applies to the Versos. The Culverin cannon were the main armament for fighting against enemy ships. They were made in many different sizes and fired balls weighing between 20 and 40 pounds. Their lengths were

30 to 32 times their bore diameter and their weight from two to three tons.

Around 1570, when a scarcity of copper prevented the manufacture of a sufficient number of bronze Culverins and other types of cannon for the Spanish ships, many began carrying larger numbers of iron cannon. The largest was called just plain *Cannon*. It fired a 40-pound ball, was 17 times its bore diameter in length and weighed 6,200 pounds. There were also Demi-Cannons, which fired balls weighing between 12 and 20 pounds, were between 12 and 20 times their bore diameters in length, and weighed between 2,300 and 3,600 pounds. During the Colonial period the maximum range of a cannon was three miles, a distance which remains today the distance from shore that the coastal states claim as their territory.

Small vessels frequently used several other types of cannon, including the Pasavolante, which fired a ball weighing between two and 15 pounds; the Moyana, which fired a ball weighing from six to 10 pounds; and the Esmeril, of which very little is known. During the 16th and 17th centuries a type of cannon named Pedrero was occasionally carried on Spanish ships, but very little is known about this cannon. Some documents mention firing balls of only a few pounds, being small in size and weight, and others mention cannon weighing as much as two tons and firing 40-pound balls. The balls they fired were always made of stone.

The principal cannon carried on English ships during the 16th century are included in the chart on following page, along with their average weights and measurements:

16th-Century English Cannon

Name	Weight (Lbs)	Length (Ft)	Caliber (Ins)	Shot Weight (Lbs)
Robinet	200	5	1 1/4	1
Falconet	500	4	2	2
Falcon	800	6	2 1/2	2 1/2
Minion	1,100	6 1/2	3 1/2	4 1/2
Saker	1,500	7	3 1/2	5
Demiculverin	3,000	10	4 1/2	9
Bastard Culverin	3,000	8 1/2	4 1/2	11
Culverin	4,000	11	5 1/2	18
Demi-Cannon	5,000	9	6 1/2	30
Cannon	7,000	12	8	60

With the exception of the Lombards, which went out of use near the end of the 16th century, the cannon described above remained in use until the beginning of the 19th century, when Carronades replaced most of the larger cannon on Spanish ships.

Spaniards apparently had a sufficient supply of bronze cannon in 1599 when all 12 galleons in the *Tierra Firme* armada carried only bronze cannon along with the *Capitañas* and *Almirantas* of both flotas. In 1605 a royal order stated that all treasure galleons and the *Capitañas* and *Almirantas* of the flotas must carry only bronze cannon, and that all merchantmen must carry a minimum of two bronze pieces. By 1644, however, only the two main flagships of the *Tierra Firme* armada carried only bronze cannon, while the other galleons carried but a few. All of the merchantmen sailing that year carried only iron cannon. In a fleet made up of 11 ships sailing to the New World in 1680, only 16 of the 467 cannon were bronze. And, in 1715 all cannon on the 12 ships returning to Spain were iron; and again on the 21 ships returning to Spain in 1733, with the exception of several small-caliber pieces.

Principal cannon carried on English ships during the 17th century are given in the following chart:

17th-Century English Cannon

Name	Weight (Lbs)	Length (Ft)	Caliber (Ins)	ShotWeight (Lbs)
Robinet	120	3	1 1/4	3/4
Falconet	210	4	2	1 1/4
Falcon	700	6	2 3/4	2 1/4
Minion	1,500	8	3	4
Saker	2,500	9 1/2	3 1/2	5 1/4
Demiculverin	3,600	10	4 1/2	9
Culverin	4,000	11	5	15
Demi-Cannon	6,000	12	6	27
Cannon	7,000	10	7	47
Cannon Royal	8,000	8	8	63

Of the above-mentioned English-made cannon, the Robinet, Falconet, Falcon, Minion, Saker, Demiculverin and Culverin were generally made of bronze. The different types and sizes of Cannon were generally made of iron.

A new type of cannon called the Carronade was introduced on English ships in 1779. Easily recognizable from those of earlier years because of its large-bore diameter and short length of only three to six feet, these pieces fired balls weighing 9, 12, 24, 32, 42, and 68 pounds. Those made before 1800 had low trunnions, and after 1800 the trunnions were centered. After 1825, however, many of them had no trunnions but were mounted with lugs on the gun carriages. From 1800 onward the Carronade replaced most of the large-caliber cannon carried on ships of all nations.

The number and types of cannon carried on English merchantmen depended on the size of the ship and their availability, as cannon were scarce in England. This also applied to English warships until about the middle of the 17th century, when the admiralty issued an order specifying the number and types of cannon that must be carried on their ships.

In 1762 a first-rater of 100 cannon carried thirty 42-pounders, twenty-eight 24-pounders, thirty-two 12-pounders, ten 8-pounders, and two 6-pounders. A second-rater of 90 cannon carried twenty-six 32-pounders, 18-pounders and 12-pounders, ten 8 pounders, and two 6-pounders. A third-rater of 74 cannon carried twenty-eight 32-pounders, thirty 24-pounders, fourteen 9-pounders, and two 6-pounders. A fourth-rater of 50 cannon carried twenty-two 24-pounders and 12-pounders, and six 6-pounders. A fifth-rater of 36 cannon carried twenty-six 12-pounders and ten 6-pounders. A sixth-rater of 28 cannon carried twenty-four 9-pounders and four 6-pounders.

The principal cannon carried on English ships during the 18th century, until the introduction of the Carronndes, are given below with their average weights and measurements.

18th-Century English Cannon

Name	Weight (Lbs)	Length (Ft)	Caliber (Ins)	Shot Weight (Lbs)
Robinet	150	3 1/2	1 3/4	1/2
Falconet	700	4 1/2	3	3
Falcon	800	6	3 1/4	4
Minion	2,000	7 1/2	3 3/4	6
Demiculverin	2,600	8	4 1/2	9
Culverin	3,200	9	4 1/2	12
18-Pound Cannon	3,900	9	5 1/3	18
24-Pound Cannon	4,600	9	5 4/5	24
32-Pound Cannon	5,500	9 1/2	6 1/2	32
42-Pound Cannon	6,500	10	7	42

Cannon on French Ships

French cannon were very similar in size, shape and weight to the English cannon, but were more lavishly marked with decorations, especially those cast in bronze. The number and types carried on their merchantmen and warships varied greatly until 1643, when the king issued an order concerning the armament on all French ships. Merchantmen sailing to the New World were required to carry the following number and sizes: a ship between 200 and 300 tons must carry six Demiculverins of 2,400-pound weight, 12 Sakers of l,600-pound weight, two Minions of 1,000-pound weight, one Falconet of 300-pound weight and one Robinet of 200-pound weight. Larger ships had to carry the smaller number and sizes of cannon, with the exception of the number and weight of the Demiculverins, which increased with the size of the ship. A 300-ton vessel carried nine Demiculverins of 3,000-pound weight, a 500-ton ship carried 16 Demiculverins of 3,200-pound weight, and a 700-ton ship carried 22 Demiculverins of the same weight.

All first and second-raters were required to carry only bronze cannon, and all smaller French warships were required to have one-quarter of their cannons made of bronze with the remainder of iron. Dutch cannon were also very similar to the English and French. They used bronze cannon almost exclusively on their ships, including the majority of their large merchantmen. Portuguese cannon differed vastly in shape from any of the others manufactured m Europe, and many of those carried on Portuguese ships were actually manufactured in India or other Portuguese possessions in the Far East.

The basic cannon projectile was the round shot, generally made of iron, but sometimes of stone or lead. The size of the shot used for each cannon was one-quarter inch smaller in diameter than the caliber of the piece. Because there was no difference in the appearance of the round shot made by all the countries, the only information that can be obtained from them establishes the caliber of

This bronze cannon from a New World shipwreck bears the royal coat of arms of Portugal and its date of manufacture, which was 1704.

the cannon carried on the shipwreck in the event that the cannon had been previously salvaged.

The following table the average weight of iron round shot in relation to its size:

Round Cannon Shot

Diameter (Inches)	Weight (Lbs & Ozs)	Diameter (Inches)	Weight (Lbs & Ozs)
2	1 & 2	5 1/4	20 & 1
2 1/4	1 & 9	5 1/2	23 & 2
2 1/2	2 & 2	5 3/4	26 & 6
2 3/4	2 & 14	6	30
3	3 & 12	6 1/4	34
3 1/4	4 & 12	6 1/2	38
3 1/2	6 & 1	6 3/4	42
3 3/4	7 & 5	7	48
4	8 & 5	7 1/4	53
4 1/4	10 & 10	7 1/2	58
4 1/2	12 & 10	7 3/4	64
4 3/4	14 & 14	8	71
5	17 & 5	8 1/4	78

Bar shot and chain shot were used primarily during sea battles to destroy the sails and rigging of enemy vessels. The first mention of bar shot was by the Dutch in 1619. Some bar shot was made by attaching an iron bar measuring six to 12 inches in length between two round shot. Other types were made with two halves of a round shot and some with round disks. Chain shot was introduced by the Dutch in 1666, with a chain replacing the iron bar of the bar shot.

Cannonballs, such as this coral-encrusted specimen that has just been salvaged by a happy diver, can provide valuable clues to help in dating a wreck.

333

Two types of antipersonnel shot were also used, grape shot and canister, sometimes called case shot. The earliest mention of grape shot was in 1556 aboard English ships. It consisted of 20 to 50 small cast-iron balls of one to two-inches in diameter held in place between two or more wood or metal disks connected to a central rod. The balls were lashed to the frame with cords or leather and the cylindrical projectile was covered with canvas and coated with wax, paint or pitch. The diameter of the projectile depended on the caliber of the cannon; its height was between six and 12 inches. Canister shot, introduced by the French in 1745, consisted of a thin cylindrical metal can containing various- shaped objects, such as glass fragments, nails, tacks, musket balls or small pebbles.

Carcass shot was an incendiary projectile, consisting of a hollow cast iron ball filled with combustible materials. When fired, flames streamed out through small holes in the side of the ball. The period when this projectile first came into use is unknown, except that it was during the second half of the 17th century.

Carronade shot also consisted of a hollow cast-iron ball but did not contain any combustible material nor have holes in it.

Weapons of many different types were carried on all ships, and it is relatively simple to identify them and establish their date and place of manufacture from studying the many excellent books available on the subject.

Even passengers were required to carry at least one hand-held weapon on ships of every flag. Crossbows were used until the end of the 16th century, but generally only small numbers of these weapons were carried aboard ships, as the arquebus or harquebuses and the musket were considered better weapons. Matchlock harquebuses, introduced in the 14th century, generally five or six feet long, weighed as much as 60 pounds and fired an iron or lead ball ranging from half an inch to an inch in diameter. The firing mechanism was an S-shaped lever pivoted to the stock near its center and forked at its upper end to hold the match. Pressing the lower end of the lever forced the match down into the flashpan, igniting the primer.

The disadvantage in using this weapon was the necessity of keeping the match lit or having the means to light it when needed. In 1517 a German invented the wheel lock with only two main parts to replace the matchlock. A steel-tooth wheel was wound up by a key to tighten a spring. By pulling the trigger, the wheel, which contained a lump of pyrite or a flint, struck the firing pan and ignited the primer. Another improvement on the firing mechanism was introduced around the end of the 16th century when the flintlock superseded the wheel lock.

In the flintlock a piece of flint held in the jaws of the cock was released by pulling the trigger of the weapon, which struck against a piece of steel, sending a shower of sparks into the priming powder pan. The flintlock remained in continuous use on all firearms until about 1820, when it was replaced by the percussion lock. Although it was invented near the end of the 16th century, some nations did not use the flintlock for many years. In France it was not used on a large scale until 1670.

Muskets, introduced in 1521, were the largest guns fired by a single man. Some were as long as ten feet and weighed over 100 pounds. A musket, because of its size and heavy recoil, had to be supported by a rest. The average size of the ball was one inch in diameter. They gradually decreased in size, and by 1690 the average musket was about five feet in length. From about 1700 onward the name "musket" was used to identify any type of firearm shot from the shoulder.

Carbines were introduced by the English during the second half of the 16th century. Similar in appearance to a musket, they were much smaller and fired a lead ball weighing less than an ounce. Pistols were first used in England in 1521 and in most other European countries soon afterward. Actually a smaller version of the harquebus, they were lighter and easier to handle, primarily invented for use by men on horseback who had only one free hand. By the middle of the 16th century they were standard equipment for all officers aboard ships. The firing mechanisms on muskets, carbines and pistols changed at the same time as those of the harquebuses.

Full suits of armor were not used aboard ships during the period covered in this book. Armored breast plates and helmets were used until the end of the sixteenth century. Archaic weapons still in use and found on some shipwrecks include boarding axes, pikes, lances and shields.

Swords, daggers, rapiers and poniards were worn by all the officers and wealthy passengers aboard ship, and many of these weapons have been discovered on shipwrecks. Cutlasses were used by the seamen and marines during battles from about the middle of the 16th century onward. Bayonets were introduced by the Spaniards in 1580, but not adopted by the French until 1647 and the English until 1690. Hand grenades were used on ships as early as 1467 and remained in use until the middle of the 19th century. They were made in many forms, but were usually round, made of various metals, glass, or ceramic and filled with gunpowder. A small hole held a fuse which was lit before the grenade was thrown.

Cleaning/Preserving

Recently a sport diver called to tell me he had discovered a shipwreck in the Bahamas and wanted me to assist him in identifying the wreck. After I asked him if he had recovered anything, he told me that he had brought up 10 silver coins and destroyed them by placing them in battery acid to remove corrosion. I groaned, for I've heard this story far too many times.

Many divers have destroyed treasure and unique artifacts in misguided efforts at cleaning and preservation. They use a sledge hammer to remove coral encrustation, or leave ancient bottles lying exposed to the air. Within a short time they have deteriorated beyond belief. A rule of thumb is to treat everything you recover from a wreck site as if it were a bottle of nitroglycerine. Bring the object up gently then place it in a bath of salt or fresh water, and *never let it dry out in the sun.* Even large objects such as iron cannon begin to disintegrate quickly when left exposed to the air.

Proper preservation is one of the weakest aspects of shipwreck exploration for both commercial salvors and archaeologists. There are fewer than 100 persons working worldwide in this specialized field, and there very few facilities where the work is done. Since most preservation and conservation laboratories in the United States are controlled by bureaucratic and academic archaeologists, treasure salvors usually have very limited access. The Florida Research and Conservation Laboratory established in 1967 has done most of the preservation work on artifacts recovered from salvors working in Florida waters.

Mel Fisher and Barry Clifford set up their own preservation laboratories where technicians developed new methods for cleaning and preserving artifacts. A number of foreign governments have sent people to train with them.

The *Vasa* project has been the most ambitious restoration program thus far attempted in this field. When the *Vasa* was raised in 1961, there were no conventional techniques available to preserve such an enormous ship and the hundreds of thousands of artifacts found in her. Preserving this ship became a proving ground in which most of the preservation methods used today were developed. Unfortunately, preservation of the ship itself has proved a dismal failure. Now three and a half centuries after she sank and almost three decades since she was brought to the surface, this 64-gun flagship is in serious trouble again. As soon as the *Vasa* was brought up, the oak hull was impregnated with polyethylene glycol (PEG) to keep the wood from shrinking as it dried. It now appears that the PEG was not applied properly and a great deal of the hull is deteriorating. Experts fear that the *Vasa*, one of Sweden's major tourist attractions, will be lost if a solution isn't found quickly. The English preservation experts charged with restoring the *Mary Rose* face a similar dilemma.

Even smaller objects preserved by experts over the years are now in deplorable states of deterioration today. Several small iron cannon found at Port Royal were turned over to the Conservation Laboratory of the Smithsonian Institution. After months of electrolytic reduction they were encased in blocks of clear fiberglass. Today only iron fragments and dust-like particles can be seen in their plastic tombs.

Preservation techniques are constantly improving, but far more research is necessary before there will be any certainty that something preserved today will last forever, or even 50 years. Although I will set forth the best and

338

latest methods for a wreck salvor to clean and preserve his finds, I strongly recommend, whenever possible, seeking the services of a preservation expert.

You may find this difficult since most preservation laboratories in universities or government agencies will handle only materials from projects in which they are directly involved. Since 1987 a commercial firm, International Artifact Conservation and Research Laboratory, Inc., of Belle Chasse, LA, (504-394-0341) has served both the private and public sectors. Their staff has extensive experience in the stabilization and conservation of both metallic and organic artifacts and uses the most current methods currently available. They have developed a number of new techniques far superior to any others available throughout the world.

Some items discovered on a shipwreck, such as gold and porcelain, do not corrode or deteriorate from their long underwater immersion and are recovered in a perfect or near perfect state of preservation. At worst they may suffer from sand abrasion in the case of glazed porcelain or minimal coral adhesions on gold. On the other hand, the majority of items to be discovered will have deteriorated in varying degrees. The purpose of this chapter is to acquaint the salvor with methods of protection after objects are recovered that will halt this deterioration and then aid in restoring and preserving them for posterity.

Most organic items like wood come under immediate attack from the teredo, fungi and different bacteria. The more these items are exposed to salt water, the more they suffer, and the quicker some of them disappear. Many of the same objects, when buried deep under sediment, will suffer less, or not at all, and on occasion can be discovered in an excellent state of preservation.

Of the various types of metals lost on a shipwreck, iron and silver suffer the most, principally from the effects of electrolysis under water. Different types of metal and salt water interact as a gigantic galvanic battery. With the salt

339

water forming the electrolyte, metals of two or more different molecular weights become opposite poles with a current of electrons flowing between. The galvanic current between the different metals will attack the metal with the highest electrode potential, converting that metal to one of its compounds. Silver converts to silver sulfide and iron to iron oxide. Cathodic protection preserves metals with the lowest electrode potential. The effects of electrolysis upon different metals occur when they are either exposed to sea water or buried under sediment on the sea floor.

Classes of Recoverable Items

Items recovered from the sea can be divided into three distinct classes:

— Those recovered in their original condition, like gold, that require no treatment at all, or only a brief immersion in fresh water to remove the salts on their exterior surfaces;

— Those that have suffered marked physical and chemical changes and can be preserved by different methods;

— Those that have suffered to such a degree that they cannot be restored to their original state. In this case, what remains of the original object can be saved by completely embedding it in plastic. In some cases nothing will remain of the original object other than a hollow form inside a coral-encrusted conglomerate, which can be recorded through x-ray photography or by making a replica of it by using the hollow form as a mold.

Any shipwreck artifact that requires preservation should be exposed to air as little as possible and must be kept wet, preferably in salt water. Since water is heavy-- and, large amounts of it are very heavy--immersion is not always practical for large objects, or when there is a great deal of material. An item can be wrapped in plastic wrap or placed in an airtight plastic bag or container. Large items are best transported from the salvage vessel to a preservation laboratory in wooden barrels or boxes containing moist sawdust.

Hard gem stones such as sapphires, rubies, emeralds and some semi-precious stones like agate do not suffer from immersion in sea water and are recovered in their natural state. Softer stones such as beryl are sometimes found scratched, due to the abrasive action of sand and other materials moving against them under water, and these scratches should be removed only by lapidary treatment.

Glass is affected in varying degrees, depending on its composition. Optical glass generally survives in a good state of preservation but is occasionally found pitted on its exterior. White-lead glass objects, such as plate glass, wine glasses, tumblers and pharmaceutical vials or medicine bottles are generally found free of calcareous deposits...though most will be covered with a thin coating of lead oxide...sometimes iron oxide when discovered in close association with iron objects.

To clean and preserve these items the following method should be used. Place the item in a 10% solution of nitric acid for the time required to remove the lead oxide. If iron oxide is present, use a 5% solution of sulfuric acid to remove the oxide, then follow through with several thorough washings in distilled water. If, after drying, the item shows signs of flaking on its exterior, it should be coated with several layers of clear plastic spray, such as Krylon.

As a rule, most bottles postdating 1750 require very little preservation. Sediment inside the bottle can be removed with careful use of a high-pressure hose or various types of tools, such as a wire or an icepick. Exterior calcareous growth can be removed by tapping gently on the bottle with a rubber mallet or by immersion in a bath consisting of 0.2% solution of sulfuric acid for several hours or as long as a week, depending on the amount of growth on it. The bottle must then be thoroughly washed in several baths of fresh water, or distilled water when available, until the glass is free of alkalis. The litmus-paper test is the best way to determine if the glass is free of alkalis. Upon drying, the surface of some bottles may tend to look dull or to develop a very thin layer of pearly iridescence in spots. No further treatment is necessary, although the iridescence, if especially fragile, may tend to flake off.

Preservation of badly decomposed glass, which is the state of most bottles predating 1750, is difficult. If the glass is not impregnated in some way, it is very likely that the exterior weathering crust will crumble away when it dries out. This may be a matter of minutes or of some months, depending on the item itself. This was one of the major preservation problems encountered during the Port Royal excavation. In consultation with Dr. Robert Brill of the Corning Glass Museum, I attempted to discover why wine bottles were recovered in a worse state of preservation than others of the same manufacture and period that were found elsewhere. The weathering crust on those at Port Royal was thicker than on other bottles of the same period, and this made them more difficult to preserve. He theorized that the heavy concentration of bauxite in the harbor sediment was the major cause. It may have created electrolysis with the lead components in the glass, causing the greater amount of deterioration.

Most bottles predating 1750 can be cleaned and preserved in the following manner. A 0.2% solution of sulfuric acid will remove the calcareous growth and stains. Depending on the fragility of the bottle, a high-pressure hose or probe can be used to remove the sediment inside the bottle. Then it must be thoroughly rinsed in distilled water until free of all alkalis. Then, without letting the bottle dry completely, it must be bathed in alcohol (wood, denatured ethyl or rubbing), which tends to remove the remaining water without causing the decomposition crust to crumble away. Then it must be air-dried for a short period and finally impregnated with several coatings of clear spray lacquers.

Through experimentation I discovered that this method did not preserve the more badly decomposed bottles, such as those recovered at Port Royal. After several months the glass began flaking under the lacquer coatings, and in many cases the bottles completely disintegrated, To prevent this, we followed the same procedure as described above, except that instead of coating the bottles with lacquer we immersed them for a week or two in a solution consisting of 50% distilled water and 50% vinyl acetate, the same material used in making the glue for bookbinding (it is marketed as padding cement). After removing the bottle, we wiped off the excess solution with a slightly damp cloth, then air-dried it in a cool area. After it was completely dried, we coated the glass with several layers of lacquer.

For mending or piecing together broken glass or bottles, there are any number of convenient epoxy cements

This chart shows the location where a treasure was buried on Anegada Island in the British Virgin Islands after it was taken from a Spanish galleon lost off this point in 1738.

343

that can be used...and, always remember that a small amount of cement works better than a large amount. The most important step in cementing glass is the cleaning of surfaces to be joined. Be careful to cement the glass correctly the first time! Once the cement sets, the bonds are permanent and cannot be loosened.

Effects on Ceramics

Different types of ceramics are affected in varying degrees by immersion in salt water. Porcelain survives the best, although its glazed exterior may have eroded. Because of its nonporous surface, porcelain is rarely found with any calcareous marine growth adhering to it. When there is growth on it, however, it can be removed by gentle tapping with a rubber tool or by bathing it in a 10% solution of nitric acid. Iron or lead-oxide stains can be removed by a bath in a 5% solution of sulfuric acid. When calcareous deposits and oxides stains are on porcelain, a sulfuric-acid bath will remove both. Thorough washing in fresh water will remove all traces of alkalis from the acids.

Glazed pottery with its waterproof vitreous layer survives much better than unglazed pottery. If the glazed layer is incomplete or imperfect, however, soluble salts may have gotten into the body of the ware and crystallized, forming efflorescence, and the glaze may flake off. If the glazed layer on the piece is intact, methods used on porcelain to remove calcareous deposits and oxide stains can be used. If the glaze is not intact, or is flaking, which occur with many delftware items, no acid should be used to remove deposits or stains. The pieces should be thoroughly bathed in fresh water to remove sea salts, then air-dried and coated with several layers of clear plastic or lacquer spray.

No acid of any type should be used on unglazed porous pottery, such as utilityware or olive-jar pottery. Calcareous deposits must be removed with small tools, then the pieces bathed for several days in several baths of fresh water to remove sea salts. To assure that these pieces are free of water, they must be dehydrated in several baths of alcohol and then coated with plastic spray. This treatment should be used only on ceramic objects that show signs of crumbling. Approximately 95% of ceramic pieces will require no treatment other than a freshwater bath to remove sea salts.

Nature will remove calcareous deposits from clay smoking pipes. After recovery they should be air-dried, which actually decreases the pipe slightly in size, causing calcareous deposits to fall off on their own. The removal of various stains on the pipes is best accomplished by washing with a mild detergent and soft brush.

Repairing or piecing together all types of ceramics is relatively simple. The joints must be first cleaned of any foreign bodies and then cemented together with Durofix or Elmer's Glue. While the glue is drying the pieces should be held in place by tape or placed in a sandbox.

All organic material recovered from salt water must be bathed in fresh water from two to four weeks, depending on its size, to remove all sea salts before preservation treatment can be attempted. If possible, the bath should consist of running water, which will flush away the sea salts as they are leached from the objects. Large items, like wooden ship's timbers, can be placed in a freshwater stream or river, provided the water is not contaminated by industrial waste. If a running-water bath cannot be provided, water should be changed at least daily.

Such organic materials as sisal or hemp fibers, beans and pods, tortoise shell, hair, textiles, leather, horn, bone or paper will generally disintegrate upon drying if the proper preservation treatment is not exercised. Sometimes organic materials such as wood or bone are completely preserved by a saturation of iron oxide which occurred while they were lying close to iron objects under water. They tend to become mineralized and hard in texture.

345

To preserve organic animal materials they must first be thoroughly dehydrated in successive baths of alcohol to remove all water. The first bath should consist of 40% alcohol and 60% water, the second of 60% alcohol and 40% water, and the third of 100% alcohol. The length of each bath depends on the size of the object...say, an hour for a small fragment of leather and several hours for a bone object weighing several pounds. Then the object must be placed in two successive baths of xylene, the first for a week and the second for four weeks. In the second bath paraffin chips should be added until a saturated solution of paraffin is obtained. After the object is removed from the second bath and allowed to solidify by air-drying, a small amount of paraffin crystals may remain on its exterior. These can be removed by heating the object in an oven until the excess crystals melt off or by brushing the object with a fine-bristle brush.

Very fragile organic animal materials, such as small objects of ivory or horn, which might suffer from treatment in the above manner, can be preserved by embedding them in clear plastic blocks after they have been dehydrated.

Organic vegetable materials such as wood, sisal and hemp fibers, textiles, paper, and beans and pods can also be preserved by the method described above for organic animal materials, but there are several other methods that can be used. The alum and glycerine process has been used with good results--especially on wood--because the alum crystallizes and replaces water in the wood, preventing it from shrinking or losing its original shape.

After all foreign matter has been removed from the object, it is immersed in a boiling solution containing equal parts, by weight, of alum, glycerine and water. As soon as the object is placed in the bath it is removed from its heat source and allowed to cool slowly. The object should remain in this bath from one to two days, depending on its size. After the object has hardened and air-dried, it should be coated with a solution of 50% turpentine and 50% linseed oil.

The polyethylene glycol process has also proven to be quite successful. The great advantage in using this process is the elimination of dehydrating the object before it is immersed in its chemical bath. Preservatives are sold commercially under the trade names of Polywax and Carbowax. Polyethylene glycol is a polymer formed by the condensation of ethylene glycol into a waxlike water-soluble preservative. The length of time that the object must remain in the chemical bath varies from four hours to several weeks, depending on the type of Polywax or Carbowax used and the size of the object.

Approximately 95% of all metal objects discovered on a shipwreck consist of iron, whose highly corrodible nature presents some of the most challenging problems for preservation. In many cases cast-iron objects corrode into a crystalline form and are so totally destroyed that only powdered oxide remains. Wrought iron objects are not as prone to corrosion, probably because they have a greater nickel content. The same applies to steel, which has a high nickel content. The amount of metal remaining in an object can best be determined by its weight or by testing with a magnet. If the object has no magnetic attraction, it is completely oxidized. When laboratory facilities are available, this can also be determined by the use of x-ray photography or a fluoroscope.

The first step in the treatment of ferrous metals--iron or steel--is removal of the exterior calcareous encrustations, which can be attempted only when a substantial amount of the original metal remains in the object. These deposits can best be removed on large objects like a cannon by tapping gently with a hammer or other hand tool. Small, delicate objects can be cleaned in ultrasonic electrical baths or chemically. Ultrasonic baths range in price from $100 upward and are easy to operate.

The chemical process consists of a bath in a solution of

10% nitric acid and 90% water, with several washes in fresh water to remove the alkalis. The object must then be treated by electrochemical reduction. It is placed in a bath consisting of 10% sodium hydroxide and 90% water and soaked for a period of four to eight weeks. The object is then removed and reimmersed in a new bath of the same solution, following which the entire object is covered with zinc chips or surrounded by zinc plates. Soon after the zinc is added to the bath the solution will begin to bubble, and this will continue throughout the two to four weeks the object is kept in the bath. Upon removal the object will be covered with a white coating, which can be removed by placing the it in another bath consisting of 5% sulfuric acid and 95% fresh water.

The next step is placing the object in a running-water bath for at least a week, then in a bath of distilled water for another week. The bath should be tested to make sure that it is free of both alkalis and chlorides. If it is not free of these elements, then more baths in distilled water are required until there are no traces. The object is then dried, preferably in a high-temperature After drying it can be coated with paraffin wax or a clear synthetic plastic or lacquer to seal its exterior and prevent further corrosion.

When little or nothing remains of the original ferrous material, an item can be treated by one of the following two methods. The object can be embedded in a plastic resin, such as Selectron 5,000. The object must first be thoroughly dehydrated, either by heat or the alcohol process, otherwise it will continue to disintegrate inside the plastic blocks. This can be a lengthy process if the mass is large, as only very thin layers of the plastic can be placed in the mold containing the object.

Finding treasure beneath the sea is but the first part of an adventure which must continue in such areas as these salvors removing coral encrustation from Spanish cannon.

An exact plaster replica of the object can be made. By x-raying the object, its size and location in the encrusted conglomerate can be determined, then the conglomerate must be cut in half by a diamond saw. The two halves will be hollow inside where the original object was and will serve as the mold into which the plaster is placed to make the replica. Another method is to drill a hole into the conglomerate and force the plaster compound into the cavity of the conglomerate. After hardening, the exterior encrustation can be removed by grinding or hand tools.

Nonferrous metals are always recovered in a far better state of preservation than ferrous and are usually easier to clean and preserve. Some of the metals are recovered in such condition that they require no treatment other than cleaning with fine steel wool and water. Gold requires no preservation treatment...it is almost always recovered as bright and shiny as the day it was lost. Occasionally gold will be tarnished, because of close underwater association with other metals. Luster can be restored, however, by soaking the gold in a bath of 10% nitric acid and 90% water. The same bath should be used to remove any calcareous deposits on gold.

Silver is affected in varying degrees under water, depending on conditions. A silver coin on the sea floor not protected by electrolysis from other metals--even other silver coins--may be converted to silver sulfide. Nothing can be done to preserve it other than casting it in plastic. When this occurs to a coin or other small silver object, it will weigh as little as one-fifth of its original weight yet may be two or three times its original thickness. Caution must be exercised in handling silver in this fragile condition. It will easily disintegrate into powder.

Old coins from shipwrecks can be very valuable, such as this rare Dutch gold piece, dated 1646 and found in Brazil, which sells for over $20,000.

When silver has been protected by electrolysis, it will survive intact, sometimes with only a superficial amount of corrosion, which can be removed by different methods. This can be accomplished by the electrochemical bath used for preserving the ferrous metals. Another method for cleaning silver is the electrolytic reduction process. The semi-corroded silver object is made the negative electrode (cathode) and is placed between two plates of sheet iron (acting as the positive electrode, or anode) in a glass or plastic container filled with a 5% solution of caustic soda, which acts as the electrolyte. Electrical current (a 6v or 12v battery) is also required. The object is connected by copper wire to the negative pole of the battery, and the iron anodes are connected to the positive pole through an ammeter and adjustable resistance unit.

When current passes into the bath, hydrogen is produced at the cathode, with the result that corrosion is gradually reduced. As the reduction progresses, chlorides are transferred from the cathode to the iron anode. The length of the process depends on the amount of corrosion on the item. The object should be removed and inspected periodically until all corrosion has been removed. When this has been completed, there will be a thin layer of insoluble oxides and metallic powder on the object which can be removed by gentle brushing under running water. Finally, the silver object should be rubbed with a paste of baking soda and water.

For cleaning and preserving large batches of silver coins (for example, 1,000 at a time) I found a better method than the electrolytic reduction process. I first wash the coins in a 12% solution of commercial hydrochloric acid and tap water for a 24 hours to remove all coral and other corrosion. For badly deteriorated "biscuit-type" coins I first remove the inactive corrosion layer using a dental tool and then place them in the acid solution for an hour. Next the coins are washed in several baths of tap water to remove all traces of the acid.

I then place the coins in a large, heavy-duty plastic container with 20 quarts of tap water, three pounds of sodium dithionite and 800 grams of caustic soda and let it soak for a week. Several times each day I shake the container for a few minutes to mix the chemical solution. At the end of a week several more washings in tap water are required. The coins will still look black and must be shined. Again a paste of water and baking soda will do the trick, and I usually follow up with a gentle polishing with quality silver polish. Since sodium dithionite is an inflammable substance and also very toxic to breathe, use it with caution.

When large amounts of silver coins or items are found together, the majority will often be in a very good state of preservation and require no more than cleaning by the paste method to remove the black silver-sulfide patina on them. Pewter is generally found in a good state of preservation. Of the pewter recovered from the sunken city of Port Royal, about 20% required very little treatment. Rubbing pewterware with a soft cloth in water and a mild detergent removed a thin black film from its surface and the luster was restored by the paste treatment. The remaining 80% were recovered with only a small amount of external corrosion and occasionally with small amounts of calcareous deposits. Both were removed by immersion in a bath consisting of a solution of 20% hydrochloric acid and 80% fresh water followed by thorough washings in running fresh water, generally for a period of several hours. Then the surface was rubbed gently with fine steel wool to remove the black patina and again placed in a bath of running water for several hours. The same paste treatment is used to restore its original luster.

On some sites, pewter is occasionally found badly corroded. In some cases the only means of preservation is embedding it in plastic. Badly corroded pewter can be cleaned and preserved in the following method. A lye bath is prepared by dissolving a pint of lye in two gallons of boiling fresh water. When the object is placed in the bath, it is removed from the heat source and allowed to cool. Generally, a period of 10 to 30 minutes is required to remove the corrosion. Caution must be observed to prevent the lye solution from contact with skin or eyes. The same procedure is then carried out as on the pewter objects cleaned by the hydrochloric-acid process. If the object is bent out of its original shape, the best time to restore it is when it is taken out of the lye bath. The metal will be warm and easily shaped which is generally done with a rubber mallet.

Lead objects suffer very little from long immersion in the sea...other than accumulating a thin coating of lead oxide on their surfaces, which is easily removed in a bath of 10% acetic acid and 90% fresh water followed by a running-water bath for several hours. Softness of this metal results in many pieces being bent and losing their original shape in the shipwreck.

Copper, brass and bronze objects are also little affected by saltwater immersion. Calcareous deposits on large objects can be removed by tapping with a rubber mallet and on smaller objects by immersion in a bath consisting of 10% nitric acid and 90% fresh water, followed by washing for a short time in running water. The acid bath is used to remove any green patina found on these objects, but this can also be accomplished with discreet use of steel wool. Since objects made entirely of magnesium, tin, aluminum, zinc or nickel will not be discovered on a shipwreck predating 1825, discussion of their preservation would not be pertinent.

Wreck Diving Politics

By now, any archaeologist who has read this far will probably be sticking pins in a Bob Marx doll!

When I began working in underwater archaeology, not only were there no resource people for me to learn from, there were few regulations regarding underwater sites. Just as thousands of people in this country living in homes built a century or even 200 years ago can do what they please with their dwellings and just as millions of Americans can buy, sell, trade or do what they will with antiques...underwater explorers interested in shipwrecks were left alone--in the American way--to pursue their work. Those who found artifacts on old wreck sites appreciated and enjoyed them...just as the owners of old homes and antiques care for their things. Museums throughout this country and abroad today display proof of the generosity of those underwater pioneers who found artifacts and shared them. Unfortunately, however, today's climate has altered radically for the underwater explorer who now faces crippling restrictions.

Lets face it. Do shipwrecks belong to a handful of purist archaeologists who spend an undue amount of time trying to prevent others from exploring, yet do virtually nothing themselves in the field of underwater archaeology? Or, do they belong to the American public and the millions of divers who want to explore these relics of the past and perhaps recover an object to furnish them years of enjoyment? This debate has been raging for years and not even passage of the Shipwreck Law two years ago has resolved the issue.

To understand the situation let me explain that at present there are over three and a half million certified scuba divers in the United States. Each year between three and four hundred thousand more join the ranks. During testimony before Congress in 1985, Robert L. Gray, the Executive Director of DEMA, stated that *41.3% of this number participate in wreck diving activities.* A subsequent survey made by PADI showed this number had increased to 53.8%. A recent survey by *Skin Diver* magazine, which has worked to protect diver's rights, found that during a one-year period over 40% of divers taking vacations were involved in wreck diving.

There is no doubt that wreck diving is today's most popular underwater activity. Yet, a mere handful of desk-bound bureaucrats and archaeologists, many of whom have never dived on a shipwreck, are obsessed with keeping everyone off all shipwrecks. Unfortunately, some of them have considerable influence in formulating laws that affect the rights of divers and shipwrecks. One archaeologist in the limelight quite often has stated on numerous occasions that no one should be permitted to work on a shipwreck unless he has a PhD degree!

The irony of this is that there are fewer than a half dozen people in this country working in underwater archaeology who have PhD's (some of which are not even in archaeology), and most of them teach in universities. They have only their summer vacations to spend under-water…usually at taxpayers expense and without much to show for their endeavors. While these PhD's collect salaries from universities and museums, they are making statements such as "no one should make money from archaeology or shipwrecks." They find it somehow immoral that anyone should profit from a shipwreck.

I heartily disagree with this philosophy.

This is not a case of sour grapes. I have been an under-water archaeologist for most of my professional life. I still consider it a very important science and will continue working in this field to the end of my days. But, my feelings about how underwater sites should be dealt with and who is capable of making contributions in this field run counter to what many of the so-called experts believe. In 1959 I was one of the original founders of the Council of Underwater Archaeology. I was on the CUA's board of advisors from that time (although I threatened to resign just about every year) until two years ago when I finally realized it was a lost cause and nothing I could do or say would change the fossilized attitudes that prevailed.

One of the main functions of the CUA when it was founded was to serve as a clearing house for information on all aspects of shipwreck work. However, my 12 associates on the advisory board interpreted this to mean that we could only share information *among ourselves.* Any association with treasure hunters or sport divers was considered a breach of professional ethics.

During the last CUA meeting I attended, I proposed

Old prints such as this whet the appetite and stir the imagination of countless sportsmen and women who believe they have the skills to participate in this exciting episode in history.

establishing an information clearing house and offered to fund it for the first year. My proposal was defeated by the majority who felt that this would just result in the plunder of shipwrecks by furnishing information to sport divers and treasure hunters. Yet, treasure hunters and sport divers are making most of the underwater discoveries. *Why not work with them?* Let's try to use all of the valuable data they can provide. Why not have projects allowing sport divers to work in fruitful association with archaeologists and other specialists to maximize contributions to underwater archaeology?

Currently so much valuable archaeological and historical information is being lost forever because of the distorted views of a handful of inflexible individuals who might be surprised to discover how productive and positive such a relationship could be. During this same CUA meeting a resolution was passed which was later adapted by SAMM (the Society of American Maritime Museums) that no object(s) recovered from the sea would be either accepted as donation(s) or bought by any museum unless recovered not only by a qualified underwater archaeologist but by one working on a non-profit expedition. They refused to consider that precious little has been recovered from the sea by *any* underwater archaeologists when compared with all that treasure hunters and sports divers have brought up!

They also ignored the sad fact that there is virtually no funding available from governmental and philanthropic sources for such underwater projects, and the future doesn't look any more promising. If their policy were somehow made retroactive and applicable to archaeological materials from land as well as underwater, museums like the Metropolitan in New York would have to close the doors on their archaeological exhibits. Less than 2% of archaeological and historical materials displayed in United States' museums was recovered by "legitimate" archaeological expeditions. Even more startling, according to a recent article in *Connoisseur* magazine, "95% of the ancient art in all American museums was *smuggled* from other countries."

Not all underwater archaeologists feel the same way as the archaeologists and bureaucrats I've been criticizing. During recent Congressional testimony, one of them stated that there were 350 underwater archaeologists in the United States, but this was a gross exaggeration in more ways than one. What this person must have been referring to was the average number of persons who turned up at the annual Conference of Underwater Archaeology. The fact is that fewer than 50 of these people have any type of degree in archaeology. The rest are individuals who are simply showing their interest in the field, the largest number being sport divers and treasure hunters.

Have They Led An Expedition?

Of the 50 or so underwater archaeologists, fewer than a dozen have ever led an underwater archaeological expedition. Several of them--believe it or not--do not even know how to dive! The chairman of the Council of Underwater Archaeology during the first 10 years of its existence didn't even swim, let alone dive. The underwater experience of his successor, who did have a PhD, was limited to diving for prehistoric shark's teeth off Florida's beaches. A number of years ago during the annual Underwater Archaeology Conference, the head underwater archaeologist of the National Park Service was forced to resign when he admitted he had not been in the water in over seven years. It is difficult to understand how people with such rigid attitudes can try to make themselves the arbiters of shipwreck exploration.

Around that same time I witnessed an event that convinced me that these people were totally unqualified to assist Congress in passing a new Shipwreck Bill. I was invited along with about 30 archaeologists, museum directors and Federal bureaucrats to attend a three-day "think tank" session. The main objective was to come up with the language to be used in the new Shipwreck Law. Three main topics to be addressed were defining what underwater archaeology is, who should be considered qualified to work on shipwrecks and which shipwrecks have archaeological value.

The session was a great disappointment...a complete fiasco. After 30 hours of intensive debate, nothing was accomplished. Some participants went so far as to proclaim that a fishing boat, lost the day before, would have archaeological potential. Others said no one with less than a master's degree in archaeology should be permitted to dive on any type of shipwreck. We even had one purist who proposed that Congress pass a law prohibiting any diving, even by archaeologists, on any shipwreck for the next 100 years. When I mentioned that all shipwrecks are constantly deteriorating underwater and that hundreds of others are destroyed by nature and man each year, his response was, "It's better to let them be destroyed than fall into the hands of treasure hunters."

There is no reasoning with some of these fanatics.

Some of the purists try to get the attention of the press with their frequent ravings about treasure hunters and sport divers who plunder and destroy shipwrecks. They claim that treasure hunters are constantly using dynamite to tear apart shipwrecks. I find this infuriating because I have never seen nor heard of a single treasure hunter using explosives. On the other hand, I personally witnessed four underwater archaeologists use dynamite on shipwreck sites off Australia, England and France. When the "prop-washes" were first introduced as an excavation tool on shipwrecks, archaeologists screamed their heads off about shipwrecks being destroyed. Today almost every one of them uses this efficient method.

Another perennial archaeological "hot button" is the

question of disposing of treasure and artifacts recovered from the sea. Now that they have convinced maritime museums not to buy or accept donations of these artifacts, they simply want them left on the bottom. Sometimes they will go to extremes, as in the case of the recent discovery of the RMS *Titanic.*

After its discovery by Dr. Robert Ballard and a team of French oceanographers, the French team returned to recover an interesting array of artifacts and some gold coins and jewelry at great cost. Several of the bureaucrats and archaeologists were greatly upset at this and a law was pushed through Congress preventing these objects from entering the United States. I'm puzzled about what rights the United States government can possibly claim over a ship of non-American origin lost 450 miles offshore? This is the same nation that during our Bicentennial Celebration failed to come up with a single penny to support archaeologists who wanted to work on Revolutionary War shipwrecks! As far as the Federal government is concerned, underwater archaeology doesn't exist.

Yet 15 years ago under another administration a law was passed stipulating that before any work is done on the Continental Shelf, cultural impact studies must be made to ensure that no shipwrecks or sites of submerged habitations exist. This was a golden opportunity for some of the bureaucrats and archaeologists. They compiled a list of those they deemed qualified archaeologists to utilize magnetometers and sonar in supervising the cultural impact surveys What resulted, and still is going on, is scandalous.

To date, despite the fact that millions of square miles of the sea floor have been surveyed, they have not reported finding *one single shipwreck!* I myself have located any number of shipwrecks in zones they have searched without reportedly finding even the trace of a wreck. The Bureau of Land Management which oversees these surveys has refused, despite repeated attempts through the Freedom of Information Act, to let me inspect their records on these surveys. Worse still, I could not get a single archaeologist to back me in this fight. One must keep in mind that most of these bureaucrats work for the Federal government, and it's not easy for them to oppose Uncle Sam. How many shipwrecks and inundated prehistoric sites have been lost because of this outrage?

There is an even more depressing development that I have been fighting almost single-handedly for over a decade. While bureaucratic archaeologists around the world rant and rave about divers destroying shipwrecks, the same governments they work for are permitting obliteration of hundreds and possibly even thousands of shipwrecks by dredging, landfill operations and construction each year. Only public outcry can stop this wanton devastation.

Wrecks Have Disappeared

A vivid example is the destruction at Cadiz, the Spanish port city which has, or had, what was considered one of the most important underwater archaeological sites in the world. Cadiz has been a seaport in continuous use for about four thousand years. More than 2,500 ships have been lost in the surrounding waters. I first dove there in 1953 and later spent three years, 1960-62, surveying the waters. I located over 150 shipwrecks dating between 1200 B.C. and 1800 A.D. Soon after I left the area, dredging and landfill operations began and are continuing today. Five years ago I returned to find that over two-thirds of the wrecks I had located no longer exist. By the end of this century I doubt if a single old shipwreck will still lie in the waters of Cadiz...but one example of hundreds of seaports throughout the world that have suffered the same fate.

Yet, archaeologists can't--or won't--do anything about this depressing situation.

Similarly on this side of the Atlantic, take any major seaport in the United States and you'll find that almost every shipwreck that existed several decades ago is now either covered by landfill or has been chewed up by the hungry jaws of a dredging machine. After a recent lecture I gave on this topic, an archaeologist asked me what I was complaining about since there are still many other shipwrecks laying offshore. If he knew anything about shipwrecks, he would know that those best preserved lie in fresh water or buried in the mud of ports and harbors.

An example of how well a ship survives in fresh water came to light several years ago when the Mississippi and several other rivers were so low that hundreds of old shipwrecks were briefly exposed. Other shipwrecks had already been chewed up by dredges. And mud, as even a school boy knows, is mainly found in harbors where ships were once preserved for centuries.

So, we have the other shipwrecks offshore and they are protected...or, so the archaeologists want us to believe. But, are they really protected? Fishermen, for example, have been dragging nets over--and tearing apart--old wrecks for centuries, scattering valuable contents all over the sea floor.

Beach replenishment, however, is the main culprit. Somewhere between 95% and 98% of old ships did not sink on the high seas. In most cases they sailed close to shore because of faulty navigation or were flung there by the fury of storms. In Florida, for example, where more than 300 pre-Civil War shipwrecks have been discovered in the past 30 years, all but about 20 have been found within 50 yards of the beach. This is the very area where dredged sand is deposited in beach replenishment efforts, with the result that any shipwreck in the zone is destroyed. The guilty party in this case is the U.S. Corps of Army Engineers who issue dredging permits with total disregard for shipwrecks. Metal detector hobbyists have a great time picking up coins and other objects from these operations. Again the official shipwreck arbiters choose to ignore this decimation of our national heritage.

Recently on the *Good Morning America* television show there was a spirited debate between a man who

363

considers himself Mr. Archaeology, and Gregg Stemm, a Tampa wreck hunter. The archaeologist, who has been working on shipwrecks off Turkey for the past 20 years, argued zealously that shipwrecks should be left to archaeologists and that everything from a site should be kept together because it takes his team around 20 to 30 years to study the materials recovered from one wreck. If this is the case...with so few underwater archaeologists working in the field, *only a few shipwrecks can ever be excavated and studied.*

Some archaeologists state emphatically that everything found on a shipwreck site has archaeological value. Apparently all archaeologists don't feel the same. For example, I once brought up intact some 40 6th-century B.C. amphoras from a shipwreck in Cadiz Bay, only to watch the museum director to whom I took them, (an archaeologist, incidentally) smash all but two into small pieces with a hammer. He explained that he only needed two examples for study and display and that the others would just take up valuable space.

"Why not sell or give them away?" I asked. He replied that it was illegal to export antiquities from Spain and that ordinary people wouldn't appreciate them in any case.

I can certainly understand why there are some shipwrecks on which everything may have archaeological importance. But I totally disagree that this is the case on every shipwreck or that it has to take decades for these objects to be studied. A galleon, for instance, may produce tens of thousands of identical coins, or a merchant ship may be carrying thousands of identical pieces of cargo. From the wrecks of such vessels a representative selection of artifacts should be set aside for study. Future studies can also be carried out using computerized drawings, and photographs and the actual artifacts may not be essential. On important shipwrecks archaeologists should be employed to gather the pertinent data and select unique items for study and this could satisfy everyone concerned.

"Publish or perish" is the theme song of the academic world, and publishing reports on underwater archaeological surveys or excavations is no exception. The bureaucrats and their cohort archaeologists are constantly harping that valuable information is being lost by the shipwreck activities of treasure hunters and sports divers who write no reports. However, they spurn any information offered by wreck divers or sport divers and refuse to participate with them on joint projects. What's more, every major treasure hunting company currently employs qualified archaeologists. In some states and many nations shipwrecks can be excavated *only* under the supervision of an archaeologist. Yet we face a major problem. The archaeological establishment has branded archaeologists who work on treasure hunts or profit-making ventures as outcasts.

Efforts by Mathewsen

For several years the Council of Underwater Archaeology refused to permit Duncan Mathewsen, a qualified archaeologist who worked for years on the *Atocha* and *Margarita* projects, from presenting reports at their annual conventions. When he threatened to sue in court, they finally relented. Now they are using new tactics claiming that there is no space to put archaeologists on the programs at their conferences. To overcome this obstacle, Mathewsen and others like him privately publish their scientific reports.

The fact is that even members of the establishment have great difficulty in getting their reports published. And those papers published in the "Proceedings," issued after each annual conference of the CUA, are generally highly condensed and drastically edited. For example, five years ago at the annual meeting in Boston I presented a 42-page paper dealing with the history and identification of anchors. When published in the Proceedings, this report that offered much needed and sought after information was condensed to a mere page and a half!

So, who really benefits from the work of archaeologists? The goal of underwater archaeology should be to contribute to a growing body of knowledge. Underwater archaeologists ought to be committed to publishing their findings and sharing the knowledge they obtain from a particular project. But if only a small part--or, in many instances, nothing--is published, just *what is underwater archaeology all about?*

In the United States about 90% of all work on Colonial shipwrecks is accomplished in Florida waters, and the State of Florida has employed full-time archaeologists ever since they initiated their program in 1964. More than 100 exploration and 50 salvage permits have been issued with all of this work supervised by state archaeologists or their assistants. An enormous amount of archaeological data has been obtained through the treasure hunting activities of various groups and individuals, but, sadly, scarcely anything to date has been published about these shipwrecks.

Two archaeologists oversaw Florida's program between 1964 and 1982, and together they only produced seven reports...three of which were actually arguments *against* the shipwreck program in Florida. Yet, as far as I know, none of the purist archaeologists have taken these two to task for not publishing the wealth of information gleaned from the Florida wrecks.

Facing
Gold and silver objects dating from the 17th century were found by a treasure hunter using only a metal detector on a coral reef off the coast of Panama.

Over
This Ming porcelain cup was washed ashore in Drake's Bay, CA, from the wreck of the Manila Galleon *San Agustin*, which was lost in 1595.

On the other hand, Duncan Mathewson and other archaeologists associated with him, all of whom are considered pariahs because they work with treasure hunters, have published dozens of excellent archaeological reports. This is the kind of hypocrisy I now also encounter since I resigned from the Council of Underwater Archaeology. As long as I was in the "inner circle" of the Council, I was considered a good--if maverick--archaeologist. Now, I have become just another dirty treasure hunter.

If the main objective of archaeology is to obtain information, then what's the difference in *how* it is obtained? Since there is virtually no funding available in the United States for qualified archaeologists to undertake their own projects, then why not, as is done elsewhere in the world, work with commercial salvors and sports divers...train them and make use of data developed through their activities? Despite the peer rebuke archaeologist face today, some have accepted this as the only solution if they want to stay in the field. Mel Fisher, Barry Clifford and others have as many as six or eight qualified archaeologists on their teams. In several instances foreign governments have sent their own underwater archaeologists to train with these commercial salvage groups.

Facing
Just finding this iron Spanish anchor on a reef off Bermuda is as much adventure as countless sports divers desire when they enter the ocean in search of a wreck.

Over
Author digs out an iron cannon he found on a beach with a metal detector, a discovery that led him to a shipwreck located just off shore.

This is the accepted norm throughout the rest of the world. Henry VIII's *Mary Rose* presents an excellent example of such an alliance. Discovery, excavation and raising of this vessel could never been accomplished without painstaking work provided by more than 250 dedicated amateur sport divers, including Prince Charles. The project was directed by Dr. Margaret Rule, who at the age of 59 learned how to dive. Dr. Rule is an outspoken individual and a dedicated archaeologist, who is severely critiqued by the establishment since she opposes much in their intransigent attitude. During a recent archaeological conference she stated, "We have over 20,000 shipwrecks around the British Isles; yet, I consider only about 20 of them to have any archaeological value." This set off a bombshell still resounding in academic circles.

The British, with their traditional appreciation of the nonprofessional who engages in cultural or scientific activity, lead the way in utilizing trained amateurs. At Fort Bovisand Diving Academy near Plymouth, Dr. Rule and other archaeologists have trained several thousand sport divers and salvors in the rudiments of underwater archaeology. Why haven't we done this in the United States where we have many skilled and intelligent amateurs, where private funding is available and where we have members of the establishment sitting around in offices with no prospect of working on a wreck site? During the past summer a total of 32 shipwreck sites were worked by salvors and sports divers in the British Isles following strict government guidelines and supervised by professional archaeologists.

Everyone benefited.

What of The Future?

The future of underwater archaeology truly hinges, to a great extent, on collaboration between professional archaeologists and non-academic divers. The motivated amateur and the commercial salvor could be encouraged to acquire basic skills needed for archaeological work through training programs such as those offered in England. As public interest in archaeology grows, the gap between trained, paid archaeologists and the educated, disciplined amateur is narrowing. The majority of members of societies interested in land archaeology are amateurs, so-called because they hold no degrees in archaeology. Yet they undertake more field work, laboratory research and publish more reports on their findings than the limited number of professionals. In an underwater excavation many non-academics can contribute specialized skills such as advanced diving techniques, use of elaborate equipment, surveying, drafting or photography...skills they may have acquired or polished in pursuit of their avocation.

Alan Albright, who for many years was the underwater archaeologist for the State of South Carolina, realized the advantage of working *with* sport divers and treasure hunters rather than against them. His objective was to study the history of his state through maritime artifacts. Divers were required to obtain a licence for a nominal fee and submit a monthly report on their activities and finds. The state returned everything recovered after a short period of study and generally even preserved artifacts for salvors at no cost. For display purposes Albright made replicas of various artifacts and in some cases divers donated objects to the state. Consequently, everyone benefited from this program which is a good example of divers and archaeologists working together.

During the heyday of treasure hunting in Florida in the 60's and 70's, relations between treasure hunting sport divers and the State of Florida were generally unsatisfactory. Everyone suffered. When Jim Miller took over as chief of the Bureau of Archaeological Research about 10 years ago, however, significant changes were made, and I now consider Florida's shipwreck program one of the best in the world.

Several years ago the state also hired a new underwater archaeologist, Dr. Roger Smith, who is doing an excellent job and is well liked by salvors and sports divers alike. Last summer Smith run a school for undergraduate university students near Pensacola where they worked on an 18th-century British shipwreck. It is hoped that the state might initiate such a program for salvors and sport divers in the near future.

Florida now has two underwater archaeological preserves and is hoping to open another soon. One is near Fort Pierce and is the site of one of the 1715 galleon, the *Urca de Lima.* The other is off Islamorada in the Florida Keys and is one of the 1733 fleet, the *San Pedro.* Divers can swim around exploring these galleons and take photographs. Ballast piles with timbers protruding and anchors and cannon lying about give a novice wreck diver his first exciting glimpse of a Spanish treasure galleon.

Every summer there are usually anywhere from 20 to 40 treasure hunting vessels at work along a 40-mile stretch of Florida coastline between Melbourne and Fort Pierce. On shore one can also see dozens of land-bound treasure hunters hard at work with metal detectors. Most of the other treasure wreck diving in Florida waters takes place in the Keys or off Cape Canaveral. Florida's east coast is believed to have a treasure wreck along every single mile.

Thus, the area is a magnet to wreck divers from around the world.

Last summer treasure hunters from more than a dozen countries worked there. On some sites as many as six vessels work at the same time. A number of divers actually work from shore by swimming out with underwater detectors and hand fanning on potential targets. Anyone can dive on shipwrecks in Florida waters, but if you want to recover anything, a permit is required or salvors must sub-lease from someone already possessing a permit. Naturally they share their finds with the permit holder and the state.

The State of Florida issues two types of permits: exploration and salvage. Both are good for a year and are renewable. Once a site has been located, the permit-holder must switch from exploration to salvage and must follow strict guidelines. Basically a permit-holder is required to gather pertinent archaeological data by keeping good records of where the finds were made (where each hole was dug) and to photograph and label all finds. Everything recovered with the exception of gold must be stored in fresh water until the end of the season when someone is sent from Tallahassee to make a complete inventory and decide which objects require preservation. Division of these finds is soon made, with the state receiving 20% of what was recovered. Most of what Florida receives ends up in museums or traveling displays. Recently the state published an excellent book with photographs of the 1,401 gold coins which it had received over the years as its share of the 1715 fleet recoveries.

If the program is working so well in both Florida and South Carolina, why not in other states. You know the answer...a consortium of short-sighted, rigid bureaucrats and archaeologists.

Wreck divers in Florida face a predicament if a new bill before the Florida Legislature passes. Bill HB-718 could virtually eliminate wreck-diving for everyone except permit holders. The bill covers the area as far out as three miles in the ocean and nine miles into the Gulf of Mexico and prohibits the use of metal detectors and the recovery of any artifact...even a Coke bottle, if it came from a shipwreck! Any violation would result in severe penalties, including confiscation of one's vessel and any vehicle or diving equipment involved, plus a mandatory civil assessment of $1,000 per object recovered. Diving clubs are fighting against this bill.

The law which affects all wreck divers in the United States is the Abandoned Shipwreck Act of 1987. Signed into law by President Reagan in April 1988, it covers the waters out to three miles offshore. Another bill has recently been presented to Congress, however, extending the limit of jurisdiction out to 200 miles. The stimulus for this proposed legislation was the discovery of the *Central America* and a number of shipwrecks in deeper water off the coast of Florida.

Prior to 1976 only 12 states had specific laws regulating shipwreck exploration. Events progressed smoothly. Then Mel Fisher filed an admiralty claim in federal court for ownership of the *Atocha*, which was outside of the waters controlled by the State of Florida but was claimed by the U.S. government. Admiralty arrests date back to British law of the 13th century and are part of international law today applying to all waters outside state and federal jurisdictions. The court ruled in Fisher's favor, declaring that the U.S. government had no right to the wreck site. The battle then began in earnest.

Encouraged by this victory, Fisher decided to challenge the State of Florida as well and placed admiralty arrests on five of the 1715 Fleet shipwrecks, which were in waters claimed by of the State. After a five-year battle finally decided in the U.S. Supreme Court, Fisher won again. A chaotic period ensued because this meant that everyone holding state permits on shipwrecks in Florida and other states lost the rights to these wrecks. Wreck divers began grabbing each other's shipwrecks by placing admiralty arrests on the sites which naturally caused a great deal of friction in the wreck-diving fraternity.

Upon enactment of the federal shipwreck law in April 1988 the U.S. government asserted title to all shipwrecks that are substantially embedded in a state's submerged lands or embedded in coralline formations protected by a state on its submerged lands, as well as any abandoned shipwreck that is included or is determined to be eligible for inclusion in the National Register of Historical Places.

Military Ships are 'Eternal'

U.S. military vessels are never officially abandoned until stricken from the Navy list. This procedure occurs when a ship is scrapped or when one is sunk and the Navy decides against salvaging it. Unless stricken officially, they are considered fully commissioned ships of the fleet.

The main problem with this law is the wording. According to government bureaucrats this law will affect only from 5 to 10% of the 50,000 shipwrecks believed to be inside the three-mile limit off U.S. shores. But who is to decide if a shipwreck is "substantially buried?" If we leave it to the establishment, all shipwrecks will be "substantially buried." Again, it will be they who decide which shipwrecks are "eligible for inclusion in the National Register of Historical Places." What is clear is that admiralty arrests can no longer be placed on shipwrecks within the three-mile limit.

Once the Shipwreck Act was passed, the Federal government transferred title to all these shipwrecks to the respective states, empowering them to manage and formulate their own laws. The Federal government retained title to abandoned shipwrecks located on public lands and military vessels still in commission. Indian tribes retain the rights to sites located off Indian lands. The act says that States are to carry out their responsibilities under the act in a manner that will protect natural resources and habitat areas, guarantee recreational exploration of shipwreck

377

sites and allow for appropriate public and private sector recovery of shipwrecks, consistent with the protection of historical values and the environmental integrity of the shipwrecks and sites.

The act directed the National Park Service to prepare and publish guidelines to assist the states in developing legislation and regulations to carry out their responsibilities under the act. The Park Service held 11 public meetings to hear citizens' views and, after a long delay, published guidelines which infuriated the entire wreck-diving community. At this time most of the states bordering bodies of waters containing shipwrecks are drafting new laws and revising older ones.

Presently 18 state or territorial laws specifically allow for commercial recovery of state-owned shipwrecks: California, Delaware, Florida, Louisiana, Maryland, Massachusetts, Michigan, Mississippi, Montana, New Hampshire, New Jersey, North Carolina, Puerto Rico, South Carolina, Rhode Island, Vermont, Virginia and Washington. The State of Texas, whose extensive coastline is sprinkled with shipwrecks, forbids any commercial salvage.

Before anyone goes after any shipwreck in state-controlled waters, it is imperative to check for applicable state laws. Keep in mind that all state-owned shipwrecks are not considered to have historic value. Some may be embedded but not considered historical, whereas other "modern wrecks" may be protected because they serve as artificial reefs. Others lying in fishing grounds or gas and oil development areas may also be off limits. Basically, each state has the right to determine which shipwrecks may be explored by sport divers, which may be exploited by commercial salvors and which are off limits to everyone.

Unfortunately, we haven't heard the last of the new Act. In a case yet to be decided, an Illinois salvor recently challenged the Abandoned Shipwreck Act as unconstitutional. Harry Zych of the American Diving and Salvage

Company of Chicago located two 19th-century shipwrecks, the *Lady Elgin* and *Seabird*, in Lake Michigan. After the State of Illinois refused to give him a salvage permit, he went to court declaring that the Admiralty Arrest Act and not the new legislation should control these sites. The outcome of this case is eagerly awaited by everyone interested in the question of jurisdiction of underwater sites.

For the past four years I have been involved in a bitter battle over the ownership of a shipwreck in California waters. In 1595 the Manila galleon *San Agustin,* en route between the Philippines and Acapulco was lost off the shore of Drake's Bay, about 25 miles northwest of San Francisco. I first went after this richly laden galleon in 1950 and found traces of her existence. Then in January 1986 I was invited by staff of the National Park Service to attempt to locate and excavate her remains. I was thrilled at the prospect of working on such a fantastic site. After a great deal of fanfare in the press, the State of California entered the picture claiming they had the rights to bestow. So, I entered into negotiations with the State Lands Commission to obtain a salvage permit. I was granted the permit in 1988 and prepared to begin the project, developing plans with the State of California to excavate the site and build a museum which would showcase the history of the fabulous Manila galleons, the largest and most richly laden treasure ships of all time.

But then the Federal government stepped into the picture claiming ownership of the site, which was ironic indeed since they had passed all rights to the states. The National Park Service, which controls the Point Reyes National Seashore adjacent to the wreck site, was behind the federal assertion of ownership. Yet another contender jumped into the ring. NOAA, the National Oceanographic and Atmospheric Agency, which has established a National Marine Sanctuary in this same area, also claims the right to grant or deny permission to work on the shipwreck site.

In June of 1989 I pinpointed the shipwreck site without disturbing the sea floor. The battle is still raging between the State and Federal governments. Until it is resolved, I am unable to start the excavation of California's oldest and most fascinating shipwreck.

Most countries claim ownership of shipwrecks in waters from anywhere from three to 200 miles offshore and their laws vary a great deal. In England anyone can search for and excavate a shipwreck without any permission at all. Recovered artifacts are turned into the Receiver of Wrecks, who holds them for a year and a day to see if anyone else makes a claim. If none is made, the British Museum in London is asked if it wishes any of the materials recovered. If the BM is interested, three independent appraisers place a value on the objects, and the museum has the option to buy them from the salvors. All remaining objects are returned to the salvors.

Other nations such as Spain, Portugal and Italy forbid all diving on shipwrecks and have severe penalties. In most countries where commercial salvage is permitted the customary split is 75% for the salvor and 25% for the country...with some nations reserving the rights to take all "unique objects." The Bahamas is one of the easiest foreign countries in which to obtain a salvage permit. No permits are required for search activities and they abide by the 75/25 split. Mexico forbids all shipwreck explorations except those by its own federal underwater archaeologists. In Canada permits are not required for search, but salvage permits must be obtained from each provisional government.

Some nations are not content with claiming shipwrecks just in their own territorial waters. The Netherlands has laid claim to all of its historical Dutch East Indiamen wrecks around the globe and has successfully defended this assertion in the International Court as it concerned shipwrecks located from Indonesia to Madeira Island. The Spanish Government has recently stated that they are also considering declaring ownership of all of the Spanish shipwrecks worldwide. This could have resounding repercussions on salvage of the hundreds of Spanish galleons, the most sought after prizes by commercial salvors.

Finding a sunken treasure on the high seas outside of a nation's territorial jurisdiction would appear to fit into the "finders-keepers" principal, but such is not the case...as the Columbus American Discovery group recently discovered. The *S.S. Central America,* one of the richest treasure ships ever lost, went down during a hurricane in 1857 approximately 160 miles off the coast of South Carolina in waters one and one-half miles deep. After a 10-year search costing over $10 million, the wreck was discovered last year by this group from Ohio. In the first season they recovered over a ton of gold ingots and rare coins. They intended to return this year to continue salvaging the treasure. No sooner had news of this discovery been released around the world, however, than 39 insurance companies, including some long-gone but "resurrected" ones, asserted claim to the treasure, stating that since they had paid claims when it was lost they now owned it. Far from making the salvors rich, the "rivers of gold coins and carpets of gold" described by project leader Thomas G. Thompson plunged them into a legal nightmare as their quest moved from the high seas to the courtroom...where they eventually won their hard-earned prize!

Bibliography

Shipwreck Locations

Anonymous, *Shipwrecks and Disasters at Sea*, 1851, London.

Bachard, Robert G., *Scuba Northeast, Shipwrecks: Rhode Island to New Jersey.*

Barrington, George, *Remarkable Voyages and Shipwrecks*, 1883, London.

Barry, James P., *Wrecks and Rescues of the Great Lakes*, 1981, San Diego.

Berg, Daniel,
Wreck Valley, 1986, New York.
Tropical Shipwrecks, 1989, East Rockaway, NY.

Berman, Bruce D., *Encyclopedia of American Shipwrecks*, 1972, Boston.

Bowen, Dana Thomas, *Shipwrecks of the Lakes*, 1952, Daytona Beach.

Boyer, Dwight, *True Tales of the Great Lakes*, 1971, New York.

Burgess, Robert
Sinkings, Salvages and Shipwrecks, 1970, New York.
Florida's Golden Galleons, 1982, New York.

Cardone, Bonnie J. & Smith, Patrick, *Shipwrecks of Southern California*, 1989, Los Angeles.

Deperthes, Jean L., *Histoire des Naufrages*, 3 vols., 1828, Paris.

Douglas, Darren, *Guide to Shipwreck Diving: Southern California, 1990, Houston.*

Duffy, James, *Shipwrecks and Empire*, 1955, Cambridge, Mass.

Duro, Fernandez Cesareo de, *Armada Española*, 9 vols., 1878, Madrid.

Farb, Richard M., *Guide to Shipwreck Diving: North Carolina*, 1990, Houston.

Farb, Roderick, *Shipwrecks: Diving the Graveyard of the Atlantic*, 1989, Houston.

Frederick, James, *Diver's Guide to River Wrecks*, 1982, New York.

Fleming, Robert M., *Primer of Shipwreck Research and Records for Skin Divers*, 1971, Milwaukee.

Gentile, Gary
Shipwrecks of New Jersey, 1987, New York.
Advanced Wreck Diving Guide, 1988, New York.

Gibbs, James Atwood
Shipwrecks of the Pacific Coast, 1957, Portland.
Disaster Log of Ships, 1971, Seattle.

Hocking, Charles
Dictionary of Disasters at Sea During the Age of Steam:1824-1962, 2 vols., 1969, London.

Hoehling, Adolph A.
Great Ship Disasters, 1971, New York.
Lost at Sea, 1984, Harrisburg, PA.

Horner, Dave
Shipwrecks, Skin Divers and Sunken Gold, 1965, New York.
The Treasure Galleons, 1971, New York.

Hudson, Kenneth, *The Book of Shipwrecks*, 1979, London.

Huntress, Keith, *Narratives of Shipwrecks and Disasters*, 1974, Ames, Iowa.

Jenney, Jim, *In Search of Shipwrecks*, 1980, New York.

Keatts, Henry
Dive into History: U-Boats, 1986, New York.
Field Reference to Sunken U-Boats, 1987, New York.
New England's Legacy of Shipwrecks, 1988, New York.

LaFrance, Jean, *Les Epaves du Saint-Laurent 1650-1760*, 1972, Montreal.

Layton, J.F., *Memorable Shipwrecks and Seafaring Adventures*, N.D., Glasgow.

Lonsdale, Adrian L. and Kaplan, H.R., *Guide to Sunken Treasure in American Waters*, 1964, Arlington, VA.

Marshall, Don B.
California Shipwrecks, 1978, Seattle.
Oregon shipwrecks, 1984, Portland.

Marx, Robert F.
Shipwrecks of the Virgin Islands 1523-1825, St.Thomas, VI.
Shipwrecks in the Waters of Puerto Rico, 1969, San Juan, PR.
Shipwrecks in Florida Waters, 1971, Melbourne FL.
Shipwrecks in Mexican Waters, 1971, Mexico City.
Shipwrecks of the Western Hemisphere 1492-1825, 1971, New York.
Spanish Treasures in Florida Waters, 1978, Boston

McDonald, Kendall
The Wreck Detectives, 1972, London.
The Treasure Divers, 1977, London.

Morris, Paul C. and Quinn, William, *Shipwrecks in New York Waters*, 1989, Orleans, MA.

Meylach, Martin, *Diving to a Flash of Gold*, 1986, Port Salerno, FL.

Neider, Charles, *Great shipwrecks and Castaways*, 1952, New York.

Nesmith, Robert I. and Potter, John S., Jr., *Treasure: How and Where to Find It*, 1968, New York.

Paine, Ralph D., *Lost Ships and Lonely Seas*, 1942, Garden City, NY.

Potter, John S., Jr., *The Treasure Diver's Guide*, Revised Edition, 1988, New York.

Quinn, William

Shipwrecks Around Cape Cod, 1973, Orleans, MA.

Shipwrecks Around New England, 1978, Orleans, MA.

Shipwrecks Around Maine, 1983, Orleans, MA.

Shipwrecks Along the Atlantic Coast, 1988, Orleans, MA.

Ratigan, William, *Great Lakes Shipwrecks and Survivals*, 1989, New York.

Rattray, Jeannette

Perils of the Port of New York, 1973, New York.

Shipwrecks, Life-Saving and Salvage on Long Island, 1978, New York.

Rieseberg, Harry E. and Mikalow, A.A., *Sunken Treasure Ships of the World*, 1965, New York.

Sands, John 0., *Yorktown's Captive Fleet*, 1983, Newport News, VA.

Scoville, Dorothy R., *Shipwrecks of Martha's Vineyard*, 1972, Gayhead, MA.

Shepard, Birse, *Lore of the Wreckers*, 1961, Boston.

Shomette, Donald G.

Shipwrecks of the Civil War, 1973, Washington, D. C.

Shipwrecks on the Chesapeake and its Tributaries 1608-1978, 1982, Centerville, MD.

Snow, Edward R.

Great Storms and Famous Shipwrecks of the New England Coast, 1943, Boston.

Pirates, Shipwrecks and Historical Chronicles, 1981, New York.

Spyglass Publications, *Snorklers' and Divers' Guide to Shipwrecks of Florida's Southeast Coast*, 1989, Miami.

Stick, David, *Graveyard of the Atlantic*, 1952, Chapel Hill, NC.

Stirling, Nord B., *Treasure Under the Sea* 1957, Garden City, NY.

Stonehouse, Frederick, *Isle Royale Shipwrecks*, 1974, Marquette, MI.

Trupp, Philip Z., *Tracking Treasure*, 1986, Washington, D.C.

Villiers, Alan J., *Wild Ocean: The Story of the North Atlantic and the Men Who Sailed It*, 1957, New York.

Voynick, Stephen M., *The Mid-Atlantic Treasure Coast: Coins, Beaches and Treasure Shipwrecks from Long Island to Maryland's Eastern Shore*, 1984, Wallingsford. PA.

Watson, Milton H., *Disasters at Sea*, 1987, London.

Wilkins, Harold T., *Hunting Hidden Treasures*, 1929, New York.

Williams, Mark, *Sunken Treasure*, 1980, London.

Wood, Walter, *Survivors' Tales of Famous Shipwrecks*, 1932, London.

Wrigley, Ronald, *Shipwrecks: Vessels That Met Tragedy on Northern Lake Superior*, 1985, Cobalt, Ontario.

Zinck, Jack, *Shipwrecks of Nova Scotia*, 1975, Windsor, Nova Scotia.

The Ships and their History

Artinano y de Galdacano, Gervasio de
La Arquitectura Naval Española, 1920, Madrid.
Historia del Comercio de Las Indias, 1917, Barcelona.

Baker, William A.
Colonial Vessels, 1962, Barre, MA.
Sloops & Shallops, 1966, Barre, Mass.

Boxer, Charles R.
The Dutch Seaborne Empire: 1600-1800, 1965, New York.
The Portuguese Seaborne Empire: 1415-1825, 1969, New York. Chaunu, Huguette and Pierre, *Seville et L'-Atlantique (1504- 1650)*, 9 vols., 1955, Paris.

Clowes, William L.*The Royal Navy*, 3 vols., 1898, Boston.

Cowburn, Philip. *The Warship in History*, 1965, New York.

Duhamel Du Monceau, Henri L., *Elemens de l'-Architecture Navale*, 1758, Paris.

Duro, Femandez Cesareo de
La Armada Española, 9 vols., 1895-1903, Madrid.
Disquisiciones Nauticas, 6 vols., 1876-81, Madrid.
Fincham, John, *A History of Naval Architecture*, 1851, London.
Hamilton, Earl J., *American Treasure and the Price Revolution in Spain, 1501-1650*, 1934, Cambridge, Mass.
Haring, Clarence H.
Trade and Navigation Between Spain and the Indies in the Time of the Hapsburgs, 1918, Cambridge, Mass.
The Buccaneers in the West Indies, 1910, Cambridge, Mass.
Landstrom, Bjorn, *The Ship*, 1961, New York.
Martinez-Hidalgo, Jose Maria, *Columbus' Ships*, 1966, Barre, Mass.
Marx, Robert F.
The Treasure Fleets of the Spanish Main, 1968, Cleveland.
The Battle of the Spanish Armada: 1588, 1965, Cleveland.   .
Morison, Samuel Eliot, *Admiral of the Ocean Sea*, 1942, Boston.
Pares, Richard, *War and Trade in the West Indies*, 1936, New York.
Parry, J. H.
The Age of Reconnaissance, 1963, London.
The Spanish Seaborne Empire, 1966, New York.
Schurz, William L., *The Manila Galleon*, 1939, New York.
Veitia Linage, Joseph de *Norte de la Contratacion de las Indias Occidentales*, 1672, Seville.

Early Salvage and Underwater Archaeology

Arnold, J. Barto, *The Nautical Archaeology of Padre Island*, 1978, New York.

Bass, George F., *Underwater Archaeology*, 1966, New York.

Blair, Clay, Jr., *Diving for Pleasure and Treasure*, 1960, Cleveland.

Bush Romero, Pablo, *Under the Waters of Mexico*, 1964, Mexico City.

Cleator, Philip Ellaby, *Underwater Archaeology*, 1973, London.

Davis, John , *Treasure, People, Ships and Dreams*, 1977, San Antonio, TX.

Davis, Robert H., *Deep Diving and Submarine Operations*, 1951, London.

Diole, Philippe, *4,000 Years Under the Sea*, 1954, New York.

Dugan, James
Man Under the Sea, 1956, New York.
Men Under Water, 1965, New York.

Dumas, Frederic, *Deep-Water Archaeology*, 1962, London.

Franzen, Anders, *The Warship Vasa*, 1960, New York.

Frost, Honor, *Under the Mediterranean*, 1963, London.

Johnstone, Paul, *The Archaeology of Ships*, 1974, London.

Karraker, Cyrus H., *The Hispañiola Treasure*, 1934, Philadelphia.

Latil, Pierre de and Rivoire, Jean, *Man and the Underwater World*, 1954, London.

Marx, Robert F.
They Dared the Deep, 1967, New York and Cleveland
Pirate Port: the Story of the Sunken City of Port Royal, 1967, New York and Cleveland.
The Underwater Dig, 1990, Houston.

Martin, Colin, *Full Fathom Five: Wrecks of the Spanish Armada*, 1975, London.

McKee, Alexander
History Under the Sea, 1968. London.
How We Found the Mary Rose, 1982, London.
Peterson, Mendel, *History Under the Sea*, 1969, Washington.
Rackl, Hanns-Wolf, *Diving Into the Past: Archaeology Underwater*, 1968, New York.
Taylor, Joan du Plat, editor, *Marine Archaeology*, 1965, London.
Throckmorton, Peter
The Lost Ships, 1964, Boston.
Shipwrecks and Archaeology, 1969, Boston.
Wilkes, Bill St. John, *Nautical Archaeology-A Handbook for Skin Divers*, 1971, New York.

Diving and Modern Salvage

Allen, Geoffrey, *The Gun of the Sacramento, 1978,* London.

Ballard, Robert D., *The Discovery of the Titanic, 1987,* New York.

Borhegyi, Suzanne de, *Ships, Shoals and Amphoras,* 1961, New York.

Carrier, Rick and Barbara, *Dive: the Complete Book of Skin Diving,* 1955, New York.

Ciampi, Elgin, *Skin Dive,* 1960, New York.

Cousteau, Capt. Jacques Yves
The Silent World, 1953, New York.
The Living Sea, 1963, New York.

Earle, Peter, *The Wreck of the Almiranta,* 1979, London.

Ellsberg, Edward
On the Bottom, 1929, New York.
Men Under the Sea, 1939, New York.

Falcon-Barker, Capt. Ted, *Roman Galley Beneath the Sea,* 1964, New York.

Garrett, Charles, *Treasure Recovery from Sand and Sea,* 1988, Dallas.

Giquere, Jon-Paul, *Salvage Laws for Weekend Divers,* 1981.

Gores, Joseph N., *Marine Salvage,* 1971, New York

Grissim, John, *The Lost Treasure of the Concepcion,* 1980, New York.

Library of Congress, A descriptive list of treasure maps and charts in the Library of Congress, 1973, Washington, D.C.

Link, Marion C., *Sea Diver, a Quest for History From the Sea,* 1959, New York.

Lyon, Eugene., *The Search for the Atocha,* 1979, N. Y.

Marx, Robert F.
Always Another Adventure, 1967, Cleveland.
Still More Adventures, 1976, New York.
The Lure of Sunken Treasure, 1973, New York.
Sea Fever, 1972, New York.
Quest for Treasure, 1982, Dallas.
Diving for Adventure, 1979, New York.
Masters, David
The Wonders of Salvage, 1924, New York.
Epics of Salvage, 1952, Boston.
Mathewson, Duncan, *Treasure of the Atocha*, 1987, New York.
Morris, Roland, *Island Treasure*, 1969, London.
Nesmith, Robert I., *Dig for Pirate Treasure*, 1958, New York.
Northeast Marine Advisory Council , *Sportsdivers Handbook for Historical Shipwrecks*, 1982, Durham, NH.
Owen, David M., *A Manual for Free Divers*, 1955, New York.
Rebikoff, Dimitri, *Free Diving*, 1956, New York.
Slack, Jack, *Finders Losers*, 1967, New York.
Stenuit, Robert, *The Deepest Days*, 1966, New York.
Tucker, Teddy, *Treasure Diving with Teddy Tucker*, 1966, Bermuda.
Wagner, Kip (as told to Taylor, L. B., Jr.), *Pieces of Eight*, 1967, New York.

Preservation

Albright, Alan, "The preservation of small water-logged wood specimens with polyethylene glycol," *Curator,* 1966, Vol. IX, No. 3, pp. 22-34.

Barkman, Lars, *The Preservation of the Vasa,* No date, Stockholm.

Caley, Earle R., "Coatings and encrustations on lead objects from the Agora and the method used for their removal," *Studies in Conservation,* 1955, Vol. 2, No. 2, pp. 49-54.

Erickson, Egon, and Tregel, Svend, *Conservation of Iron Recovered from the Sea,* 1966, Copenhagen.

Graham, John Meredith, *American Pewter,* 1949, Brooklyn.

Katsev, Michael, and Doornick, Fredrick van, "Replicas of iron tools from a Byzantine shipwreck," *Studies in Conservation,* August 1966, Vol. 11, No. 3, pp. 133-42.

Organ, R. M., "The conservation of fragile metallic objects," *Studies in Conservation,* November 1961, Vol. 6, No. 4, pp. 135-36.

Pittsburgh Plate Glass Company, "Embedding Objects in Selectron 5000 Resins," 1946, Pittsburgh.

Plenderleith, H. J., *The Conservation of Antiquities and Works of Art,* 1956, London.

(The most comprehensive work on the subject.)

Smith, James B., Jr., and Ellis, John P., "The preservation of underwater archaeological specimens in plastic," *Curator,* 1963, Vol. VI, No. 1, pp. 32-36.

Thomas M. W., and Dunton, John V. N., *Treatment for Cleaning and Preserving Excavated Iron Objects,* 1954, Williamsburg, Va.

Townsend, Samuel P., "Heat methods of preserving cast iron artifacts recovered from salt water," Report presented at the Third Conference on Underwater Archaeology, Miami, FL, March 23-25, 1967.

Werner, A. E., "Consolidation of fragile objects," *Studies in Conservation*, November, 1961, Vol. 6, No. 4, pp. 133-35.

Identification of Artifacts

Artillery

Foulkes, Charles, *The Gun Founders of England*, 1937, Cambridge, England.

Gibbon, John, *The Artillerists Manual*, 1863, New York.

Grant, Michael, *Armada Guns*, 1961, London.

Hime, Henry W. L., *The Origin of Artillery*, 1915, London.

Hogg, Oliver F. G., *English Artillery 1326-1716*, 1963, London.

Manucy, Albert, *Artillery Through the Ages*, 1949, Washington, D.C.

Mountaine, William, *The Practical Sea-gunners' Companion or an Introduction to the Art of Gunnery*, 1747, 3rd edition, London.

Muller, John, *A Treatise of Artillery*, 1780, 3rd edition, London.

Museo del Ejercito, Catalogo del Museo del Ejercito, 4 vols., 1956, Madrid.

Robins, Benjamin, *New Principles of Gunnery*, 1742, London.

Saint-Remy, Pierre Surirey de, *Memoires d'artillerie*, 2 vols., 1741, The Hague, Holland.

Smith, George, *An Universal Military Dictionary*, 1779, London.

Streete, Thomas, *The Use and Effects of the Gunne* (sic), 1674, London.

Thomas, Capt., *A Treatise on Gunpowder*, 1789, London.

Vigon, Jorge, *Historia de la Artilleria Española*, 3 vols., 1947, Madrid.

Weapons

Greener, W. W., *The Gun and its Development*, 9th edition, 1967, New York.

Jackson, H. J., *European Hand Firearms of the 16th, 17th & 18th Centuries.*

Peterson, Harold L.
The Treasury of the Gun 1962, New York.
Arms and Armor in Colonial America, 1526-1783
Daggers and Fighting Knives of the Western World.

Stone, George Cameron, *A Glossary of the Construction, Decoration and Use of Arms and Armor in all Countries and in all Times*, 1934, New York.

(The most comprehensive work on the subject.)

Tunis, Edwin, *Weapons: A Pictorial History*, 1954, Cleveland and New York.

Wilkinson, Frederick, *Swords and Daggers*, 1968, New York.

Navigation Instruments

Brewington, M. V., *Navigating Instruments*, 1963, Salem, Mass.

Garcia France, Salvador, *Instrumentos Nauticos en el Museo Naval*, 1959, Madrid.

Mountaine, William, and Wakely, Andrew, *The Mariner's Compass Rectified*, 1754, London.

Waters, David W., *The Art of Navigation in England in Elizabethan and Early Stuart Times*, 1958, London.

Zinner, Ernst, *Astronomische Instrumente*, 1967, Munich.

Clay Smoking Pipes

Brongars, G. A., *Nicotiana Tabacum*, 1964, Amsterdam.

Dunhill, Alfred, *The Pipe Book*, 1924, New York.

Harrington, J. C., "Dating stem fragments of 17th and 18th century tobacco pipes," Bull. Arch. Soc., 1954, Vol. 4.

Marx, Robert F.
"Clay smoking pipes recovered from the sunken city of Port Royal: May 1, 1966-September 3, 1967," March 1968.
"Clay smoking pipes recovered from the sunken city of Port Royal: October 1, 1967-March 31, 1968," August 1968.
(Both reports were published by the Jamaica National Trust Commission, Kingston, Jamaica.)

Oswald, Adrian, *English Clay Tobacco Pipes*, 1967, London.

Glassware and Bottles

Buckley, Francis, *The Glass Trade in England in the 17th Century*, 1914, London.

Corning Glass Museum, *Glass from the Corning Glass Museum*, 1965, Corning, N.Y.

Frothingham, Alice Wilson, *Hispanic Glass*, 1941, New York.

Harrington, J. C., *Glassmaking at Jamestown*, 1953, Richmond, Va.

Hayes, E. Barrington, *Glass Through the Ages*, 1966, Baltimore.

Honey, W. B., *Glass*, 1946, London.

Hume, Ivor Noel
"Dating English glass wine bottles," *Wine and Spirit Trade Record*, February 1955.
Here Lies Virginia, 1963, New York.

Lee, Ruth Webb, *Victorian Glass*, 1939, Framington, Mass.

Marx, Robert F.

"Wine glasses recovered from the sunken city of Port Royal: May 1, 1966-March 31, 1968," Jamaica National Trust Commission, Kingston, Jamaica, May, 1968.

"Glass bottles recovered from the sunken city of Port Royal, Jamaica: May 1, 1966-March 31, 1968," Caribbean Research Institute, St. Thomas, VI, January, 1969.

McKearin, Helen and George, *Two Hundred Years of American Blown Glass*, 1956, New York.

Rider, Dennis, *A History of Glass Bottles*, 1956, London.

Ruggles-Brise, Sheelah, *Sealed Bottles*, 1949, London.

Gold Plate

Castro, J. P. de, *The Law and Practice of Marking Gold and Silver Ware*, 1935, London.

Heal, A., *The London Goldsmiths, 1200-1800*, 1935, Cambridge, England.

Hill, H. D., *Antique Gold Boxes, Their Lore and Their Lure*, 1953. New York.

Jackson, C. J., *English Goldsmiths and Their Marks*, 1949, London.

Jones, E. A., *Old English Gold Plate*, 1907, London.

Prideaux, W. S., *Memorials of the Goldsmiths' Company, 1335- 1815*, 2 vols, 1896-97, London.

Silverware

Cripps, W. J., *Old English Plate, Ecclesiastical, Decorative and Domestic: Its Makers and Marks*, 1926, London.

Jackson, C. J., *An Illustrated History of English Plate, Ecclesiastical and Secular*, 2 vols., 1926, London.

Jones, E. A., *Old Silver of Europe and America*, 1928, London and New York.

Wyler, S. B., *The Book of Old Silver: English, American, and Foreign*, 1947, New York.

Pewterware

Bell, Malcolm, *Old Pewter*, 1905, New York.

Cotterell, Howard H., *Old Pewter: Its Makers and Marks*, 1929, London.

(The most comprehensive work on the subject.)

Markham, C. A., *Pewter Marks and Old Pewterware*, 1909, London.

Welch, C., *History of the Worshipful Company of Pewterers of London*, 1902, London.

Pottery and Porcelain

Chaffers, William, *The New Collector's Handbook of Marks and Monograms on Pottery and Porcelain*, 1914, London.

Cushion, J. P., and Honey, W. B., *Handbook of Pottery and Porcelain Marks*, 1956, London.

Frothingham, Alice Wilson
Talavera Pottery, 1944, New York.
Lustreware of Spain, 1951, New York.

Garner, Frederic H., *English Delftware*, 1948, New York.

Godden, Geoffrey A., *British Pottery and Porcelain*, 1966, New York.

Goggin, John M.
"The Spanish olive jar, an introductory study,". Yale University publications in Anthropology, No. 62, 1960, New Haven.
Spanish Majolica in the New World: Types of the 16th to 18th Centuries, 1968, New Haven.

Savage, George, *Porcelain Through the Ages*, 1963, Baltimore.

Shepard, Anna O., *Ceramics for the Archaeologist*, 1965, Washington, D.C.

Thorn, C. Jordan, *Handbook of Old Pottery and Porcelain Marks,* 1965, New York.

Towner, Donald C., *English Cream-Colored Earthenware,* 1957, London.

Watkins, Lura W., *Early New England Potters and their Wares,* 1950, Cambridge, Mass.

Wills, Geoffrey, *The Book of English China,* 1964, New York.

Spanish Coinage

Beals, Gary, *Numismatic Terms of Spain and Spanish America,* 1966, San Diego.

Dasi, Tomas, *Estudio de los Reales de a Ocho,* 5 vols., 1950, Valencia, Spain.

Harris, Robert P., *Pillars and Portraits,* 1968, San Jose, California.

Lopez-Chaves y Sanchez, Leopoldo
Catalogo de la Onza Española, 1961, Madrid.
Catalogo de la Media Onza o Doblon de a Cuatro, 1961, Madrid.
Catalogo de las Onzas de la America Independiente, 1961, Madrid.

Nesmith, Robert I., *The Coinage of the First Mint of the Americas at Mexico City,* 1955, New York.

Pradeau, Alberto F., *Numismatic History of Mexico from the Pre-Columbian Epoch to 1823,* 1938, Los Angeles.

Yriarte, Jose de., *Catalogo de los Reales de a Ocho Españoles,* 1955, Madrid.

Coinage of Other Nations

Brooke, George C., *English Coins From the 7th Century to the Present Day,* 1932, London.

Ciani, Louis, *Catalogue de Monnaies Francaises,* 3 vols., 1926-31, Paris.

Dieudonne, A., *Monnaies Royales Francaises*, 1916, Paris.
Lindheim, Leon, *Facts and Fiction About Coins*, 1967, Cleveland and New York.
Peck, C. Wilson, *English Copper, Tin and Bronze Coins: 1558- 1958*, 1960, London.
Santos, Leitao & Cie., *Catalogo de Moedas Brasileiras de 1643 a 1944*, No date, Rio de Janeiro.
Wood, Howland, *The Coinage of the West Indies, and the Sou Marque*, 1915, New York.
Yeoman, R. S.
A Catalog of Modern World Coins, 1965, Chicago.
A Guide Book of United States Coins, 1965, Chicago.

Brass and Copper Objects

Marx, Robert F., "Brass and copper items recovered from the sunken city of Port Royal: May 1, 1966-March 31, 1968," Jamaica National Trust Commission, Kingston, Jamaica, May 1968.
Wills, G., *Collecting Copper and Brass*, 1954, Glasgow. Privately published.

Miscellaneous Reference Books

Bradford, Ernle, *Four Centuries of European Jewelry*, 1953, Feltham, England.
Bruton, E., *Clocks and Watches*, 1965, London.
Hume, Ivor Noel, *A Guide to Artifacts of Colonial America*, 1970, New York.

(This comprehensive book is useful in the identification of hundreds of different types of artifacts, such as bells, buckles, buttons, cooking vessels, cutlery, locks and padlocks, and tools.)

Mercer, Henry C., *Ancient Carpenters' Tools*, 1960, Doylestown, Pa.

Ram Books

Please send the following books:

☐ Buried Treasure of the U.S. $10.95
☐ Treasure Recovery from Sand & Sea $14.95
☐ The New Successful Coin Hunting $10.95
☐ Modern Treasure Hunting $12.95
☐ Modern Electronic Prospecting . . . .$ 9.95
☐ Modern Metal Detectors $14.95
☐ Treasure Hunting Pays Off . . . .$ 6.95
☐ Weekend Prospecting . . . .$ 3.95
☐ Gold Panning Is Easy . . . .$ 6.95

True Treasure Tales

☐ Secret of John Murrell's Vault . . . .$ 2.95
☐ Missing Nez Perce Gold . . . .$ 2.95

Garrett Guides to Treasure ($1 each)
(No shipping charge when shipping/handling is paid for any other book)

☐ An Introduction to Metal Detectors
☐ Find Wealth in the Surf
☐ Find Wealth on the Beach
☐ Metal Detectors Can Help You Find Coins
☐ Find More Treasure With The Right Detector
☐ You Can Avoid Detector Problems
☐ Use the Super Sniper
☐ Find An Ounce of Gold A Day
☐ Money Caches are Waiting To Be Found

Ram Publishing Company
P.O. Drawer 38649
Dallas, TX 75238

Please add $1 for
each book ordered
(maximum of $3)
for handling charges.

Total for items $_____

8.25% Tax (Texas residents) $_____

Handling Charge $_____

TOTAL $_____

☐ Enclosed check or money order

I prefer to order through

☐ MasterCard
☐ Visa

_____

Credit Card Number

_____

Expiration Date   **Phone Number (8 a.m. to 4 p.m.)**

_____

Signature (Credit Card orders must be signed.)

_____

NAME

_____

ADDRESS (For Shipping)

_____

CITY, STATE, ZIP